Chuang Tzu
Mystic, Moralist, and Social Reformer

Zhuangzi

Chuang Tzu: Mystic, Moralist, and Social Reformer

Copyright © 2023 Bibliotech Press
All rights reserved

The present edition is a reproduction of previous publication of this classic work. Minor typographical errors may have been corrected without note; however, for an authentic reading experience the spelling, punctuation, and capitalization have been retained from the original text.

ISBN: 979-8-88830-341-2

CONTENTS

Introduction iv
Note on the Philosophy of Chuang Tzǔ, by Canon Moore   X

CHAPTERS

I	Transcendental Bliss	1
II	The Identity of Contraries	6
III	Nourishment of the Soul	16
IV	Man among Men	18
V	The Evidence of Virtue Complete	26
VI	The Great Supreme	31
VII	How to Govern	42
VIII	Joined Toes	46
IX	Horses' Hoofs	49
X	Opening Trunks	51
XI	On Letting Alone	55
XII	The Universe	62
XIII	The Tao of God	72
XIV	The Circling Sky	79
XV	Self-Conceit	87
XVI	Exercise of Faculties	89
XVII	Autumn Floods	91
XVIII	Perfect Happiness	100
XIX	The Secret of Life	104
XX	Mountain Trees	112
XXI	T'ien Tzǔ Fang	119
XXII	Knowledge travels North	126
XXIII	Kêng Sang Ch'u	134
XXIV	Hsü Wu Kuei	142
XXV	Tsê Yang	152
XXVI	Contingencies	160
XXVII	Language	165
XXVIII	On Declining Power	169
XXIX	Robber Chê	176
XXX	On Swords	185
XXXI	The Old Fisherman	187
XXXII	Lieh Tzǔ	192
XXXIII	The Empire	198

Introduction

Chuang Tzŭ[1] belongs to the third and fourth centuries before Christ. He lived in the feudal age, when China was split up into a number of States owning a nominal allegiance to the royal, and weakly, House of Chou.

He is noticed by the historian Ssŭ-ma Ch'ien, who flourished at the close of the second century B.C., as follows:—

Chuang Tzŭ was a native of Mêng.[2] His personal name was Chou. He held a petty official post at Ch'i-yüan in Mêng.[3] He lived contemporaneously with Prince Hui of the Liang State and Prince Hsüan of the Ch'i State. His erudition was most varied; but his chief doctrines are based upon the sayings of Lao Tzŭ.[4] Consequently, his writings, which extend to over 100,000 words, are mostly allegorical.[5]

He wrote The Old Fisherman, Robber Chê, and Opening Trunks, with a view to asperse the Confucian school and to glorify the mysteries of Lao Tzŭ.[6] Wei Lei Hsü, Kêng Sang Tzŭ, and the like, are probably unsubstantial figments of his imagination.[7] Nevertheless, his literary and dialectic skill was such that the best scholars of the age proved unable to refute his destructive criticism of the Confucian and Mihist schools.[8]

His teachings were like an overwhelming flood, which spreads at its own sweet will. Consequently, from rulers and ministers downwards, none could apply them to any definite use.[9]

Prince Wei of the Ch'u State, hearing of Chuang Tzŭ's good report, sent messengers to him, bearing costly gifts, and inviting him to become Prime Minister. At this Chuang Tzŭ smiled and said to the messengers, "You offer me great wealth and a proud position indeed; but have you never seen a sacrificial ox?—When after being fattened up for several years, it is decked with embroidered trappings and led to the altar, would it not willingly then change places with some uncared-for pigling?... Begone! Defile me not! I would rather disport myself to my own enjoyment in the mire than be slave to the ruler of a State. I will never take office. Thus I shall remain free to follow my own inclinations."[10]

---

[1] Pronounce Chwongdza.
[2] In the modern province of An-hui.
[3] Hence he is often spoken of in the book language as "Ch'i-yüan."
[4] Pronounce Lowdza. The low as in allow. See p. vii.
[5] Of an imaginative character, in keeping with the visionary teachings of his master.
[6] See chs. xxxi, xxix, and x, respectively.
[7] The second of these personages is doubtless identical, though the name is differently written, with the Kêng Sang Ch'u of ch. xxiii. The identity of the first name has not been satisfactorily settled.
[8] See p. 8.
[9] This last clause is based upon a famous passage in the Lun Yü:—The perfect man is not a mere thing; i.e., his functions are not limited. The idea conveyed is that Chuang Tzŭ's system was too far-reaching to be practical.
[10] See p. 197.

To enable the reader to understand more fully the writings of Chuang Tzŭ, and to appreciate his aim and object, it will be necessary to go back a few more hundred years.

In the seventh century B.C., lived a man, now commonly spoken of as Lao Tzŭ. He was the great Prophet of his age. He taught men to return good for evil, and to look forward to a higher life. He professed to have found the clue to all things human and divine.

He seems to have insisted that his system could not be reduced to words. At any rate, he declared that those who spoke did not know, while those who knew did not speak.

But to accommodate himself to conditions of mortality, he called this clue TAO, or The Way, explaining that the word was to be understood metaphorically, and not in a literal sense as the way or road upon which men walk.

The following are sentences selected from the indisputably genuine remains of Lao Tzŭ, to be found scattered here and there in early Chinese literature:—

All the world knows that the goodness of doing good is not real goodness.

When merit has been achieved, do not take it to yourself. On the other hand, if you do not take it to yourself, it shall never be taken from you.

By many words wit is exhausted. It is better to preserve a mean.

Keep behind, and you shall be put in front. Keep out, and you shall be kept in.

What the world reverences may not be treated with irreverence.

Good words shall gain you honour in the market-place. Good deeds shall gain you friends among men.

He who, conscious of being strong, is content to be weak,—he shall be a cynosure of men.

The Empire is a divine trust, and may not be ruled. He who rules, ruins. He who holds by force, loses.

Mighty is he who conquers himself.

He who is content, has enough.

To the good I would be good. To the not-good I would also be good, in order to make them good.

If the government is tolerant, the people will be without guile. If the government is meddling, there will be constant infraction of the law.

Recompense injury with kindness.

The wise man's freedom from grievance is because he will not regard grievances as such.

Of such were the pure and simple teachings of Lao Tzŭ. But it is upon the wondrous doctrine of Inaction that his claim to immortality is founded:—

Do nothing, and all things will be done.

I do nothing, and my people become good of their own accord.

Abandon wisdom and discard knowledge, and the people will be benefited an hundredfold.

The weak overcomes the strong, the soft overcomes the hard. All the world knows this; yet none can act up to it.

The softest things in the world override the hardest. That which has no substance enters where there is no fissure. And so I know that there is advantage in Inaction.

Such doctrines as these were, however, not likely to appeal with force to the sympathies of a practical people. In the sixth century B.C., before Lao Tzŭ's death, another Prophet arose. He taught his countrymen that duty to one's neighbour comprises the whole duty of man. Charitableness of heart, justice, sincerity, and fortitude,—sum up the ethics of Confucius. He knew nothing of a God, of a soul, of an unseen world. And he declared that the unknowable had better remain untouched.

Against these hard and worldly utterances, Chuang Tzŭ raised a powerful cry. The idealism of Lao Tzŭ had seized upon his poetic soul, and he determined to stem the tide of materialism in which men were being fast rolled to perdition.

He failed, of course. It was, indeed, too great a task to persuade the calculating Chinese nation that by doing nothing, all things would be done. But Chuang Tzŭ bequeathed to posterity a work which, by reason of its marvellous literary beauty, has always held a foremost place. It is also a work of much originality of thought. The writer, it is true, appears chiefly as a disciple insisting upon the principles of a Master. But he has contrived to extend the field, and carry his own speculations into regions never dreamt of by Lao Tzŭ.

It may here be mentioned that the historian Ssŭ-ma Ch'ien, already quoted, states in his notice of Lao Tzŭ that the latter left behind him a small volume in 5,000 and odd characters. Ssŭ-ma Ch'ien does not say, nor does he give the reader to understand, that he himself had ever seen the book in question. Nor does he even hint (see p. v.) that Chuang Tzŭ drew his inspiration from a book, but only from the "sayings" of Lao Tzŭ.

Confucius never mentions this book. Neither does Mencius, China's "Second Sage," who was born about one hundred years after the death of the First.

But all this is a trifle compared with the fact that Chuang Tzŭ himself never once alludes to such a book; although now, in this nineteenth century, there are some, happily few in number, who believe that we possess the actual work of Lao Tzŭ's pen. It is, perhaps, happier still that this small number cannot be said to include within it the name of a single native scholar of eminence. In fact, as far as I know, the whole range of Chinese literature yields but the name of one such individual who has ever believed in the genuineness of the so-called Tao-Tê-Ching.[11] Even he would probably have remained unknown to fame, had he not been brother to Su Tung-p'o.[12]

---

[11] The Canon of Tao, and of Tê, the exemplification thereof. See p.57. I have discussed the claims of this work at some length in The Remains of Lao Tzŭ: Hong Kong, 1886.

[12] The brilliant philosopher, statesman, poet, &c., of the Sung dynasty (A.D. 1036-1101).

Chuang Tzŭ, indeed, puts into the mouth of Lao Tzŭ sayings which are now found in the Tao-Tê-Ching, mixed up with a great many other similar sayings which are not to be found there. But he also puts sayings, which now appear in the Tao-Tê-Ching, into the mouth of Confucius (p. 125)! And even into the mouth of the Yellow Emperor (p. 127), whose date is some twenty centuries earlier than that of Lao Tzŭ himself!!

Two centuries before the Christian era, an attempt was made to destroy, with some exceptions, the whole of Chinese literature, in order that history might begin anew from the reign of the First Emperor of united China. The extent of the actual mischief done by this "Burning of the Books" has been greatly exaggerated. Still, the mere attempt at such a holocaust gave a fine chance to the scholars of the later Han dynasty (A.D. 25-221), who seem to have enjoyed nothing so much as forging, if not the whole, at any rate portions, of the works of ancient authors. Some one even produced a treatise under the name of Lieh Tzŭ, a philosopher mentioned by Chuang Tzŭ, not seeing that the individual in question was a creation of Chuang Tzŭ's brain!

And the Tao-Tê-Ching was undoubtedly pieced together somewhere about this period, from recorded sayings and conversations of Lao Tzŭ.[13]

Chuang Tzŭ's work has suffered in like manner. Several chapters are clearly spurious, and many episodes have been interpolated by feeble imitators of an inimitable style.

The text, as it now stands, consists of thirty-three chapters. These are a reduction from fifty-three, which appear to have been in existence in the fourth century A.D.[14] The following is the account given in the Imperial Catalogue of the first known edition:—

Chuang Tzŭ, with Commentary, in 10 books. By Kuo Hsiang of the Chin dynasty (A.D. 265-420).

The Shih-shuo-hsin-yü[15] *states that Kuo Hsiang stole his work from Hsiang Hsiu.*[16] *Subsequently, Hsiang Hsiu's edition was issued, and the two were in circulation together. Hsiang Hsiu's edition is now lost, while Kuo Hsiang's remains.*

Comparison with quotations from Hsiang Hsiu's work, as given in Chuang Tzŭ Explained, by Lu Tê-ming, shows conclusive evidence of plagiarism. Nevertheless, Kuo Hsiang contributed a certain amount of independent revision, making it impossible for us to regard the whole as from the hand of Hsiang Hsiu. Consequently, it now passes under the name of Kuo Hsiang.

---

[13] A curious parallelism will be found in Supernatural Religion, vol. i, p. 460:—
"No period in the history of the world ever produced so many spurious works as the first two or three centuries of our era. The name of every Apostle, or Christian teacher, not excepting that of the great Master, was freely attached to every description of religious forgery."
[14] On the authority of the I-wên-chih.
[15] A work of the fifth century A.D.
[16] Of the Han dynasty. Mayers puts him a little later, viz., A.D. 275.

Since Kuo Hsiang's time, numberless editions with ever-varying interpretations have been produced to delight and to confuse the student. Of these, I have chosen six, representative as nearly as possible of different schools of thought. Their editors are:—

1.—*Kuo Hsiang of the Chin dynasty. (a) As given in the Shih Tzŭ Ch'üan Shu, or Complete Works of the Ten Philosophers. (b) As edited by Tan Yüan-ch'un, of the Ming dynasty, with his own valuable notes.*
2.—*Lü Hui-ch'ing of the Sung dynasty.*
3.—*Lin Hsi-yi of the Sung dynasty.*
4.—*Wang Yü of the Sung dynasty. Son of the famous Wang An-shih.*
5.—*Hsing Tung, a Taoist priest of the Ming dynasty.*
6.—*Lin Hsi-chung, of the Ming and Ch'ing dynasties.*

Where there is a consensus of opinion, I have followed such interpretation without demur. But where opinions differ, I have not hesitated to accept that interpretation which seemed to me to be most in harmony with the general tenor of Chuang Tzŭ's philosophy. And where all commentators fail equally, as they sometimes do, to yield anything at all intelligible, I have then ventured to fall back upon what Chuang Tzŭ himself would have called the "light of nature." Always keeping steadily in view the grand precept of Lin Hsi-chung, that we should attempt to interpret Chuang Tzŭ neither according to Lao Tzŭ, nor according to Confucius, nor according to Buddha, but according to Chuang Tzŭ himself.

Of the thirty-three existing chapters, the first seven are called "inside" chapters, the next fifteen "outside," and the remaining eleven "miscellaneous."

The meaning of "inside" and "outside" is a matter of dispute. Some Chinese critics have understood these terms in the obvious sense of esoteric and exoteric. But it is simpler to believe with others that the titles of the first seven chapters are taken from the inside or subject-matter, while the outside chapters are so named because their titles are derived casually from words which happen to stand at the beginning or outside of each.

Compared with the "miscellaneous," these latter seem to have been classed together as elucidating a single principle in terms more easy of apprehension; while the "miscellaneous" chapters embrace several distinct trains of thought, and are altogether more abstruse. The arrangement is unscientific, and it was probably this which caused Su Tung-p'o to decide that division into chapters belongs to a later age. He regards chaps. xxix-xxxii as spurious, although Ssŭ-ma Ch'ien alludes to two of these as Chuang Tzŭ's work. It has indeed been held that the inside chapters alone (i-vii) are from Chuang Tzŭ's own pen. But most of the other chapters, exclusive of xxix-xxxi, contain unmistakable traces of a master hand. Ch. xvii, by virtue of an exquisite imagery, has earned for its author the affectionate sobriquet of "Chou of the Autumn Floods."

Chuang Tzŭ, it must be remembered, has been for centuries classed as a heterodox writer. His work was an effort of reaction against the materialism of Confucian teachings. And in the course of it he was anything but sparing of terms. Confucius is dealt with in language which no modern literate can approve. But the beauty and vigour of the language are facts admitted by all. He is constantly quoted in the great standard lexicon which passes under the name of K'ang Hsi.

But no acquaintance with the philosophy of Chuang Tzŭ would assist the candidate for honours at the competitive examinations which are the portals to official place and power. Consequently, Chuang Tzŭ is studied chiefly by older men, who have retired from office, or who have been disappointed in their career. Those too who are dominated by a religious craving for something better than mortality, find in his pages much agreeable solace against the troubles of this world, with an implied promise of another and a better world to come.

It has been publicly announced that translations of Lao Tzŭ and Chuang Tzŭ are to appear among the Sacred Books of the East.[17]

Now to include the Tao-Tê-Ching in such a series would be already a doubtful step. Apart from spuriousness, it can only by a severe stretch of courtesy be termed a "sacred book." It undoubtedly contains many of Lao Tzŭ's sayings, but it also undoubtedly contains much that Lao Tzŭ never said and never could have said. It illustrates rather that period when the pure Tao of Lao Tzŭ began to be corrupted by alchemistic research and gropings after the elixir of life. It was probably written up in self-defence against the encroachments of Buddhism, in those early days of religious struggle when China was first flooded with the "sacred books" of the West. It is not seriously recognised as the Canon of ancient Taoism. Among the Taoists of to-day, not one in ten thousand has more than heard its name. For modern Taoism is but a hybrid superstition,—a mixture of ancient nature-worship and Buddhistic ceremonial, with Tao as the style of the firm. Its teachings are farther removed from the Tao of Lao Tzŭ than Ritualism from the Christianity of Christ.

As to Chuang Tzŭ, his work can in no sense be called "sacred." Unless indeed we modify somewhat the accepted value of terms, and reckon the works of Aristotle among the "sacred" books of the Greeks. Chuang Tzŭ was scarcely the founder of a school. He was not a Prophet, as Lao Tzŭ was, nor can he fairly be said ever to have been regarded by genuine Taoists as such.

When, many centuries later, the light of Lao Tzŭ's real teachings had long since been obscured, then a foolish Emperor conferred upon Chuang Tzŭ's work the title of Holy Canon of Nan-hua.[18] But this was done solely to secure for the follies of the age the sanction of a great name. Not to mention that Lieh Tzŭ's alleged work, and many other similar forgeries have also been equally honoured. So that if works like these are to be included among the Sacred Books of the East, then China alone will be able to supply matter for translation for the next few centuries to come.

Partly of necessity, and partly to spare the general reader, I have relegated to a supplement all textual and critical notes involving the use of Chinese characters. This supplement will be issued as soon as possible

---

[17] The China Review, vol. xvi, p. 195.
[18] In A.D. 742.

after my return to China. It will not form an integral part of the present work, being intended merely to assist students of the language in verifying the renderings I have here seen fit to adopt. As a compromise I have supplied a kind of running commentary, introduced, in accordance with the Chinese system, into the body of the text. It is hoped that this will enable any one to understand the drift of Chuang Tzŭ's allusions, and to follow arguments which are usually subtle and oft-times obscure.

Only one previous attempt has been made to place Chuang Tzŭ in the hands of English readers.[19] In that case, the knowledge of the Chinese language possessed by the translator was altogether too elementary to justify such an attempt.[20]

HERBERT A. GILES

Note on the Philosophy of Chaps i-vii

By the Rev. AUBREY MOORE

Tutor of Keble and Magdalen Colleges, Oxford; Hon. Canon of Christ Church, &c.

The translator of Chuang Tzŭ has asked me to append a note on the philosophy of chs. i-vii. It is difficult to see how one who writes not only in ignorance of Chinese modes of thought, but with the preconceptions of Western philosophy, can really help much towards the understanding of an admittedly obscure system, involving terms and expressions on which Chinese scholars are not yet agreed. But an attempt to point out parallelisms of thought and reasoning between East and West may be of use in two ways. It may stimulate those who are really competent to understand both terms in the comparison to tell us where the parallelism is real and where it is only apparent; and it may help to accustom ordinary readers to look for and expect resemblances in systems in which an earlier age would have seen nothing but contrasts.

---

[19] The Divine Classic of Nan-hua. By Frederic Henry Balfour, F.R.G.S., Shanghai and London, 1881.
[20] One example will suffice. In ch. xxiii (see p. 141) there occurs a short sentence which means, "A one-legged man discards ornament, his exterior not being open to commendation."
Mr. Balfour translated this as follows:—"Servants will tear up a portrait, not liking to be confronted with its beauties and its defects."

There was a time when historians of Greek philosophy used to point out what were considered to be the characteristics of Greek thought, and then to put down to "Oriental influence" anything which did not at once agree with these characteristics. How and through what channels this "Oriental influence" was exercised, it was never easy to determine, nor was it always thought worthy of much discussion. In recent times, however, a greater knowledge of Eastern systems has familiarised us with much which, on the same principle, ought to be attributed to "Greek influence." And the result has been that we have learned to put aside theories of derivation, and to content ourselves with tracing the evolution of reason and of rational problems, and to expect parallelisms even where the circumstances are widely different.

One instance may be worth quoting in illustration. We used to be told that the Greek mind, in its speculation and its art, was characterised by its love of order, harmony, and symmetry, in contrast with the monstrous creations of the Oriental imagination, and the "colossal ugliness of the Pyramids"; and it was said with reason that the Aristotelian doctrine of "the mean" was the ripe fruit of the practical inquiries of the Greeks, and was the ethical counterpart of their artistic development. But in 1861 we were introduced by Dr. Legge to a Confucianist work, attributed to Tzŭ Tzŭ, grandson of Confucius and a contemporary of Socrates, and entitled The Doctrine of the Mean,[21] which is there represented as the true moral way in which the perfect man walks, while all else go beyond or fall short of it. Yet even those who discovered the doctrine of the Trinity in the Tâo-Tê-Ching have not, we believe, suggested that Aristotle had private access to the Li Chi.

We may then, without bringing any charge of piracy or plagiarism against either, point out some parallels between Chuang Tzŭ and a great Greek thinker.

Chuang Tzŭ's first chapter is mainly critical and destructive, pointing out the worthlessness of ordinary judgments, and the unreality of sense knowledge. The gigantic Rukh, at the height of 90,000 li, is a mere mote in the sunbeam. For size is relative. The cicada, which can just fly from tree to tree, laughs with the dove at the Rukh's high flight. For space also is relative. Compared with the mushroom of a day, P'êng Tsu is as old as Methuselah; but what is his age to that of the fabled tree, whose spring and autumn make up 16,000 years? Time, then, is relative too. And though men wonder at him who could "ride upon the wind and travel for many days," he is but a child to one who "roams through the realms of For-Ever."

This doctrine of "relativity," which is a commonplace in Greek as it is in modern philosophy, is made the basis, both in ancient and modern times, of two opposite conclusions. Either it is argued that all sense knowledge is relative, and sense is the only organ of knowledge, therefore real knowledge is impossible; or else the relativity of sense knowledge

---

[21] In 1885 this treatise was republished by Dr. Legge in its place as Bk. xxviii of the Lî Kî of Li Chi (Sacred Books of the East, vols. xxvii, xxviii), with a new title The State of Equilibrium and Harmony. But the parallelism with the Aristotelian doctrine is as obvious as ever.

leads men to draw a sharp contrast between sense and reason and to turn away from the outward in order to listen to the inward voice. The one alternative is scepticism, the other idealism. In Greek thought the earliest representatives of the former are the Sophists, of the latter Heracleitus.

There is no doubt to which side of the antithesis Chuang Tzǔ belongs. His exposure of false and superficial thinking looks at first like the destruction of knowledge. Even Socrates was called a Sophist because of his destructive criticism and his restless challenging of popular views. But Chuang Tzǔ has nothing of the sceptic in him. He is an idealist and a mystic, with all the idealist's hatred of a utilitarian system, and the mystic's contempt for a life of mere external activity. "The perfect man ignores self; the divine man ignores action; the true sage ignores reputation" (p. 2). The Emperor Yao would have abdicated in favour of a hermit, but the hermit replies that "reputation is but the shadow of reality," and will not exchange the real for the seeming. But greater than Yao and the hermit is the divine being who dwells on the mysterious mountain in a state of pure, passionless inaction.

For the sage, then, life means death to all that men think life, the life of seeming or reputation, of doing or action, of being or individual selfhood. This leads on to the "budget of paradoxes" in chap. II. As in the moral and active region we escape from the world and self, and are able to reverse and look down upon the world's judgments, so in the speculative region we get behind and beyond the contradictions of ordinary thinking, and of speech which stereotypes abstractions. The sage knows nothing of the distinction between subjective and objective. It exists only ex analogiâ hominis. "From the standpoint of Tao" all things are one. People "guided by the criteria of their own mind," see only the contradiction, the manifoldness, the difference; the sage sees the many disappearing in the One, in which subjective and objective, positive and negative, here and there, somewhere and nowhere, meet and blend. For him, "a beam and a pillar are identical. So are ugliness and beauty, greatness, wickedness, perverseness, and strangeness. Separation is the same as construction: construction is the same as destruction" (p. 9). The sage "blends everything into one harmonious whole, rejecting the comparison of this and that. Rank and precedence, which the vulgar prize, the sage stolidly ignores. The universe itself may pass away, but he will flourish still" (p. 13). "Were the ocean itself scorched up, he would not feel hot. Were the milky way frozen hard he would not feel cold. Were the mountains to be riven with thunder, and the great deep to be thrown up by storm, he would not tremble" (pp. 12-13).

> *Si fractus illabatur orbis,*
> *Impavidum ferient ruinæ.*

He is "embraced in the obliterating unity of God," and passing into the realm of the Infinite finds rest therein (p. 14).

It is impossible in reading this chapter on "The Identity of Contraries" not to be reminded of Heracleitus. The disparagement of sense knowledge, and the contempt for common views is indeed equally marked in Eleaticism, and there is much in Chuang Tzŭ which recalls Parmenides,[22] so far as the contrast between the way of truth and the way of error, the true belief in the One and the popular belief in the Many, is concerned. But it seems to me that the "One" of Chuang Tzŭ is not the dead Unit of Eleaticism, which resulted from the thinking away of differences, but the living Unity of Heracleitus, in which contraries co-exist. Heracleitus, indeed, seems to have been a man after Chuang Tzŭ's own heart, not only in his obscurity, which won for him the title of ὁ σκοτεινὸς, but in his indifference to worldly position, shown in the fact that, like the Emperor Yao, he abdicates in his brother's favour (Diog. Laert. ix. 1), and in his supercilious disregard for the learned like Hesiod and Pythagoras and Xenophanes and Hecataeus,[23] no less than for the common people[24] of his day.

"Listen," says Heracleitus, "not to me, but to reason, and confess the true wisdom that 'All things are One.'"[25] "All is One, the divided and the undivided, the begotten and the unbegotten, the mortal and the immortal, reason and eternity, father and son, God and justice."[26] "Cold is hot, heat is cold, that which is moist is parched, that which is dried up is wet."[27] "Good and evil are the same."[28] "Gods are mortal, men immortal: our life is their death, our death their life."[29] "Upward and downward are the same."[30] "The beginning and the end are one."[31] "Life and death, sleeping and waking, youth and age are identical."[32]

This is what reason tells the philosopher. "All is One." The world is a unity of opposing forces (παλίντροπος ἁρμονίη κόσμου ὅκωσπερ λύρας καὶ τόξου).[33] "Join together whole and not whole, agreeing and different, harmonious and discordant. Out of all comes one: out of one all."[34] "God is day-night, winter-summer, war-peace, repletion-want."[35] The very rhythm of nature is strife. War, which men hate and the poets would banish, "is the father and lord of all."[36] But "men are without understanding, they hear and hear not,"[37] or "they hear and understand not."[38] For they trust to their

---

[22] See the fragments in Ritter and Preller's *Hist. Phil. Græc.* § 93 and § 94 A. B. Seventh edition.
[23] Heracl. Eph. Rell. Bywater, xvi.
[24] ὀχλολοίδορος Ἡράκλειτος Timon ap. Diog. Laert. ix. i.
[25] Οὐκ ἐμεῦ ἀλλὰ τοῦ λόγου ἀκουσάντας ὁμολογέειν σοφόν ἐστι ἓν πάντα εἶναι. Heracl. Eph. Rell. i.
[26] Hippolytus Ref. haer. ix. 9.
[27] Heracl. Eph. Rell. xxxix.
[28] Ibid., lvii.
[29] Ibid., lxvii.
[30] Ibid., lxix.
[31] Ibid., lxx.
[32] Ibid., lxxviii.
[33] Ibid., xlv.
[34] Ibid., lix.
[35] Ibid., xxxvi.
[36] Ibid., xliv.
[37] Ibid., v.
[38] Heracl. Eph. Rell. iv.

senses, which are "false witnesses."[39] They see the contradictions, but know not that "the different is at unity with itself."[40] They cannot see the "hidden harmony, which is greater than the harmony which is seen."[41] For they live in the external, the commonplace, the relative, and never rise above the life of the senses. "The sow loves the mire."[42] "The ass prefers fodder to gold."[43] And men love their "private conceits" instead of clinging to the universal reason which orders all things,[44] and which even the sun obeys.[45]

Of the fragments which remain to us of Heracleitus, the greater number belong to the region of logic and metaphysics, while Chuang Tzŭ devotes much space to the more practical side of the question. He not only ridicules those who trust their senses, or measure by utilitarian standards, or judge by the outward appearance;—he teaches them how to pass from the seeming to the true. The wonderful carver, who could cut where the natural joints are,[46] is one who sees not with the eye of sense but with his mind. When he is in doubt he "falls back upon eternal principles"; for he is "devoted to Tao" (chap. iii). There is something of humour, as well as much of truth, in the rebuke which Confucius, speaking pro hâc vice as a disciple of Lao Tzŭ, administers to his self-confident follower who wanted to "be of use." "Cultivate fasting;—not bodily fasting, but the fasting of the heart." Tao can only abide in the life which has got rid of self. So the Duke of Shê is reminded that there is something higher than duty,[47] viz., destiny, the state, that is, in which conscious obedience has given way to that which is instinctive and automatic. The parable of the trees (p. 23), with its result in the survival of the good-for-nothing, is again a reversal of popular outside judgments. For as the first part of the chapter had taught the uselessness of trying to be useful, so the last part teaches the usefulness of being useless. And the same thought is carried on in the next chapter, which deals with the reversal of common opinion as to persons. Its motto is:—Judge not by the appearance. Virtue must prevail and outward form be forgotten. The loathsome leper Ai T'ai To is made Prime Minister by the wise Duke Ai. The mutilated criminal is judged by Lao Tzŭ to be a greater man than Confucius. For the criminal is mutilated in body by man, while Confucius, though men know it not, by the judgment of God is πεπηρωμένος πρὸς ἀρετήν.

---

[39] Ibid., xlv.
[40] Ibid., xlvii.
[41] Ibid., iii.
[42] Ibid., liv., and notes.
[43] Ibid., li.
[44] Ibid., xci, xix.
[45] Ibid., xxix.
[46] Cf. Plat. Phaedr. 265: κατ' ἄρθρα ᾗ πέφυκεν καὶ μὴ ἐπιχειρεῖν καταγνύναι μέρος μηδὲν κακοῦ μαγείρου τρόπῳ χρώμενος.
[47] Cf. Herbert Spencer's well-known paradox,—"The sense of duty or moral obligation is transitory, and will diminish as fast as moralisation increases."—Data of Ethics, p. 127.

This protest of Chuang Tzŭ against externality, and judging only by the outward appearance, might easily be translated into Christian language. For Christianity also teaches inwardness, and, in common with all idealism, resents the delimitation of human life and knowledge to "the things which are seen." In its opposition to a mere practical system like Confucianism, Taoism must have appealed to those deeper instincts of humanity to which Buddhism appealed some centuries later. In practice, Confucianism was limited to the finite. Action, effort, benevolence, unselfishness,—all these have a place in it, and their theatre is the world as we know it. Its last word is worldly wisdom; not selfishness, but an enlarged prudentialism. To the Taoist such a system savours of "the rudiments of the world." Its "charity and duty," its "ceremonies and music," are the "Touch not, taste not, handle not," of an ephemeral state of being, and perish in the using. And the sage seeks for the Absolute, the Infinite, the Eternal. He seeks to attain to Tao.

It is here that we reach (in chaps. vi, vii) what properly constitutes the mysticism of Chuang Tzŭ. Heracleitus is not a mystic, though he is the founder of a long line, which through Plato, and Dionysius the Areopagite and John the Scot in the ninth century, and Meister Eckhart in the thirteenth, and Jacob Böhme in the sixteenth, reaches down to Hegel. Heracleitus despises the world and shuns it; but he has not yet made flight from the world a dogma. Even Plato, when in a well-known passage in the Theaetetus,[48] he counsels flight from the present state of things, explains that he means only "flee from evil and become like God." Still less has Heracleitus got so far as to aim at self-absorption in God. In Greek thought the attempt to get rid of consciousness, and to become the unconscious vehicle of a higher illumination, is unknown till the time of Philo. Yet this is the teaching of Chuang Tzŭ. "The true sage takes his refuge in God, and learns that there is no distinction between subject and object. This is the very axis of Tao" (p. 14). Abstraction from self, then, is the road which leads to Tao (chap. vi). The pure of old did not love life and hate death. They were content to be passive vehicles of Tao. They had reached the state of sublime indifference, they had become "oblivious of their own existence." Everything in them was spontaneous; nothing the result of effort. "They made no plans; therefore failing, they had no cause for regret; succeeding, no cause for congratulation" (p. 31). "They cheerfully played their allotted parts, waiting patiently for the end." They were free, for they were in perfect harmony with creation (p. 32). For them One and not One are One; God and Man. For they had attained to Tao, and Tao is greater than God. "Before heaven and earth were, Tao was. It has existed without change from all time. Spiritual beings draw their spirituality therefrom; while the universe became what we see it now. To Tao the zenith is not high, nor the nadir low; no point of time is long ago, nor by lapse of ages has it grown old" (p. 35). The great legislators obtained TAO, and laid

---

[48] Theaet. 176. A. διὸ καὶ πειρᾶσθαι χρὴ ἐνθένδε ἐκεῖσε φεύγειν ὅ τι τάχιστα. φυγὴ δὲ ὁμοίωσις Θεῷ κατὰ τὸ δυνατόν. ὁμοίωσις δὲ δίκαιον καὶ ὅσιον μετὰ φρονήσεως γενέσθαι.

down eternal principles. The sun and moon, and the Great Bear are kept in their courses by Tao.

"*Thou dost preserve the stars from wrong;
And the most ancient heavens, through thee, are fresh and strong.*"

He who would attain to Tao must get rid of the thought of "charity and duty," of "music and ceremonies," of body and mind. The flowers and the birds do not toil, they simply live. That is Tao. And for man a state of indifference and calm, the ἀταραξία not of the sceptic but of the mystic, a passive reflecting of the Eternal, is the ideal end. "The perfect man employs his mind as a mirror. It grasps nothing, it refuses nothing. It receives but does not keep. And thus he can triumph over matter without injury to himself." (See p. 45.)

It would of course be presumption to attempt to assign a meaning to Tao, and still more to discover an equivalent in Western thought. But it may be lawful to say that Heraclitus often speaks of Λόγος as Chuang Tzŭ speaks of Tao. It is Necessity (ἀνάγκη), or Fate (εἱμαρμένη), or Mind (γνώμη), or Justice (Δικὴ). In nature it appears as balance and equipoise; in the State as Law; in man as the universal Reason, which is in him but not of him. Sometimes it is identified with the mysterious name of Zeus, which may not be uttered;[49] sometimes like the Ἀνάγκη of the Greek poets, it is supreme over gods and men. If it is hard to say what is the relation of Tao to God, it is not less hard to define the relation of Λόγος to Zeus. To speak of Chuang Tzŭ and Heraclitus as pantheists is only to say that, so far as we can translate their language into ours, that name seems less inappropriate than Theist or Deist. But it is doubtful whether the distinction between Pantheism and Theism would have been intelligible to either philosopher, and certain that if they could have understood it, they would have denied to it reality. Both held the immanence of the Eternal Principle in all that is. Both taught that the soul is an emanation from the Divine, and both, though in very different degrees, seem to teach that a life is perfect in proportion as it becomes one with that from which it came, and loses what is individual in it.

In Chuang Tzŭ, as in all mystics, there is an element of antinomianism. That "good and evil are the same," may contain a deep truth for the sage, but "take no heed of time, nor of right and wrong" (p. 1) is, to say the least, dangerous teaching for the masses. The mystic's utterances will not bear translation into the language of the world, and to take them au pied de la lettre can hardly fail to produce disastrous results. This is why antinomianism always dogs the heels of mysticism. And this may perhaps help to explain the debased Taoism of to-day. But of this I know nothing.

It would be interesting to know whether in the undisputed utterances of Lao Tzŭ (i. e. putting on one side the Tâo-Tê-Ching),

---

[49] Heracl. Eph. Rell. lxv.

Quietism and the glorification of Inaction are as prominent as they are in Chuang Tzŭ. One would be prepared à priori to find that they are not. Lao Tzŭ was born at the end of the seventh century B.C., and was, therefore, some fifty years older than Confucius, with whom in 517 B.C., he is said to have had an interview.[50] By the time of Chuang Tzŭ, who was possibly contemporary with Mencius, and therefore some two or three centuries after Lao Tzŭ, Confucianism had become to some extent the established religion of China, and Taoism, like Republicanism in the days of the Roman Empire, became a mere opposition de salon. Under such circumstances any elements of mysticism latent in Lao Tzŭ's system would develop rapidly. And the antagonism between the representatives of Lao Tzŭ and Confucius would proportionately increase. But philosophy does not become mystical and take refuge in flight until it abandons all hope of converting the world. When effort is useless, the mind idealises Inaction, and seeks a metaphysical basis for it. For mysticism and scepticism flourish in the same atmosphere though in different soils, both, though in different ways, implying the abandonment of the rational problem. The Sceptic, the Agnostic or Positivist of to-day, declares it insoluble, and settles down content to take things as they are; the mystic retires into himself, and dreams of a state of being which is the obverse of the world of fact.

The triumph of Confucianism in the centuries which intervened between Lao Tzŭ and Chuang Tzŭ would account for the antagonism between Taoism and Confucianism as we find it. But it fails to account for the way in which Confucius is sometimes represented as playing into the hands of Taoism. On p. 39 f. n. the translator explains it as a literary coup de main. Dr. Chalmers, quoted by Dr. Legge,[51] says that both Chuang Tzŭ and Lieh Tzŭ introduced Confucius into their writings "as the lords of the Philistines did the captive Samson on their festive occasions, 'to make sport for them.'" But there is not a hint of this given in the text, though throughout one long chapter (chap. iv) we find Confucius giving a Taoist refutation of Confucianist doctrines when defended by his own pupil Yen Hui. It might seem like an attempt to draw a distinction between Confucius and Confucianism, though elsewhere Confucius is ridiculed as wanting in sense.

May not the explanation be as follows?—

(i.) *Lao Tzŭ and Confucius were probably much nearer to one another philosophically than the Taoism of Chuang Tzŭ and the Confucianism of Mencius. The passages in which Confucius talks Taoism would, on this hypothesis, represent a traditional survival of their real relations to one another. The episode of Confucius' visit to Lao Tzŭ "to ask about the Tao," would, whether it records a fact or not, tend in the same direction.*

(ii.) *From the first we may assume that the one took an ideal, the other a practical and utilitarian view of Tao "the Way"; Confucius finding*

---

[50] Chuang Tzŭ, chap. xiv, p. 83.
[51] Encycl. Met., Art. "Lao Tzŭ."

it in social duties and the work of practical life, Lao Tzŭ in the hidden and the inward, the "interior life," as Christian mystics would call it. Thus the historian Ssŭ-ma Ch'ien[52] says, "Lao Tzŭ cultivated the Tao and virtue, his chief aim in his studies being how to keep himself concealed and unknown. Seeing the decay of the dynasty he withdrew himself out of sight, and no one knows where he died."

(iii.) The divergence between the two views, the ideal and the actual, the mystical and the practical, would increase with time, each intensifying the other by opposition and reaction, until the practical won its way to security, and the mystical got left out in the cold, perhaps persecuted, certainly suspected, and treated as heterodox, and naturally retaliating by scornful criticism of the dominant view. When this stage is reached, Mencius regards Lao Tzŭ as a heresiarch, while Chuang Tzŭ often treats Confucius with contempt and ridicule. For "the Way that is walked upon is not the Way," and "the Tao which shines forth is not Tao" (p. 12). But Confucianism being "established," the Taoists are now "dissenters," and not being strong enough to disestablish Confucianism become more and more mystical, and content themselves with a policy of protest.

If there is little direct evidence for this theory as to the relations of Taoism and Confucianism, there is a curious parallel in Western thought. When Plato was known only in a neo-Platonic disguise, and Aristotle judged by the Organon, it was possible for partisans to represent the two philosophers as typical opposites, and to assume that "every one is born a Platonist or an Aristotelian," forgetting that Aristotle was Plato's pupil, and both were followers of Socrates. Later on, when Aristotelianism became "established" as the Christian philosophy, Platonism, which survived in the more mystical schoolmen, fell under suspicion, and not unfrequently justified the suspicion by developing in the direction of Pantheism. It was not till the thirteenth century that the world appealed from Platonists and Aristotelians to Plato and Aristotle, and discovered that the divergent streams flowed from neighbouring springs. Such an appeal, it is to be feared, is hardly possible in the case of Lao Tzŭ and Confucius, especially as the authenticity of the Tao-Tê-Ching is still in controversy among Sinologues.

My object, however, in this note, which has grown out of all proportion, was not to suggest a theory as to the possible relations of Lao Tzŭ and Confucius, but to point out what seemed to be a remarkable parallel between the teaching of Chuang Tzŭ and Heracleitus. In doing this I have accepted Mr. Giles's translation as an ultimate fact, for the simple reason that I do not know a single Chinese character. So far, therefore, as the translation prejudices or prejudges questions of Chinese scholarship, I must leave the defence to the translator. It is also possible, and more than possible, that my Western preconceptions may have biassed my judgment

---

[52] Quoted by Dr. Legge, loc. cit.

of Chuang Tzŭ's philosophical teaching. Recent attempts[53] to draw a parallel between the life of Gautama and the life of Christ have shown how easy it is unconsciously to read between the lines, and find parallelisms where they do not exist. If I have been guilty in the same way, then, with Socrates in the Republic, I say, "I can but suffer the penalty of ignorance; and that penalty is, to be taught by those who know."

A. L. M.
Chuang Tzŭ

---

[53] E.g. Mr. Edwin Arnold's Light of Asia, and still more Professor Seydel's Das Evangelium von Jesu in seinen Verhältnissen zu Buddha-Sage and Buddha-Lehre. On the other side of the question, cf. Dr. Kellogg's The Light of Asia and The Light of the World. London, 1885. And an article in the Nineteenth Century for July, 1888, on Buddhism, by the Bishop of Colombo.

CHAPTER I

Transcendental Bliss

Argument:—Space infinite—Time infinite—Relativity of magnitudes, physical and moral—The magnitude absolute—Usefulness as a test of value—The usefulness of the useless.

In the northern ocean there is a fish, called the Leviathan, many thousand li in size. This leviathan changes into a bird, called the Rukh, whose back is many thousand li in breadth. With a mighty effort it rises, and its wings obscure the sky like clouds.

At the equinox, this bird prepares to start for the southern ocean, the Celestial Lake. And in the Record of Marvels we read that when the rukh flies southwards, the water is smitten for a space of three thousand li around, while the bird itself mounts upon a typhoon to a height of ninety thousand li, for a flight of six months' duration.

Just so are the motes in a sunbeam blown aloft by God. For whether the blue of the sky is its real colour, or only the result of distance without end, the effect to the bird looking down would be just the same as to the motes.

Distance being relative. The rukh at an altitude of 90,000 li (three li to a mile) is no more than a mote in a sunbeam a few feet from the ground.

If there is not sufficient depth, water will not float large ships. Upset a cupful into a small hole, and a mustard-seed will be your boat. Try to float the cup, and it will stick, from the disproportion between water and vessel.

So with air. If there is not a sufficient depth, it cannot support large birds. And for this bird a depth of ninety thousand li is necessary; and then, with nothing save the clear sky above, and no obstacle in the way, it starts upon its journey to the south.

A cicada laughed, and said to a young dove, "Now, when I fly with all my might, 'tis as much as I can do to get from tree to tree. And sometimes I do not reach, but fall to the ground midway. What then can be the use of going up ninety thousand li in order to start for the south?"

He who goes to Mang-ts'ang,
A short distance into the country.
taking three meals with him, comes back with his stomach as full as when he started. But he who travels a hundred li must grind flour enough for a night's halt. And he who travels a thousand li must supply himself with provisions for three months. Those two little creatures,—what should they know? Small knowledge has not the compass of great knowledge any more than a short year has the length of a long year.

How can we tell that this is so? The mushroom of a morning knows not the alternation of day and night. The chrysalis knows not the alternation of spring and autumn. Theirs are short years.

But in the State of Ch'u there is a tortoise whose spring and autumn are each of five hundred years' duration. And in former days there was a large tree which had a spring and autumn each of eight thousand years' duration. Yet, P'êng Tsu

The Methusaleh of China. His age has not been agreed upon by Chinese writers, but the lowest computation gives him a life of eight hundred years.

is still, alas! an object of envy to all.

It was on this very subject that the Emperor T'ang

B.C. 1766.

spoke to Chi, as follows:—"At the barren north there is a great sea, the Celestial Lake. In it there is a fish, several thousand li in breadth, and I know not how many in length. It is called the Leviathan. There is also a bird, called the Rukh, with a back like Mount T'ai,

China's most famous mountain, situated in the province of Shantung.

and wings like clouds across the sky. Upon a typhoon it soars up to a height of ninety thousand li, beyond the clouds and atmosphere, with only the clear sky above it. And then it directs its flight towards the south pole.

"A quail laughed, and said: Pray, what may that creature be going to do? I rise but a few yards in the air, and settle again after flying around among the reeds. That is the most I can manage. Now, where ever can this creature be going to?"

The repetition of this story, coupled with its quotation from the Record of Marvels, is considered to give an air of authenticity to Chuang Tzŭ's illustration, which the reader might otherwise suppose to be of his own invention.

Such, indeed, is the difference between small and great. Take, for instance, a man who creditably fills some small office, or who is a pattern of virtue in his neighbourhood, or who influences his prince to right government of the State,—his opinion of himself will be much the same as that quail's. The philosopher Yung laughs at such a one. He, if the whole world flattered him, would not be affected thereby, nor if the whole world blamed him would he lose his faith in himself. For Yung can distinguish between the intrinsic and the extrinsic, between honour and shame,—and such men are rare in their generation. But even he has not established himself.

Beyond the limits of an external world. His achievements are after all only of the earth, earthy.

There was Lieh Tzŭ again.

A personage of whom nothing is really known. He is considered by the best authorities to have been of Chuang Tzŭ's own creation. This, however, did not prevent some enterprising scholar, probably of the Han dynasty, from discovering a treatise which still passes under Lieh Tzŭ's name.

He could ride upon the wind, and travel whithersoever he wished, staying away as long as fifteen days. Among mortals who attain happiness, such a man is rare. Yet although Lieh Tzŭ was able to dispense with walking, he was still dependent upon something.

Sc. the wind.

But had he been charioted upon the eternal fitness of Heaven and Earth, driving before him the elements as his team while roaming through the realms of For-Ever,—upon what, then, would he have had to depend?

That is, nourished upon the doctrines of inaction, the continuity of life and death, etc., which will be dealt with in later chapters.

Thus it has been said, "The perfect man ignores self; the divine man ignores action; the true Sage ignores reputation."

His—for the three are one—is a bliss "beyond all that the minstrel has told." Material existences melt into thin air; worldly joys and sorrows cease for him who passes thus into the everlasting enjoyment of a transcendental peace.

The Emperor Yao

B.C. 2356. His reign, coupled with that of Shun who succeeded him, may be regarded as the Golden Age of China's history. See p. 4.

wished to abdicate in favour of Hsü Yu,

A worthy hermit.

saying, "If, when the sun and moon are shining, you persist in lighting a torch, is not that a misapplication of fire? If, when the rainy season is at its height, you still continue to water the ground, is not this a waste of labour? Now, sir, do you assume the reins of government, and the empire will be at peace. I am but a dead body, conscious of my own deficiency. I beg you will ascend the throne."

"Ever since you, sire, have directed the administration," replied Hsü Yu, "the empire has enjoyed tranquillity. Supposing, therefore, that I were to take your place now, should I gain any reputation thereby? Besides, reputation is but the shadow of reality; and should I trouble myself about the shadow? The tit, building its nest in the mighty forest, occupies but a single twig. The tapir slakes its thirst from the river, but drinks enough only to fill its belly. To you, sire, belongs the reputation: the empire has no need for me. If a cook is unable to dress his funeral sacrifices, the boy who impersonates the corpse may not step over the wines and meats and do it for him."

This illustrates rejection of reputation by the true Sage. See ch. vii.

Chien Wu said to Lien Shu,

Both fictitious personages.

"I heard Chieh Yü utter something unjustifiably extravagant and without either rhyme or reason.

This was an individual, named Lu T'ung, who feigned madness in order to escape an official career. For his interview with Confucius, see ch. iv, ad fin.

I was greatly startled at what he said, for it seemed to me boundless as the Milky Way, though very improbable and removed from the experiences of mortals."

"What was it?" asked Lien Shu.

"He declared," replied Chien Wu, "that on the Miao-ku-shê mountain

Which is as fabulous as the story.
there lives a divine man whose flesh is like ice or snow, whose demeanour is that of a virgin, who eats no fruit of the earth, but lives on air and dew, and who, riding on clouds with flying dragons for his team, roams beyond the limits of mortality. This being is absolutely inert. Yet he wards off corruption from all things, and causes the crops to thrive. Now I call that nonsense, and do not believe it."

"Well," answered Lien Shu, "you don't ask a blind man's opinion of a picture, nor do you invite a deaf man to a concert. And blindness and deafness are not physical only. There is blindness and deafness of the mind, diseases from which I fear you yourself are suffering. The good influence of that man fills all creation. Yet because a paltry generation cries for reform, you would have him condescend to the details of an empire!

Not seeing that the greater contains the less.
"Objective existences cannot harm him. In a flood which reached to the sky, he would not be drowned. In a drought, though metals ran liquid and mountains were scorched up, he would not be hot. Out of his very dust and siftings you might fashion two such men as Yao and Shun. And you would have him occupy himself with objectives!"

Illustrating the inaction of the divine man.
A man of the Sung State carried some sacrificial caps into the Yüeh State, for sale. But the men of Yüeh used to cut off their hair and paint their bodies, so that they had no use for such things. And so, when the Emperor Yao, the ruler of all under heaven and pacificator of all within the shores of ocean, paid a visit to the four sages of the Miao-ku-shê mountain, on returning to his capital at Fên-yang, the empire existed for him no more.

This illustrates the rejection of self by the perfect man. Yao had his eyes opened to the hollowness and uselessness of all mortal possessions. He ceased, therefore, to think any more of himself, and per consequens of the empire.

Hui Tzŭ

A celebrated schoolman, contemporary with and antagonistic to Chuang Tzŭ. For an account of his theories, see ch. xxxiii.
said to Chuang Tzŭ, "The Prince of Wei gave me a seed of a large-sized kind of gourd. I planted it, and it bore a fruit as big as a five-bushel measure. Now had I used this for holding liquids, it would have been too heavy to lift; and had I cut it in half for ladles, the ladles would have been ill adapted for such purpose. It was uselessly large, so I broke it up."

"Sir," replied Chuang Tzŭ, "it was rather you who did not know how to use large things. There was a man of Sung who had a recipe for salve for chapped hands, his family having been silk-washers for generations. Well, a stranger who had heard of it, came and offered him 100 oz. of silver for this recipe; whereupon he called together his clansmen and said, 'We have never made much money by silk-washing. Now, we can make 100 oz. in a single day. Let the stranger have the recipe.'

"So the stranger got it, and went and informed the Prince of Wu who was just then at war with the Yüeh State. Accordingly, the Prince used it in a naval battle fought at the beginning of winter with the Yüeh State, the result being that the latter was totally defeated.

They suffered from chapped hands, while their rivals of the Wu State were protected by their patent salve.

The stranger was rewarded with territory and a title. Thus, while the efficacy of the salve to cure chapped hands was in both cases the same, its application was different. Here, it secured a title; there, a capacity for washing silk.

"Now as to your five-bushel gourd, why did you not make a boat of it, and float about over river and lake? You could not then have complained of its not holding anything! But I fear you are rather woolly inside."

Like it. This, of course, is a sneer. Hui Tzŭ could not see that the greatness of a thing depends upon the greatness of its application.

Hui Tzŭ said to Chuang Tzŭ, "Sir, I have a large tree, of a worthless kind. Its trunk is so irregular and knotty that it cannot be measured out for planks; while its branches are so twisted as to admit of no geometrical subdivision whatever. It stands by the roadside, but no carpenter will look at it. And your words, sir, are like that tree;—big and useless, not wanted by anybody."

"Sir," rejoined Chuang Tzŭ, "have you never seen a wild cat, crouching down in wait for its prey? Right and left it springs from bough to bough, high and low alike,—until perchance it gets caught in a trap or dies in a snare. On the other hand, there is the yak with its great huge body. It is big enough in all conscience, but it cannot catch mice.

The adaptability of a thing is oft-times its bane. The inability of the yak to catch mice saves it from the snare which is fatal to the wild cat.

"Now if you have a big tree and are at a loss what to do with it, why not plant it in the domain of non-existence,

Beyond the limits of our external world. Referring to the conditions of mental abstraction in which alone true happiness is to be found.

whither you might betake yourself to inaction by its side, to blissful repose beneath its shade?

"Why does the horizon hold me fast, with my joy and grief in this centre?"—Emerson.

There it would be safe from the axe and from all other injury; for being of no use to others, itself would be free from harm."

Illustrating the advantage of being useless. That which is small and useful is thus shown to be inferior to that which is large and useless.

CHAPTER II

The Identity of Contraries

> *Argument:—Contraries spring from our subjective individuality—Identity of subjective and objective—The centre where all distinctions are merged in One—How to reach this point—Speech an obstacle—The negative state—Light out of darkness—Illustrations.*

Tzŭ Ch'i of Nan-kuo sat leaning on a table. Looking up to heaven, he sighed and became absent, as though soul and body had parted.

Yen Ch'êng Tzŭ Yu, who was standing by him, exclaimed, "What are you thinking about that your body should become thus like dry wood, your mind like dead ashes? Surely the man now leaning on the table is not he who was here just now."

"My friend," replied Tzŭ Ch'i, "your question is apposite. To-day I have buried myself.... Do you understand?... Ah! perhaps you only know the music of Man, and not that of Earth. Or even if you have heard the music of Earth, you have not heard the music of Heaven."

"Pray explain," said Tzŭ Yu.

"The breath of the universe," continued Tzŭ Ch'i, "is called wind. At times, it is inactive. But when active, every aperture resounds to the blast. Have you never listened to its growing roar?

"Caves and dells of hill and forest, hollows in huge trees of many a span in girth;—these are like nostrils, like mouths, like ears, like beam-sockets, like goblets, like mortars, like ditches, like bogs. And the wind goes rushing through them, sniffing, snoring, singing, soughing, puffing, purling, whistling, whirring, now shrilly treble, now deeply bass, now soft, now loud; until, with a lull, silence reigns supreme. Have you never witnessed among the trees such a disturbance as this?"

"Well, then," enquired Tzŭ Yu, "since the music of earth consists of nothing more than holes, and the music of man of pipes and flutes,—of what consists the music of Heaven?"

"The effect of the wind upon these various apertures," replied Tzŭ Ch'i, "is not uniform. But what is it that gives to each the individuality, to all the potentiality, of sound?

"Great knowledge embraces the whole:

Sees both "the upper and under side of the medal of Jove" at once.

small knowledge, a part only. Great speech is universal:

Speech, according to Chuang Tzŭ's ideal, always covers the whole ground in question, leaving no room for positive and negative to appear in antagonism.

small speech is particular.

"For whether when the mind is locked in sleep or whether when in waking hours the body is released, we are subject to daily mental perturbations,—indecision, want of penetration, concealment, fretting fear, and trembling terror. Now like a javelin the mind flies forth, the arbiter of right and wrong.

Thus recognising contraries.

Now like a solemn covenanter it remains firm, the guardian of rights secured.

Adhering to an opinion formed.

Then, as under autumn and winter's blight, comes gradual decay, a passing away, like the flow of water, never to return. Finally, the block when all is choked up like an old drain,—the failing mind which shall not see light again.

"Joy and anger, sorrow and happiness, caution and remorse, come upon us by turns, with ever-changing mood. They come like music from hollowness, like mushrooms from damp. Daily and nightly they alternate within us, but we cannot tell whence they spring. Can we then hope in a moment to lay our finger upon their very Cause?

"But for these emotions I should not be. But for me, they would have no scope. So far we can go; but we do not know what it is that brings them into play. 'Twould seem to be a soul; but the clue to its existence is wanting. That such a Power operates, is credible enough, though we cannot see its form. It has functions without form.

As will be gathered later on, Chuang Tzŭ conceives of the soul as an emanation from God, passing to and from this earth through the portals of Life and Death.

"Take the human body with all its manifold divisions. Which part of it does a man love best? Does he not cherish all equally, or has he a preference? Do not all equally serve him? And do these servitors then govern themselves, or are they subdivided into rulers and subjects? Surely there is some soul which sways them all.

"But whether or not we ascertain what are the functions of this soul, it matters but little to the soul itself. For coming into existence with this mortal coil of mine, with the exhaustion of this mortal coil its mandate will also be exhausted. To be harassed by the wear and tear of life, and to pass rapidly through it without possibility of arresting one's course,—is not this pitiful indeed? To labour without ceasing, and then, without living to enjoy the fruit, worn out, to depart, suddenly, one knows not whither,—is not that a just cause for grief?

"What advantage is there in what men call not dying? The body decomposes, and the mind goes with it. This is our real cause for sorrow. Can the world be so dull as not to see this? Or is it I alone who am dull, and others not so?

"If we are to be guided by the criteria of our own minds, who shall be without a guide?

The mind should be a tabula rasa, free from all judgments or opinions of its own as to the external world, and ready only to accept things as they are, not as they appear to be.

What need to know of the alternations of passion,

As above described.

when the mind thus affords scope to itself?—verily even the minds of fools! Whereas, for a mind without criteria

As it should be.
to admit the idea of contraries, is like saying, I went to Yüeh to-day, and got there yesterday.
One of Hui Tzŭ's paradoxes. See ch. xxxiii.
Or, like placing nowhere somewhere,—topography which even the Great Yü
The famous engineer of antiquity (B.C. 2205), who drained the empire of a vast body of water and arranged its subdivision into nine provinces.
would fail to understand; how much more I?

"Speech is not mere breath. It is differentiated by meaning. Take away that, and you cannot say whether it is speech or not. Can you even distinguish it from the chirping of young birds?

"But how can Tao be so obscured that we speak of it as true and false? And how can speech be so obscured that it admits the idea of contraries? How can Tao go away and yet not remain?
Being omnipresent.
How can speech exist and yet be impossible?
See p. 6.
"Tao is obscured by our want of grasp. Speech is obscured by the gloss of this world.
I.e. by the one-sided meanings attached to words and phrases.
Hence the affirmatives and negatives of the Confucian and Mihist schools,
Mih Tzŭ was a philosopher of the fourth century B.C., who propounded various theories which were vigorously attacked by the Confucianists under Mencius. We shall hear more of him by-and-by.
each denying what the other affirmed and affirming what the other denied. But he who would reconcile affirmative with negative and negative with affirmative,
The "union of impossibilities," which Emerson credits to Plato alone.
must do so by the light of nature.
I.e. Have no established mental criteria, and thus see all things as ONE.

"There is nothing which is not objective: there is nothing which is not subjective. But it is impossible to start from the objective. Only from subjective knowledge is it possible to proceed to objective knowledge. Hence it has been said,
By Hui Tzŭ.
'The objective emanates from the subjective; the subjective is consequent upon the objective. This is the Alternation Theory.' Nevertheless, when one is born, the other dies. When one is possible, the other is impossible. When one is affirmative the other is negative. Which being the case, the true sage rejects all distinctions of this and that. He takes his refuge in God, and places himself in subjective relation with all things.
It was to this end that Tzŭ Ch'i "buried himself."

"And inasmuch as the subjective is also objective, and the objective also subjective, and as the contraries under each are indistinguishably blended, does it not become impossible for us to say whether subjective and objective really exist at all?

What is positive under the one will be negative under the other. Yet as subjective and objective are really one and the same, their positives and negatives must also be one and the same.

It is as though we were to view them through a kind of mental Pseudoscope, by which means each would appear to be the other.

"When subjective and objective are both without their correlates, that is the very axis of Tao. And when that axis passes through the centre at which all Infinities converge, positive and negative alike blend into an infinite One. Hence it has been said that there is nothing like the light of nature.

Probably an allusion to Lao Tzŭ's "Use the light that is within you to revert to your natural clearness of sight." We should then be able to view things in their true light. See Tao-Tê-Ching, ch. lii., and The Remains of Lao Tzŭ, p. 34.

"To take a finger in illustration of a finger not being a finger is not so good as to take something which is not a finger. To take a horse in illustration of a horse not being a horse is not so good as to take something which is not a horse.

"So with the universe and all that in it is. These things are but fingers and horses in this sense. The possible is possible: the impossible is impossible. Tao operates, and given results follow. Things receive names and are what they are. They achieve this by their natural affinity for what they are and their natural antagonism to what they are not. For all things have their own particular constitutions and potentialities. Nothing can exist without these.

These last few sentences are repeated in ch. xxvii. ad init.

"We can never know anything but phenomena. Things are what they are, and their consequences will be what they will be."—J. S. Mill.

"Therefore it is that, viewed from the standpoint of Tao, a beam and a pillar are identical.

The horizontal with the vertical.

So are ugliness and beauty, greatness, wickedness, perverseness, and strangeness. Separation is the same as construction: construction is the same as destruction. Nothing is subject either to construction or to destruction, for these conditions are brought together into One.

"Only the truly intelligent understand this principle of the identity of all things. They do not view things as apprehended by themselves, subjectively; but transfer themselves into the position of the things viewed.

Avoiding the fallacious channels of the senses.

And viewing them thus they are able to comprehend them, nay, to master them;—and he who can master them is near. So it is that to place oneself in subjective relation with externals, without consciousness of their objectivity,—this is Tao. But to wear out one's intellect in an obstinate adherence to the individuality of things, not recognising the fact that all things are One,—this is called Three in the Morning."

"What is Three in the Morning?" asked Tzǔ Yu.

"A keeper of monkeys," replied Tzǔ Ch'i, "said with regard to their rations of chestnuts that each monkey was to have three in the morning and four at night. But at this the monkeys were very angry, so the keeper said they might have four in the morning and three at night, with which arrangement they were all well pleased. The actual number of the chestnuts remained the same, but there was an adaptation to the likes and dislikes of those concerned. Such is the principle of putting oneself into subjective relation with externals.

"Wherefore the true Sage, while regarding contraries as identical, adapts himself to the laws of Heaven. This is called following two courses at once.

He is thus prevented from trying to walk through walls, etc., as later Taoists have professed themselves able to do, of course with a view to gull the public and enrich themselves. "God," says Locke, "when he makes the prophet, does not unmake the man."

So Carlyle in his essay on Novalis:—"To a Transcendentalist, matter has an existence but only as a Phenomenon.... It is a mere relation, or rather the result of a relation between our living souls and the great First Cause."

"The knowledge of the men of old had a limit. It extended back to a period when matter did not exist. That was the extreme point to which their knowledge reached.

"The second period was that of matter, but of matter unconditioned.

By time or space. "Being, in itself," says Herbert Spencer, "out of relation, is itself unthinkable." Principles of Psychology, iii. p. 258.

"The third epoch saw matter conditioned, but contraries were still unknown. When these appeared, Tao began to decline. And with the decline of Tao, individual bias arose.

"Have then these states of falling and rising real existences? Surely they are but as the falling and rising of Chao Wên's music,—the consequences of his playing.

Chao Wên played the guitar. Shih K'uang wielded the bâton.

To keep time.

Hui Tzǔ argued. Herein these three men excelled, and in the practice of such arts they passed their lives.

"Hui Tzǔ's particular views being very different from those of the world in general, he was correspondingly anxious to enlighten people. But he did not enlighten them as he should have done,

By the cultivation and passive manifestation of his own inward light.

and consequently ended in the obscurity of the 'hard and white.'

Hui Tzǔ regarded such abstractions as hardness and whiteness as separate existences, of which the mind could only be conscious separately, one at a time.

Subsequently, his son searched his works for some clue, but never succeeded in establishing the principle. And indeed if such were possible to be established, then even I am established; but if not, then neither I nor anything in the universe is established!

"Therefore what the true Sage aims at is the light which comes out of darkness. He does not view things as apprehended by himself, subjectively, but transfers himself into the position of the things viewed. This is called using the light.

"There remains, however, Speech. Is that to be enrolled under either category of contraries, or not? Whether it is so enrolled or not, it will in any case belong to one or the other, and thus be as though it had an objective existence. At any rate, I should like to hear some speech which belongs to neither category.

Contraries being disposed of, there remains the vehicle Speech, i.e. the actual terms in which it is stated that contraries have ceased to be.

"If there was a beginning, then there was a time before that beginning. And a time before the time which was before the time of that beginning.

"If there is existence, there must have been non-existence. And if there was a time when nothing existed, then there must have been a time before that—when even nothing did not exist. Suddenly, when nothing came into existence, could one really say whether it belonged to the category of existence or of non-existence? Even the very words I have just now uttered,—I cannot say whether they have really been uttered or not.

I.e. The words in the text, denying the existence of contraries.

"There is nothing under the canopy of heaven greater than the tip of an autumn spikelet. A vast mountain is a small thing. Neither is there any age greater than that of a child cut off in infancy. P'êng Tsu himself died young. The universe and I came into being together; and I, and everything therein, are One.

"If then all things are One, what room is there for Speech? On the other hand, since I can utter these words, how can Speech not exist?

"If it does exist, we have One and Speech = two; and two and one = three. From which point onwards even the best mathematicians will fail to reach:
Tao.
how much more then will ordinary people fail?

"Hence, if from nothing you can proceed to something, and subsequently reach three, it follows that it would be still more easy if you were to start from something. To avoid such progression, you must put yourself into subjective relation with the external.

"Before conditions existed, Tao was. Before definitions existed, Speech was. Subjectively, we are conscious of certain delimitations which are,—
>Right and Left
>Relationship and Obligation
>Division and Discrimination
>Emulation and Contention
>These are called the Eight Predicables.

Not, of course, in the strict logical sense.

For the true Sage, beyond the limits of an external world, they exist, but are not recognised. By the true Sage, within the limits of an external world, they are recognised, but are not assigned. And so, with regard to the wisdom of the ancients, as embodied in the canon of Spring and Autumn,

Confucius' history of his native State. Now one of the canonical books of China.

the true Sage assigns, but does not justify by argument. And thus, classifying he does not classify; arguing, he does not argue."

"How can that be?" asked Tzŭ Yu.

"The true Sage," answered Tzŭ Ch'i, "keeps his knowledge within him, while men in general set forth theirs in argument, in order to convince each other. And therefore it is said that in argument he does not manifest himself.

Others try to establish their own subjective view. The true Sage remains passive, aiming only at the annihilation of contraries.

"Perfect Tao does not declare itself. Nor does perfect argument express itself in words. Nor does perfect charity show itself in act. Nor is perfect honesty absolutely incorruptible. Nor is perfect courage absolutely unyielding.

"For the Tao which shines forth is not Tao. Speech which argues falls short of its aim. Charity which has fixed points loses its scope. Honesty which is absolute is wanting in credit. Courage which is absolute misses its object. These five are, as it were, round, with a strong bias towards squareness. Therefore that knowledge which stops at what it does not know, is the highest knowledge.

"Who knows the argument which can be argued without words?—the Tao which does not declare itself as Tao? He who knows this may be said to be of God. To be able to pour in without making full, and pour out without making empty, in ignorance of the power by which such results are accomplished,—this is accounted Light."

Of old, the Emperor Yao said to Shun, "I would smite the Tsungs, and the Kueis, and the Hsü-aos. Ever since I have been on the throne I have had this desire. What do you think?"

"These three States," replied Shun, "are paltry out-of-the-way places. Why can you not shake off this desire? Once upon a time, ten suns came out together, and all things were illuminated thereby. How much more then should virtue excel suns?"

Illustrating the use of "light." Instead of active force, substitute the passive but irresistible influence of virtue complete. The sun caused the traveller to lay aside his cloak when the north wind succeeded only in making him draw it tighter around him.

Yeh Ch'üeh asked Wang I,

A disciple and tutor of remote antiquity. Said to have been two of the four Sages on the Miao-ku-shê mountain mentioned in ch. i.

saying, "Do you know for certain that all things are subjectively the same?"

"How can I know?" answered Wang I. "Do you know what you do not know?"

"How can I know?" replied Yeh Ch'üeh. "But can then nothing be known?"

"How can I know?" said Wang I. "Nevertheless, I will try to tell you.

How can it be known that what I call knowing is not really not knowing, and that what I call not knowing is not really knowing? Now I would ask you this. If a man sleeps in a damp place, he gets lumbago and dies. But how about an eel? And living up in a tree is precarious and trying to the nerves;—but how about monkeys? Of the man, the eel, and the monkey, whose habitat is the right one, absolutely? Human beings feed on flesh, deer on grass, centipedes on snakes, owls and crows on mice. Of these four, whose is the right taste, absolutely? Monkey mates with monkey, the buck with the doe; eels consort with fishes, while men admire Mao Ch'iang and Li Chi,

Beauties of the fifth and seventh centuries B.C., respectively. The commentators do not seem to have noted the very obvious anachronism here involved.

at the sight of whom fishes plunge deep down in the water, birds soar high in the air, and deer hurry away.

For shame at their own inferiority.

Yet who shall say which is the correct standard of beauty? In my opinion, the standard of human virtue, and of positive and negative, is so obscured that it is impossible to actually know it as such."

"If you then," asked Yeh Ch'üeh, "do not know what is bad for you, is the Perfect Man equally without this knowledge?"

"The Perfect Man," answered Wang I, "is a spiritual being. Were the ocean itself scorched up, he would not feel hot. Were the Milky Way frozen hard, he would not feel cold. Were the mountains to be riven with thunder, and the great deep to be thrown up by storm, he would not tremble. In such case, he would mount upon the clouds of heaven, and driving the sun and the moon before him, would pass beyond the limits of this external world, where death and life have no more victory over man;—how much less what is bad for him?"

Chü Ch'iao addressed Chang Wu Tzŭ

A disciple and tutor of antiquity.

as follows:—"I heard Confucius say, 'The true sage pays no heed to mundane affairs. He neither seeks gain nor avoids injury. He asks nothing at the hands of man. He adheres, without questioning, to Tao. Without speaking, he can speak; and he can speak and yet say nothing. And so he roams beyond the limits of this dusty world. These,' added Confucius, 'are wild words.'

Han Fei Tzŭ tells us that Lao Tzŭ, whose doctrines Confucius seems to be here deriding, said exactly the opposite of this; viz: "The true Sage is beforehand in his attention to mundane affairs," i.e. "takes time by the forelock." Neither utterance, however, appears in the Tao-Tê-Ching. See The Remains of Lao Tzŭ, p. 44.

Now to me they are the skilful embodiment of Tao. What, Sir, is your opinion?"

"Points upon which the Yellow Emperor doubted," replied Chang Wu Tzŭ, "how should Confucius know?

Lao Tzŭ and the Yellow Emperor have always been mixed up in the heads of Taoist writers, albeit separated by a chasm of some two thousand years. Confucius is here evidently dealing with the actual doctrines of Lao Tzŭ.

You are going too fast. You see your egg, and expect to hear it crow. You look at your cross-bow, and expect to have broiled duck before you. I will say a few words to you at random, and do you listen at random.

"How does the Sage seat himself by the sun and moon, and hold the universe in his grasp? He blends everything into one harmonious whole, rejecting the confusion of this and that. Rank and precedence, which the vulgar prize, the Sage stolidly ignores. The revolutions of ten thousand years leave his Unity unscathed. The universe itself may pass away, but he will flourish still.

"How do I know that love of life is not a delusion after all? How do I know but that he who dreads to die is not as a child who has lost the way and cannot find his home?

"The lady Li Chi was the daughter of Ai Fêng.

A border chieftain.

When the Duke of Chin first got her, she wept until the bosom of her dress was drenched with tears. But when she came to the royal residence, and lived with the Duke, and ate rich food, she repented of having wept. How then do I know but that the dead repent of having previously clung to life?

"Those who dream of the banquet, wake to lamentation and sorrow. Those who dream of lamentation and sorrow wake to join the hunt. While they dream, they do not know that they dream. Some will even interpret the very dream they are dreaming; and only when they awake do they know it was a dream. By and by comes the Great Awakening, and then we find out that this life is really a great dream. Fools think they are awake now, and flatter themselves they know if they are really princes or peasants. Confucius and you are both dreams; and I who say you are dreams,—I am but a dream myself. This is a paradox. Tomorrow a sage may arise to explain it; but that tomorrow will not be until ten thousand generations have gone by.

"Granting that you and I argue. If you beat me, and not I you, are you necessarily right and I wrong? Or if I beat you and not you me, am I necessarily right and you wrong? Or are we both partly right and partly wrong? Or are we both wholly right and wholly wrong? You and I cannot know this, and consequently the world will be in ignorance of the truth.

"Who shall I employ as arbiter between us? If I employ some one who takes your view, he will side with you. How can such a one arbitrate between us? If I employ some one who takes my view, he will side with me. How can such a one arbitrate between us? And if I employ some one who either differs from, or agrees with, both of us, he will be equally unable to decide between us. Since then you, and I, and man, cannot decide, must we not depend upon Another?

Upon God, in whose infinity all contraries blend indistinguishably into One.

Such dependence is as though it were not dependence. We are embraced in the obliterating unity of God. There is perfect adaptation to whatever may eventuate; and so we complete our allotted span.

"But what is it to be embraced in the obliterating unity of God? It is this. With reference to positive and negative, to that which is so and that which is not so,—if the positive is really positive, it must necessarily be different from its negative: there is no room for argument. And if that which is so really is so, it must necessarily be different from that which is not so: there is no room for argument.

"Take no heed of time, nor of right and wrong. But passing into the realm of the Infinite, take your final rest therein."

Our refuge is in God alone, the Infinite Absolute. Contraries cannot but exist, but they should exist independently of each other without antagonism. Such a condition is found only in the all-embracing unity of God, wherein all distinctions of positive and negative, of right and wrong, of this and of that, are obliterated and merged in One.

Herbert Spencer says, "The antithesis of subject and object, never to be transcended while consciousness lasts, renders impossible all knowledge of the Ultimate Reality in which subject and object are united." Principles of Psychology, i. p. 272.

The Penumbra said to the Umbra, "At one moment you move: at another you are at rest. At one moment you sit down: at another you get up. Why this instability of purpose?" "I depend," replied the Umbra, "upon something which causes me to do as I do; and that something depends in turn upon something else which causes it to do as it does. My dependence is like that of a snake's scales or of a cicada's wings.

Which do not move of their own accord.

How can I tell why I do one thing, or why I do not do another?"

Showing how two or more may be the phenomena of one.

Once upon a time, I, Chuang Tzŭ, dreamt I was a butterfly, fluttering hither and thither, to all intents and purposes a butterfly. I was conscious only of following my fancies as a butterfly, and was unconscious of my individuality as a man. Suddenly, I awaked, and there I lay, myself again. Now I do not know whether I was then a man dreaming I was a butterfly, or whether I am now a butterfly dreaming I am a man. Between a man and a butterfly there is necessarily a barrier. The transition is called Metempsychosis.

Showing how one may appear to be either of two.

CHAPTER III

Nourishment of the Soul

Argument:—Life too short—Wisdom unattainable—Accommodation to circumstances—Liberty paramount—Death a release—The soul immortal.

My life has a limit, but my knowledge is without limit. To drive the limited in search of the limitless, is fatal; and the knowledge of those who do this is fatally lost.

In striving for others, avoid fame. In striving for self, avoid disgrace. Pursue a middle course. Thus you will keep a sound body, and a sound mind, fulfil your duties, and work out your allotted span.

Prince Hui's cook was cutting up a bullock. Every blow of his hand, every heave of his shoulders, every tread of his foot, every thrust of his knee, every whshh of rent flesh, every chhk of the chopper, was in perfect harmony,—rhythmical like the dance of the Mulberry Grove, simultaneous like the chords of the Ching Shou.

Commentators are divided in their identifications of these ancient morceaux.

"Well done!" cried the Prince. "Yours is skill indeed."

"Sire," replied the cook; "I have always devoted myself to Tao. It is better than skill. When I first began to cut up bullocks, I saw before me simply whole bullocks. After three years' practice, I saw no more whole animals.

Meaning that he saw them, so to speak, in sections.

And now I work with my mind and not with my eye. When my senses bid me stop, but my mind urges me on, I fall back upon eternal principles. I follow such openings or cavities as there may be, according to the natural constitution of the animal. I do not attempt to cut through joints: still less through large bones.

For a curious parallelism, see Plato's Phædrus, 265.

"A good cook changes his chopper once a year,—because he cuts. An ordinary cook, once a month,—because he hacks. But I have had this chopper nineteen years, and although I have cut up many thousand bullocks, its edge is as if fresh from the whetstone. For at the joints there are always interstices, and the edge of a chopper being without thickness, it remains only to insert that which is without thickness into such an interstice.

These words help to elucidate a much-vexed passage in ch. xliii of the Tao-Tê-Ching. See The Remains of Lao Tzŭ, p. 30.

By these means the interstice will be enlarged, and the blade will find plenty of room. It is thus that I have kept my chopper for nineteen years as though fresh from the whetstone.

"Nevertheless, when I come upon a hard part where the blade meets with a difficulty, I am all caution. I fix my eye on it. I stay my hand, and gently apply my blade, until with a hwah the part yields like earth crumbling to the ground. Then I take out my chopper, and stand up, and look around, and pause, until with an air of triumph I wipe my chopper and put it carefully away."

"Bravo!" cried the Prince. "From the words of this cook I have learnt how to take care of my life."

Meaning that which informs life, sc. the soul.

When Hsien, of the Kung-wên family, beheld a certain official, he was horrified, and said, "Who is that man? How came he to lose a foot? Is this the work of God, or of man?

"Why, of course," continued Hsien, "it is the work of God, and not of man. When God brought this man into the world, he wanted him to be unlike other men. Men always have two feet. From this it is clear that God and not man made him as he is.

It was by God's will that he took office with a view to personal aggrandisement. That he got into trouble and suffered the common punishment of loss of feet, cannot therefore be charged to man.

"Now, wild fowl get a peck once in ten steps, a drink once in a hundred. Yet they do not want to be fed in a cage. For although they would thus be able to command food, they would not be free."

And had our friend above kept out of the official cage he would still have been independent as the fowls of the air.

When Lao Tzŭ died, Ch'in Shih went to mourn. He uttered three yells and departed.

A disciple asked him saying, "Were you not our Master's friend?"

"I was," replied Ch'in Shih.

"And if so, do you consider that a sufficient expression of grief at his loss?" added the disciple.

"I do," said Ch'in Shih. "I had believed him to be the man of all men, but now I know that he was not. When I went in to mourn, I found old persons weeping as if for their children, young ones wailing as if for their mothers. And for him to have gained the attachment of those people in this way, he too must have uttered words which should not have been spoken, and dropped tears which should not have been shed, thus violating eternal principles, increasing the sum of human emotion, and forgetting the source from which his own life was received. The ancients called such emotions the trammels of mortality. The Master came, because it was his time to be born; he went, because it was his time to die. For those who accept the phenomenon of birth and death in this sense, lamentation and sorrow have no place. The ancients spoke of death as of God cutting down a man suspended in the air. The fuel is consumed, but the fire may be transmitted, and we know not that it comes to an end."

The soul, according to Chuang Tzŭ, if duly nourished and not allowed to wear itself out with the body in the pursuits of mortality, may become immortal and return beatified to the Great Unknown whence it came.

CHAPTER IV

Man Among Men

Argument:—Man must fall in with his mortal environment—His virtue should be passive, not active—He should be rather than do—Talents a hindrance—But of petty uselessness great usefulness is achieved.

Yen Hui went to take leave of Confucius.
A disciple of the Sage. Also known as Tzŭ Yüan.
"Whither are you bound?" asked the Master.
"I am going to the State of Wei," was the reply.
"And what do you propose to do there?" continued Confucius.
"I hear," answered Yen Hui, "that the Prince of Wei is of mature age, but of an unmanageable disposition. He behaves as if the State were of no account, and will not see his own faults. Consequently, the people perish; and their corpses lie about like so much undergrowth in a marsh. They are at extremities. And I have heard you, Sir, say that if a State is well governed it may be neglected; but that if it is badly governed, then we should visit it.
In the Lun Yü, Confucius says exactly the opposite of this.
The science of medicine embraces many various diseases. I would test my knowledge in this sense, that perchance I may do some good to that State."
"Alas!" cried Confucius, "you will only succeed in bringing evil upon yourself. For Tao must not be distributed. If it is, it will lose its unity. If it loses its unity, it will be uncertain; and so cause mental disturbance,—from which there is no escape.

"The sages of old first got Tao for themselves, and then got it for others. Before you possess this yourself, what leisure have you to attend to the doings of wicked men? Besides, do you know what Virtue results in and where Wisdom ends? Virtue results in a desire for fame; Wisdom ends in contentions. In the struggle for fame men crush each other, while their wisdom but provokes rivalry. Both are baleful instruments, and may not be incautiously used.

"Besides, those who, before influencing by their own solid virtue and unimpeachable sincerity, and before reaching the heart by the example of their own disregard for name and fame, go and preach charity and duty to one's neighbour to wicked men,—only make these men hate them for their very goodness' sake. Such persons are called evil speakers. And those who speak evil of others are apt to be evil spoken of themselves. That, alas! will be your end.

"On the other hand, if the Prince loves the good and hates the bad, what object will you have in inviting him to change his ways? Before you have opened your mouth to preach, the Prince himself will have seized the opportunity to wrest the victory from you. Your eye will fall, your expression fade, your words will stick, your face will change, and your heart will die within you. It will be as though you took fire to quell fire, water to quell water, which is popularly known as 'pouring oil on the flames.' And if you begin with concessions, there will be no end to them. Neglect this sound advice, and you will be the victim of that violent man.

"Of old, Chieh murdered Kuan Lung Fêng, and Chou slew Prince Pi Kan. Their victims were both men who cultivated virtue themselves in order to secure the welfare of the people. But in doing this they offended their superiors; and therefore, because of that very moral culture, their superiors got rid of them, in order to guard their own reputations.

Chieh and Chou are the two typical tyrants of Chinese history.

"Of old, Yao attacked the Ts'ung-chih and Hsü-ao countries, and Yü attacked the Yu-hu country. Homes were desolated and families destroyed by the slaughter of the inhabitants. Yet they fought without ceasing, and strove for victory to the last. These are instances known to all. Now if the Sages of old failed in their efforts against this love of fame, this desire for victory,—are you likely to succeed? But of course you have a scheme. Tell it to me."

"Gravity of demeanour," replied Yen Hui, "and dispassionateness; energy and singleness of purpose,—will this do?"

"Alas!" said Confucius, "that will not do. If you make a show of being perfect and obtrude yourself, the Prince's mood will be doubtful. Ordinarily, he is not opposed, and so he has come to take actual pleasure in trampling upon the feelings of others. And if he has thus failed in the practice of routine virtues, do you expect that he will take readily to higher ones? You may insist, but without result. Outwardly you will be right, but inwardly wrong. How then will you make him mend his ways?"

"Just so," replied Yen Hui. "I am inwardly straight, and outwardly crooked, completed after the models of antiquity.

"He who is inwardly straight is a servant of God. And he who is a servant of God knows that the Son of Heaven

The Emperor.

and himself are equally the children of God. Shall then such a one trouble whether man visits him with evil or with good? Man indeed regards him as a child; and this is to be a servant of God.

(1) Children are everywhere exempt.—This is the first limb of a threefold argument.

"He who is outwardly crooked is a servant of man. He bows, he kneels, he folds his hands;—such is the ceremonial of a minister. What all men do, shall I dare not to do? What all men do, none will blame me for doing. This is to be a servant of man.

(2) The individual is not punished for the faults of the community.

"He who is completed after the models of antiquity is a servant of the Sages of old. Although I utter the words of warning and take him to task, it is the Sages of old who speak, and not I. Thus my uprightness will not bring me into trouble, the servant of the Sages of old.—Will this do?"

(3) The responsibility rests, not with the mouthpiece, but with the authors of the doctrines enunciated.

"Alas!" replied Confucius, "No. Your plans are too many, and are lacking in prudence. However, your firmness will secure you from harm; but that is all. You will not influence him to such an extent that he shall seem to follow the dictates of his own heart."

"Then," said Yen Hui, "I am without resource, and venture to ask for a method."

Confucius said, "FAST.... Let me explain. You have a method, but it is difficult to practise. Those which are easy are not from God."

"Well," replied Yen Hui, "my family is poor, and for many months we have tasted neither wine nor flesh. Is not that fasting?"

"The fasting of religious observance it is," answered Confucius, "but not the fasting of the heart."

"And may I ask," said Yen Hui, "in what consists the fasting of the heart?"

"Cultivate unity," replied Confucius.

Make of the mind as it were an undivided indivisible ONE.

"You hear not with the ears, but with the mind; not with the mind, but with your soul.

The vital fluid which informs your whole being; in fact, "with your whole self."

But let hearing stop with the ears. Let the working of the mind stop with itself. Then the soul will be a negative existence, passively responsive to externals. In such a negative existence, only Tao can abide. And that negative state is the fasting of the heart."

"Then," said Yen Hui, "the reason I could not get the use of this method is my own individuality. If I could get the use of it, my individuality would have gone. Is this what you mean by the negative state?"

"Exactly so," replied the Master. "Let me tell you. If you can enter this man's domain without offending his amour propre, cheerful if he hears you, passive if he does not; without science, without drugs, simply living there in a state of complete indifference,—you will be near success. It is easy to stop walking: the trouble is to walk without touching the ground. As an agent of man, it is easy to deceive; but not as an agent of God. You have heard of winged creatures flying. You have never heard of flying without wings. You have heard of men being wise with wisdom. You have never heard of men wise without wisdom.

Wise of God, without the wisdom of man.

"Look at that window. Through it an empty room becomes bright with scenery; but the landscape stops outside. Were this not so, we should have an exemplification of sitting still and running away at one and the same time.

An empty room would contain something,—a paradox like that in the text.

"In this sense, you may use your ears and eyes to communicate within, but shut out all wisdom from the mind.

Let the channels of your senses be to your mind what a window is to an empty room.

And there where the supernatural

Something which is and yet is not, like the landscape seen in, and yet not in, a room.

can find shelter, shall not man find shelter too? This is the method for regenerating all creation.

By passive, not by active, virtue.

It was the instrument which Yü and Shun employed. It was the secret of the success of Fu Hsi and Chi Chü. Shall it not then be adopted by mankind in general?"

Who stand much more in need of regeneration than such worthies as were these ancient Emperors.

Tzŭ Kao, Duke of Shê,

A district of the Ch'u State.

being about to go on a mission to the Ch'i State, asked Confucius, saying, "The mission my sovereign is sending me on is a most important one. Of course, I shall be received with all due respect, but they will not take the same interest in the matter that I shall. And as an ordinary person cannot be pushed, still less a Prince, I am in a state of great alarm.

"Now you, Sir, have told me that in all undertakings great and small, Tao alone leads to a happy issue. Otherwise that, failing success, there is to be feared punishment from without, and with success, punishment from within; while exemption in case either of success or non-success falls only to the share of those who possess the virtue required.

I.e. those to whom the issue, as regards their own reward or punishment, is a matter of the completest indifference.

The term virtue, here as elsewhere unless specially notified, should be understood in the sense of exemplification of Tao.

"Well, I am not dainty with my food; neither am I always wanting to cool myself when hot. However, this morning I received my orders, and this evening I have been drinking iced water. I am so hot inside. Before I have put my hand to the business I am suffering punishment from within; and if I do not succeed I am sure to suffer punishment from without. Thus I get both punishments, which is really more than I can bear. Kindly tell me what there is to be done."

"There exist two sources of safety," Confucius replied. "One is Destiny: the other is Duty. A child's love for its parents is destiny. It is inseparable from the child's life. A subject's allegiance to his sovereign is duty. Beneath the canopy of heaven there is no place to which he can escape from it. These two sources of safety may be explained as follows. To serve one's parents without reference to place but only to the service, is the acme of filial piety. To serve one's prince without reference to the act but only to the service, is the perfection of a subject's loyalty. To serve one's own heart so as to permit neither joy nor sorrow within, but to cultivate resignation to the inevitable,—this is the climax of Virtue.

"Now a minister often finds himself in circumstances over which he has no control. But if he simply confines himself to his work, and is utterly oblivious of self, what leisure has he for loving life or hating death? And so you may safely go.

"But I have yet more to tell you. All intercourse, if personal, should be characterised by sincerity. If from a distance, it should be carried on in loyal terms. These terms will have to be transmitted by some one. Now the transmission of messages of good- or ill-will is the hardest thing possible. Messages of good-will are sure to be overdone with fine phrases; messages of ill-will with harsh ones. In each case the result is exaggeration, and a consequent failure to carry conviction, for which the envoy suffers. Therefore it was said in the Fa-yen,

Name of an ancient book.

'Confine yourself to simple statements of fact, shorn of all superfluous expression of feeling, and your risk will be small.'

"In trials of skill, at first all is friendliness; but at last it is all antagonism. Skill is pushed too far. So on festive occasions, the drinking which is in the beginning orderly enough, degenerates into riot and disorder. Festivity is pushed too far. It is in fact the same with all things: they begin with good faith and end with contempt. From small beginnings come great endings.

"Speech is like wind to wave. Action is liable to divergence from its true goal. By wind, waves are easily excited. Divergence from the true goal is fraught with danger. Thus angry feelings rise up without a cause. Specious words and dishonest arguments follow, as the wild random cries of an animal at the point of death. Both sides give way to passion. For where one party drives the other too much into a corner, resistance will always be provoked without apparent cause. And if the cause is not apparent, how much less will the ultimate effect be so?

"Therefore it is said in the Fa-yen, 'Neither deviate from nor travel beyond your instructions.

"Travel beyond your instructions," is literally, "urge a settlement."

To pass the limit is to go to excess.'

"To deviate from, or to travel beyond instructions, may imperil the negotiation. A settlement to be successful must be lasting. It is too late to change an evil settlement once made.

"Therefore let yourself be carried along without fear, taking refuge in no alternative to preserve you from harm on either side. This is the utmost you can do. What need for considering your obligations? Better leave all to Destiny, difficult as this may be."

It is passing strange that this exposition of the laissez-aller inaction doctrine of Tao should be placed in the mouth of Confucius, who is thus made in some measure to discredit his own teachings. The commentators, however, see nothing anomalous in the position here assigned to the Sage.

Yen Ho

A philosopher from the Lu State.

was about to become tutor to the eldest son of Prince Ling of the Wei State. Accordingly he observed to Chü Poh Yü,

Prime Minister of the Wei State.

"Here is a man whose disposition is naturally of a low order. To let him take his own unprincipled way is to endanger the State. To try to restrain him is to endanger one's personal safety. He has just wit enough to see faults in others, but not to see his own. I am consequently at a loss what to do."

"A good question indeed," replied Chü Poh Yü, "You must be careful, and begin by self-reformation. Outwardly you may adapt yourself, but inwardly you must keep up to your own standard. In this there are two points to be guarded against. You must not let the outward adaptation penetrate within, nor the inward standard manifest itself without. In the former case, you will fall, you will be obliterated, you will collapse, you will lie prostrate. In the latter case, you will be a sound, a name, a bogie, an uncanny thing. If he would play the child, do you play the child too. If he cast aside all sense of decorum, do you do so too. As far as he goes, do you go also. Thus you will reach him without offending him.

"Don't you know the story of the praying mantis? In its rage it stretched out its arms to prevent a chariot from passing, unaware that this was beyond its strength, so admirable was its energy! Be cautious. If you are always offending others by your superiority, you will probably come to grief.

"Do you not know that those who keep tigers do not venture to give them live animals as food, for fear of exciting their fury when killing the prey? Also, that whole animals are not given, for fear of exciting the tigers' fury when rending them? The periods of hunger and repletion are carefully watched in order to prevent such outbursts. The tiger is of a different species from man; but the latter too is manageable if properly managed, unmanageable if excited to fury.

"Those who are fond of horses surround them with various conveniences. Sometimes mosquitoes or flies trouble them; and then, unexpectedly to the animal, a groom will brush them off, the result being that the horse breaks his bridle, and hurts his head and chest. The intention is good, but there is a want of real care for the horse. Against this you must be on your guard."

A certain artisan was travelling to the Ch'i State. On reaching Ch'ü-yüan, he saw a sacred li tree,

A worthless species of oak.

large enough to hide an ox behind it, a hundred spans in girth, towering up ten cubits over the hill top, and carrying behind it branches, many tens of the smallest of which were of a size for boats. Crowds stood gazing at it, but our artisan took no notice, and went on his way without even casting a look behind. His apprentice however gazed his fill, and when he caught up his master, said, "Ever since I have handled an adze in your service, I have never seen such a splendid piece of timber as that. How was it that you, sir, did not care to stop and look at it?"

"It's not worth talking about," replied his master. "It's good for nothing. Make a boat of it,—'twould sink. A coffin,—'twould rot. Furniture,—'twould soon break down. A door,—'twould sweat. A pillar,—'twould be worm-eaten. It is wood of no quality, and of no use. That is why it has attained its present age."

When the artisan reached home, he dreamt that the tree appeared to him in a dream and spoke as follows:—"What is it that you compare me with? Is it with the more elegant trees?—The cherry-apple, the pear, the orange, the pumelo, and other fruit-bearers, as soon as their fruit ripens are stripped and treated with indignity. The great boughs are snapped off, the small ones scattered abroad. Thus do these trees by their own value injure their own lives. They cannot fulfil their allotted span of years, but perish prematurely in mid-career from their entanglement with the world around them. Thus it is with all things. For a long period my aim was to be useless. Many times I was in danger, but at length I succeeded, and so became useful as I am to-day. But had I then been of use, I should not now be of the great use I am. Moreover, you and I belong both to the same category of things. Have done then with this criticism of others. Is a good-for-nothing fellow whose dangers are not yet passed a fit person to talk of a good-for-nothing tree?"

When our artisan awaked and told his dream, his apprentice said, "If the tree aimed at uselessness, how was it that it became a sacred tree?"

Which of course may be said to be of use.

"What you don't understand," replied his master, "don't talk about. That was merely to escape from the attacks of its enemies. Had it not become sacred, how many would have wanted to cut it down! The means of safety adopted were different from ordinary means,

In order to reach the somewhat extraordinary goal of uselessness. and to test these by ordinary canons leaves one far wide of the mark."

Tzŭ Ch'i of Nan-poh

Said to be identical with the individual mentioned at the beginning of ch. ii.

was travelling on the Shang mountain when he saw a large tree which astonished him very much. A thousand chariot teams could have found shelter under its shade.

"What tree is this?" cried Tzŭ Ch'i. "Surely it must have unusually fine timber." Then looking up, he saw that its branches were too crooked for rafters; while as to the trunk he saw that its irregular grain made it valueless for coffins. He tasted a leaf, but it took the skin off his lips; and its odour was so strong that it would make a man as it were drunk for three days together.

"Ah!" said Tzŭ Ch'i. "This tree is good for nothing, and that is how it has attained this size. A wise man might well follow its example."

And so escape danger from his surroundings.

In the State of Sung there is a place called Ching-shih, where thrive the beech, the cedar, and the mulberry. Such as are of a one-handed span or so in girth are cut down for monkey-cages. Those of two or three two-handed spans are cut down for the beams of fine houses. Those of seven or eight such spans are cut down for the solid sides of rich men's coffins.

To this day, the very best kinds of wood are still reserved for the "planks of old age."

Thus they do not fulfil their allotted span of years, but perish in mid-career beneath the axe. Such is the misfortune which overtakes worth.

For the sacrifices to the River God, neither bulls with white cheeks, nor pigs with large snouts, nor men suffering from piles, were allowed to be used. This had been revealed to the soothsayers, and these characteristics were consequently regarded as inauspicious. The wise, however, would regard them as extremely auspicious.

Readers of Don Juan will recollect how the master's mate had reason to share his view.

There was a hunchback named Su. His jaws touched his navel. His shoulders were higher than his head. His hair knot looked up to the sky. His viscera were upside down. His buttocks were where his ribs should have been. By tailoring, or washing, he was easily able to earn his living. By sifting rice he could make enough to support a family of ten.

In all of which occupations a man would necessarily stoop.

When orders came down for a conscription, the hunchback stood unconcerned among the crowd. And similarly, in matters of public works, his deformity shielded him from being employed.

On the other hand, when it came to donations of grain, the hunchback received as much as three chung,

An ancient measure of uncertain capacity.

and of firewood, ten faggots. And if physical deformity was thus enough to preserve his body until its allotted end, how much more would not moral and mental deformity avail!

A moral and mental deviation would be still more likely to condemn a man to that neglect from his fellows which is so conducive to our real welfare.

When Confucius was in the Ch'u State, the eccentric Chieh Yü passed his door, saying, "O phœnix, O phœnix, how has thy virtue fallen!—

By thus issuing forth out of due season.

unable to wait for the coming years or to go back into the past.

When you might be, or might have been, of use. The idea conveyed is that Confucianism was unsuited to its age. See Lun-yü, ch. xviii.

If Tao prevails on earth, prophets will fulfil their mission. If Tao does not prevail, they will but preserve themselves. At the present day they will but just escape.

"The honours of this world are light as feathers, yet none estimate them at their true value. The misfortunes of this life are weighty as the earth itself, yet none can keep out of their reach. No more, no more, seek to influence by virtue. Beware, beware, move cautiously on! O ferns, O ferns, wound not my steps! Through my tortuous journey wound not my feet! Hills suffer from the trees they produce. Fat burns by its own combustibility. Cinnamon trees furnish food: therefore they are cut down. The lacquer tree is felled for use. All men know the use of useful things; but they do not know the use of useless things."

CHAPTER V

The Evidence of Virtue Complete

Argument:—Correspondence between inward virtue and outward influence—The virtuous man disregards externals—The possession of virtue causes oblivion of outward form—Neglect of the human—Cultivation of the divine.

In the State of Lu there was a man, named Wang T'ai, who had had his toes cut off. His disciples were as numerous as those of Confucius. Ch'ang Chi
One of the latter.
asked Confucius, saying, "This Wang T'ai has been mutilated, yet he divides with you, Sir, the teaching of the Lu State. He neither preaches nor discusses; yet those who go to him empty, depart full. He must teach the doctrine which does not find expression in words;
The doctrine of Tao. These words occur in chs. ii and xliii of the Tao-Tê-Ching. See The Remains of Lao Tzŭ, p. 7.
and although his shape is imperfect, his mind is perhaps complete. What manner of man is this?"

"He is a prophet," replied Confucius, "whose instruction I have been late in seeking. I will go and learn from him. And if I,—why not those who are not equal to me? And I will take with me, not the State of Lu only, but the whole world."

"The fellow has been mutilated," said Ch'ang Chi, "and yet people call him Master. He must be very different from the ordinary run. But how does he use his mind in this sense?"

"Life and Death are all powerful," answered Confucius, "but they cannot affect it.
The mind, or soul, which is immortal. See ch. iii.
Heaven and earth may collapse, but that will remain. If this is found to be without flaw, it will not share the fate of all things. It can cause other things to change, while preserving its own constitution intact."

"How so?" asked Ch'ang Chi.

"From the point of view of difference," replied Confucius, "we distinguish between the liver and the gall, between the Ch'u State and the Yüeh State. From the point of view of sameness, all things are ONE. Such is the position of Wang T'ai. He does not trouble about what reaches him through the senses of hearing and sight, but directs his whole mind towards the very climax of virtue. He beholds all things as though ONE, without observing their discrepancies. And thus the discrepancy of his toes is to him as would be the loss of so much mud."

"He devotes himself in fact to himself," said Ch'ang Chi, "and uses his wisdom to perfect his mind, until it becomes perfect. But how then is it that people make so much of him?"

His virtue being wholly, as it were, of a selfish order.

"A man," replied Confucius, "does not seek to see himself in running water, but in still water. For only what is itself still can instil stillness into others.

"The grace of earth has reached only to pines and cedars;—winter and summer alike they are green. The grace of God has reached to Yao and to Shun alone;—the first and foremost of all creation. Happily they were able to regulate their own lives and thus regulate the lives of all mankind.

"By nourishment of physical courage, the sense of fear may be so eliminated that a man will, single-handed, brave a whole army. And if such a result can be achieved in search of fame, how much more by one who extends his sway over heaven and earth and influences all things; and who, lodging within the confines of a body with its channels of sight and sound, brings his knowledge to know that all things are ONE, and that his soul endures for ever! Besides, he awaits his appointed hour, and men flock to him of their own accord. He makes no effort to attract them."

That men thus gather around him is the outward sign or evidence of his inward virtue complete.

Shên T'u Chia had had his toes cut off. Subsequently, he studied under Poh Hun Wu Jen at the same time as Tzŭ Ch'an of the Chêng State. The latter said to him, "When I leave first, do you remain awhile. When you leave first, I will remain behind."

Tzŭ Ch'an was a model minister of the sixth century B.C. Under his guidance the people of the Chêng State became so virtuous that doors were not locked at night, nor would any one pick up lost articles left lying in the road. He was hardly likely to be ashamed of walking out with a mutilated criminal.

Next day, when they were again together in the lecture-room, Tzŭ Ch'an said, "When I leave first, do you remain awhile. When you leave first, I will remain. I am now about to go. Will you remain or not? I notice you show no respect to a Minister of State. Perhaps you think yourself my equal?"

"Dear me!" replied Shên T'u Chia, "I didn't know we had a Minister of State in the class. Perhaps you think that because you are one you should take precedence over the rest. Now I have heard that if a mirror is perfectly bright, dust and dirt will not collect on it. That if they do, it is because the mirror was not bright. He who associates for long with the wise will be without fault. Now you have been improving yourself at the feet of our Master, yet you can utter words like these. Is not the fault in you?"

"You are a fine fellow, certainly," retorted Tzŭ Ch'an, "you will be emulating the virtue of Yao next. To look at you, I should say you had enough to do to attend to your own shortcomings!"

A sneer at his want of toes.

"Those who disguise their faults," said Shên T'u Chia, "so as not to lose their toes, are many in number. Those who do not disguise their faults, and so fail to keep them, are few. To recognise the inevitable and to quietly acquiesce in Destiny, is the achievement of the virtuous man alone. He who should put himself in front of the bull's-eye when Hou I

A Chinese Tell.

was shooting, would be hit. If he was not hit, it would be destiny. Those with toes who laugh at me for having no toes are many. This used to make me angry. But since I have studied under our Master, I have ceased to trouble about it. It may be that our Master has so far succeeded in purifying me. At any rate I have been with him nineteen years without being aware of the loss of my toes. Now you and I are engaged in studying the internal. Do you not then commit a fault by thus dragging me back to the external?"

At this Tzǔ Ch'an began to fidget, and changing countenance, begged Shên T'u Chia to say no more.

There was a man of the Lu State who had been mutilated,—Shu Shan No-toes. He came walking on his heels to see Confucius; but Confucius said, "You did not take care, and so brought this misfortune upon yourself. What is the use of coming to me now?"

"In my ignorance," replied No-toes, "I made free with my body and lost my toes. But I come with something more precious than toes which I now seek to keep. There is no man, but Heaven covers him: there is no man, but Earth supports him;—and I thought that you, sir, would be as Heaven and Earth. I little expected to hear these words from you."

"I must apologise," said Confucius. "Pray walk in and let us discuss." But No-toes walked out.

"There!" said Confucius to his disciples. "There is a criminal without toes who seeks to learn in order to make atonement for his previous misdeeds. And if he, how much more those who have no misdeeds for which to atone?"

No-toes went off to Lao Tzǔ and said, "Is Confucius a sage, or is he not? How is it he has so many disciples? He aims at being a subtle dialectician, not knowing that such a reputation is regarded by real sages as the fetters of a criminal."

"Why do you not meet him with the continuity of life and death, the identity of can and can not," answered Lao Tzǔ, "and so release him from these fetters?"

"He has been thus punished by God," replied No-toes. "It would be impossible to release him."

A sneer at Confucius. No-toes himself had only been punished by man.

Duke Ai of the Lu State said to Confucius, "In the Wei State there is a leper, named Ai T'ai T'o. The men who live with him like him and make no effort to get rid of him. Of the women who have seen him, many have said to their parents, Rather than be another man's wife, I would be his concubine.

"He never preaches at people, but puts himself into sympathy with them. He wields no power by which he may protect men's bodies. He has at his disposal no appointments by which to gratify their hearts. He is loathsome to a degree. He sympathises, but does not instruct. His knowledge is limited to his own State. Yet males and females alike all congregate around him.

"So thinking that he must be different from ordinary men, I sent for him, and saw that he was indeed loathsome to a degree. Yet we had not been many months together ere my attention was fixed upon his conduct. A year had not elapsed ere I trusted him thoroughly; and as my State wanted a Prime Minister, I offered the post to him. He accepted it sullenly, as if he would much rather have declined. Perhaps he didn't think me good enough for him! At any rate, he took it; but in a very short time he left me and went away. I grieved for him as for a lost friend, and as though there were none left with whom I could rejoice. What manner of man is this?

"When I was on a mission to the Ch'u State," replied Confucius, "I saw a litter of young pigs sucking their dead mother. After a while they looked at her, and then they all left the body and went off. For their mother did not look at them any more, nor did she any more seem to be of their kind. What they loved was their mother; not the body which contained her, but that which made the body what it was.

"When a man is killed in battle, his arms are not buried with him.
He has no further use for weapons.
A man whose toes have been cut off does not value a present of boots. In each case the function of such things is gone.

"The concubines of the Son of Heaven do not cut their nails or pierce their ears.
For fear of injuring their persons.
He who has a marriageable daughter keeps her away from menial work. To preserve her beauty is quite enough occupation for her. How much more so for a man of perfect virtue?
Who should trouble himself only about the internal.

"Now Ai T'ai T'o says nothing, and is trusted. He does nothing, and is sought after. He causes a man to offer him the government of his own State, and the only fear is lest he should decline. Truly his talents are perfect and his virtue without outward form!"

"What do you mean by his talents being perfect?" asked the Duke.

"Life and Death," replied Confucius, "existence and non-existence, success and non-success, poverty and wealth, virtue and vice, good and evil report, hunger and thirst, warmth and cold,—these all revolve upon the changing wheel of Destiny. Day and night they follow one upon the other, and no man can say where each one begins. Therefore they cannot be allowed to disturb the harmony of the organism, nor enter into the soul's domain. Swim however with the tide, so as not to offend others. Do this day by day without break, and live in peace with mankind. Thus you will be ready for all contingencies, and may be said to have your talents perfect."

"And virtue without outward form; what is that?"

"In a water-level," said Confucius, "the water is in a most perfect state of repose. Let that be your model. The water remains quietly within, and does not overflow. It is from the cultivation of such harmony that virtue results. And if virtue takes no outward form, man will not be able to keep aloof from it."

Mankind will be regenerated thereby, in the same way that evenness is imparted by the aid of water to surfaces, although the water is all the time closed up and does not overflow.

Some days afterwards Duke Ai told Min Tzŭ,
One of Confucius' disciples.
saying, "When first I took the reins of government in hand, I thought that in caring for my people's lives I had done all my duty as a ruler. But now that I have heard what a perfect man is, I fear that I have not been succeeding, but foolishly using my body and working destruction to my State. Confucius and I are not prince and minister, but merely friends with a care for each other's moral welfare."

A certain hunchback, named Wu Ch'un, whose heels did not touch the ground, had the ear of Duke Ling of Wei. The Duke took a great fancy to him; and as for well-formed men, he thought their necks were too short.

Another man, with a goitre as big as a large jar, had the ear of Duke Huan of Ch'i. The Duke took a great fancy to him; and as for well-formed men, he thought their necks were too thin.

Thus it is that virtue should prevail and outward form be forgotten. But mankind forgets not that which is to be forgotten, forgetting that which is not to be forgotten. This is forgetfulness indeed! And thus with the truly wise, wisdom is a curse, sincerity like glue, virtue only a means to acquire, and skill nothing more than a commercial capacity. For the truly wise make no plans, and therefore require no wisdom. They do not separate, and therefore require no glue. They want nothing, and therefore need no virtue. They sell nothing, and therefore are not in want of a commercial capacity. These four qualifications are bestowed upon them by God and serve as heavenly food to them. And those who thus feed upon the divine have little need for the human. They wear the forms of men, without human passions. Because they wear the forms of men, they associate with men. Because they have not human passions, positives and negatives find in them no place. Infinitesimal indeed is that which makes them man: infinitely great is that which makes them divine!

Hui Tzŭ said to Chuang Tzŭ, "Are there then men who have no passions?"

Chuang Tzŭ replied, "Certainly."

"But if a man has no passions," argued Hui Tzŭ, "what is it that makes him a man?"

"Tao," replied Chuang Tzŭ, "gives him his expression, and God gives him his form. How should he not be a man?"

"If then he is a man," said Hui Tzŭ, "how can he be without passions?"

"What you mean by passions," answered Chuang Tzŭ, "is not what I mean. By a man without passions I mean one who does not permit good and evil to disturb his internal economy, but rather falls in with whatever happens, as a matter of course, and does not add to the sum of his mortality."

The play of passion would tend to create conditions which otherwise would not exist.

"But whence is man to get his body," asked Hui Tzŭ, "if there is to be no adding to the sum of mortality?"

This is of course a gibe. Hui Tzŭ purposely takes Chuang Tzŭ's words à double entente.

"Tao gives him his expression," said Chuang Tzŭ, "and God gives him his form. He does not permit good and evil to disturb his internal economy. But now you are devoting your intelligence to externals, and wearing out your mental powers. You prop yourself against a tree and mutter, or lean over a table with half-closed eyes.

> *God has made you a shapely sight,*
> *Yet your only thought is the hard and white."*

Chang Tzŭ puts his last sentence into doggerel, the more effectively to turn the tables against Hui Tzŭ, whose paradoxical theories he is never tired of ridiculing. See ch. ii.

CHAPTER VI

The Great Supreme

Argument:—*The human and the divine—The pure men of old—Their qualifications—Their self-abstraction—All things as ONE—The known and the unknown—Life a boon—Death a transition—Life eternal open to all—The way thither—Illustrations.*

He who knows what God is, and who knows what Man is, has attained. Knowing what God is, he knows that he himself proceeded therefrom. Knowing what Man is, he rests in the knowledge of the known, waiting for the knowledge of the unknown. Working out one's allotted span, and not perishing in mid career,—this is the fulness of knowledge.

God is a principle which exists by virtue of its own intrinsicality, and operates spontaneously, without self-manifestation.

It is in the human that the divine finds expression. Man emanates from God, and should therefore be on earth, in this brief life of ours, what God is for all eternity in the universe.

Herein, however, there is a flaw. Knowledge is dependent upon fulfilment. And as this fulfilment is uncertain, how can it be known that my divine is not really human, my human really divine?

Not until death lifts the veil can we truly know that this life is bounded at each end by an immortality to which the soul finally reverts.

> *"Heaven from all creatures hides the book of Fate,*
> *All but the page prescribed, their present state."*

We must have pure men, and then only can we have pure knowledge.

"Pure" must be understood in the sense of transcendent.

But what is a pure man?—The pure men of old acted without calculation, not seeking to secure results. They laid no plans. Therefore, failing, they had no cause for regret; succeeding, no cause for congratulation. And thus they could scale heights without fear; enter water without becoming wet; fire, without feeling hot. So far had their wisdom advanced towards Tao.

"The world-spirit is a good swimmer, and storms and waves cannot drown him."—Emerson.

The pure men of old slept without dreams, and waked without anxiety. They ate without discrimination, breathing deep breaths. For pure men draw breath from their uttermost depths; the vulgar only from their throats.

"Uttermost depths" is literally "heels," but all the best commentators take the sentence to mean that pure men breathe with their whole being, and not as it were superficially, from the throat only.

This passage is probably responsible for the trick of taking deep inhalations of morning air, practised (not without scientific foundation) by the followers of the debased Taoism of modern times. Other tricks for prolonging life, such as swallowing the saliva three times in every two hours, etc., are more open to adverse criticism. See the T'ai-Hsi-Ching.

Out of the crooked, words are retched up like vomit. If men's passions are deep, their divinity is shallow.

The pure men of old did not know what it was to love life or to hate death. They did not rejoice in birth, nor strive to put off dissolution. Quickly come, and quickly go;—no more. They did not forget whence it was they had sprung, neither did they seek to hasten their return thither. Cheerfully they played their allotted parts, waiting patiently for the end. This is what is called not to lead the heart astray from Tao,

By admitting play of passion in the sense condemned in ch. v. which would hinder the mind from resting quietly in the knowledge of the known.

nor to let the human seek to supplement the divine.

But to wait patiently for the knowledge of the unknown.

And this is what is meant by a pure man.

Such men are in mind absolutely free; in demeanour, grave; in expression, cheerful. If it is freezing cold, it seems to them like autumn; if blazing hot, like spring. Their passions occur like the four seasons.

Each at its appointed time.

They are in harmony with all creation, and none know the limit thereof.

These last few words occur in the Tao-Tê-Ching, ch. lviii. See The Remains of Lao Tzŭ, p. 40. Also, with a variation, in ch. xxii of this work.

And so it is that a perfect man can destroy a kingdom and yet not lose the hearts of the people, while the benefits he hands down to ten thousand generations do not proceed from love of his fellow-man.

Whatever he does is spontaneous, and therefore natural, and therefore in accordance with right.

He who delights in man, is himself not a perfect man. His affection is not true charity.

Charity is the universal love of all creation which admits of no particular manifestations.

Depending upon opportunity, he has not true worth.

True worth is independent of circumstances. It is a quality which is always unconsciously operating for good, and needs no opportunity to call it into existence.

He who is not conversant with both good and evil is not a superior man.

The good, to practise; the evil, to avoid.

He who disregards his reputation is not what a man should be.

As a mere social unit.

He who is not absolutely oblivious of his own existence can never be a ruler of men.

Thus Hu Pu Hsieh, Wu Kuang, Poh I, Shu Ch'i, Chi Tzǔ Hsü Yü, Chi T'o, and Shên T'u Ti, were the servants of rulers, and did the behests of others, not their own.

A list of ancient worthies whose careers had been more or less unsuccessful. Of the first and second little is known, except that the ears of the latter were seven inches long.

The third and fourth were brothers and are types of moral purity. Each refused the throne of their State, because each considered his brother more entitled thereto. Finally, they died of starvation on the mountains rather than submit to a change of the Imperial dynasty. More will be heard of these two later on.

The fifth smeared his body all over with lacquer, so that no one should come near him. Of the sixth, nothing is recorded; and of the seventh, only that he tied a stone around his neck and jumped into a river. See the Fragmenta at the end of the works of Shih Tzǔ.

The pure men of old did their duty to their neighbours, but did not associate with them.

Among them, but not of them.

They behaved as though wanting in themselves, but without flattering others. Naturally rectangular, they were not uncompromisingly hard. They manifested their independence without going to extremes. They appeared to smile as if pleased, when the expression was only a natural response.

As required by the exigencies of society.

Their outward semblance derived its fascination from the store of goodness within. They seemed to be of the world around them, while proudly treading beyond its limits. They seemed to desire silence, while in truth they had dispensed with language.

See ch. v.

They saw in penal laws a trunk;

A natural basis of government.

in social ceremonies, wings;

To aid man's progress through life.
in wisdom, a useful accessory; in morality, a guide. For them penal laws meant a merciful administration; social ceremonies, a passport through the world; wisdom, an excuse for doing what they could not help; and morality, walking like others upon the path.

Instead of at random across country. At such an early date was uniformity a characteristic of the Chinese people.

And thus all men praised them for the worthy lives they led.

For what they cared for could be reduced to ONE, and what they did not care for to ONE also. That which was ONE was ONE, and that which was not ONE was likewise ONE. In that which was ONE, they were of God; in that which was not ONE, they were of Man. And so between the human and the divine no conflict ensued. This was to be a pure man.

Life and Death belong to Destiny. Their sequence, like day and night, is of God, beyond the interference of man, an inevitable law.

A man looks upon God as upon his father, and loves him in like measure. Shall he then not love that which is greater than God?

Sc. Tao.

A man looks upon a ruler of men as upon some one better than himself, for whom he would sacrifice his life. Shall he not then do so for the Supreme Ruler of Creation?

Sc. Tao, the omnipresent, omnipotent Principle which invests even God himself with the power and attributes of divinity.

The careful student of pure Taoism will find however that the distinction between Tao and God is sometimes so subtle as altogether to elude his intelligence.

When the pond dries up, and the fishes are left upon dry ground, to moisten them with the breath or to damp them with spittle is not to be compared with leaving them in the first instance in their native rivers and lakes. And better than praising Yao and blaming Chieh would be leaving them both and attending to the development of Tao.

Tao gives me this form, this toil in manhood, this repose in old age, this rest in death. And surely that which is such a kind arbiter of my life is the best arbiter of my death.

A boat may be hidden in a creek, or in a bog, safe enough.

The text has "or a mountain in a bog," which taken with the context seems to me to be nonsense. Yet all the commentators labour to explain away the difficulty, instead of making the obvious change of "mountain" into "boat," to which change the forms of the two Chinese characters readily lend themselves. In over two thousand years of literary activity, it seems but rarely to have occurred to the Chinese that a textus receptus could contain a copyist's slip.

But at midnight a strong man may come and carry away the boat on his back. The dull of vision do not perceive that however you conceal things, small ones in larger ones, there will always be a chance of losing them.

The boat is figurative of our mortal coil which cannot be hidden from decay.

But if you conceal the whole universe in the whole universe, there will be no place left wherein it may be lost. The laws of matter make this to be so.

To have attained to the human form must be always a source of joy. And then, to undergo countless transitions, with only the infinite to look forward to,—what incomparable bliss is that! Therefore it is that the truly wise rejoice in that which can never be lost, but endures alway.

The soul which as Tao, is commensurate only with time and space.

For if we can accept early death, old age, a beginning, and an end,

As inseparable from Destiny,—already a step in the right direction.

why not that which informs all creation and is of all phenomena the Ultimate Cause?

The long chain of proximate causes reaches finality in Tao. Here we have the complete answer to such queries as that propounded to the Umbra by the Penumbra at the close of ch. ii.

Tao has its laws, and its evidences. It is devoid both of action and of form. It may be transmitted, but cannot be received.

So that the receiver can say he has it.

It may be obtained, but cannot be seen. Before heaven and earth were, Tao was. It has existed without change from all time. Spiritual beings drew their spirituality therefrom, while the universe became what we can see it now. To Tao, the zenith is not high, nor the nadir low; no point in time is long ago, nor by lapse of ages has it grown old.

To the infinite all terms and conditions are relative.

Hsi Wei obtained Tao, and so set the universe in order.

A legendary ruler of remote antiquity. In what sense he set the universe in order has not been authentically handed down.

Fu Hsi obtained it, and was able to establish eternal principles.

The first in the received list of Chinese sovereigns (B.C. 2852). This monarch is said to have invented the art of writing and to have taught his people to cook.

The Great Bear obtained it, and has never erred from its course. The sun and moon obtained it, and have never ceased to revolve. K'an P'i obtained it, and established the K'un-lun mountains.

The divinity of the sacred mountains here mentioned.

P'ing I obtained it, and rules over the streams. Chien Wu obtained it, and dwells on Mount T'ai.

See ch. i.

The Yellow Emperor obtained it, and soared upon the clouds to heaven.

The most famous of China's legendary rulers (B.C. 2697). He is said among other things to have invented wheeled vehicles, and generally to have given a start to the civilisation of his people. Some of Lao Tzǔ's sayings have been attributed to him; and by some he has been regarded as the first promulgator of Tao.

Chuan Hsü obtained it, and dwells in the Dark Palace.

A legendary ruler (B.C. 2513), of whose Dark Palace nothing is known.

Yü Ch'iang obtained it, and fixed himself at the North Pole.

As its presiding genius.

Hsi Wang Mu obtained it, and settled at Shao Kuang; since when, no one knows; until when, no one knows either.

A lady,—or a place, for accounts vary,—around whose name innumerable legends have gathered.

P'êng Tsu obtained it, and lived from the time of Shun until the time of the Five Princes.

From 2255 to the 7th century B.C. See ch. i.

Fu Yüeh obtained it, and as the Minister of Wu Ting

A monarch of the Yin dynasty, B.C. 1324.

got the empire under his control. And now, charioted upon one constellation and drawn by another, he has been enrolled among the stars of heaven.

Nan Po Tzǔ K'uei

Probably the individual mentioned in chs. ii. and iv.

said to Nü Yü,

By one authority said to be a woman.

"You are old, Sir, and yet your countenance is like that of a child. How is this?"

Nü Yü replied, "I have learnt Tao."

"Could I get Tao by studying it?" asked the other.

"I fear not," said Nü Yü. "You are not the sort of man. There was Pu Liang I. He had all the qualifications of a sage, but not Tao. Now I had Tao, though none of the qualifications. But do you imagine that much as I wished it I was able to teach Tao to him so that he should be a perfect sage? Had it been so, then to teach Tao to one who has the qualifications of a sage would be an easy matter. No, Sir. I imparted as though withholding; and in three days, for him, this sublunary state had ceased to exist.

With all its paltry distinctions of sovereign and subject, high and low, good and bad, etc.

When he had attained to this, I withheld again; and in seven days more, for him, the external world had ceased to be. And so again for another nine days, when he became unconscious of his own existence. He became first etherealised, next possessed of perfect wisdom, then without past or present, and finally able to enter there where life and death are no more,—where killing does not take away life, nor does prolongation of life add to the duration of existence.

In Tao life and death are One.

In that state, he is ever in accord with the exigencies of his environment;

Literally, there is no sense in which he is not accompanying or meeting, destroying or constructing. That is, in spite of his spiritual condition as above described, he can still adapt himself naturally to life among his fellow-men. The retirement of a hermit is by no means necessary to the perfection of the pure man.

and this is to be Battered but not Bruised. And he who can be thus battered but not bruised is on the way to perfection."

"And how did you manage to get hold of all this?" asked Nan Po Tzŭ K'uei.

"I got it from books," replied Nü Yü; "and the books got it from learning, and learning from investigation, and investigation from cö-ordination,
Of eye and mind.
and cö-ordination from application, and application from desire to know, and desire to know from the unknown, and the unknown from the great void, and the great void from infinity!"

Four men were conversing together, when the following resolution was suggested:—"Whosoever can make Inaction the head, Life the backbone, and Death the tail, of his existence,—that man shall be admitted to friendship with us." The four looked at each other and smiled; and tacitly accepting the conditions, became friends forthwith.

By-and-by, one of them, named Tzŭ Yü, fell ill, and another, Tzŭ Ssŭ, went to see him. "Verily God is great!" said the sick man. "See how he has doubled me up. My back is so hunched that my viscera are at the top of my body. My cheeks are level with my navel. My shoulders are higher than my neck. My hair grows up towards the sky. The whole economy of my organism is deranged. Nevertheless, my mental equilibrium is not disturbed." So saying, he dragged himself painfully to a well, where he could see himself, and continued, "Alas, that God should have doubled me up like this!"

"Are you afraid?" asked Tzŭ Ssŭ.

"I am not," replied Tzŭ Yü. "What have I to fear? Ere long I shall be decomposed. My left shoulder will become a cock, and I shall herald the approach of morn. My right shoulder will become a cross-bow, and I shall be able to get broiled duck. My buttocks will become wheels; and with my soul for a horse, I shall be able to ride in my own chariot. I obtained life because it was my time: I am now parting with it in accordance with the same law. Content with the natural sequence of these states, joy and sorrow touch me not. I am simply, as the ancients expressed it, hanging in the air, unable to cut myself down, bound with the trammels of material existence. But man has ever given way before God: why, then, should I be afraid?"

"What comes from God to us, returns from us to God."—Plato.

By-and-by, another of the four, named Tzŭ Lai, fell ill, and lay gasping for breath, while his family stood weeping around. The fourth friend, Tzŭ Li, went to see him. "Chut!" cried he to the wife and children; "begone! you balk his decomposition." Then, leaning against the door, he said, "Verily, God is great! I wonder what he will make of you now. I wonder whither you will be sent. Do you think he will make you into a rat's liver
The Chinese believe that a rat has no liver.
or into the shoulders of a snake?"

"A son," answered Tzŭ Lai, "must go whithersoever his parents bid him. Nature is no other than a man's parents.
The term "Nature" stands here as a rendering of Yin and Yang, the

Positive and Negative Principles of Chinese cosmogony, from whose interaction the visible universe results.

If she bid me die quickly, and I demur, then I am an unfilial son. She can do me no wrong. Tao gives me this form, this toil in manhood, this repose in old age, this rest in death. And surely that which is such a kind arbiter of my life is the best arbiter of my death.

"Suppose that the boiling metal in a smelting-pot were to bubble up and say, 'Make of me an Excalibur;' I think the caster would reject that metal as uncanny. And if a sinner like myself were to say to God, 'Make of me a man, make of me a man;' I think he too would reject me as uncanny. The universe is the smelting-pot, and God is the caster. I shall go whithersoever I am sent, to wake unconscious of the past, as a man wakes from a dreamless sleep."

Tzŭ Sang Hu, Mêng Tzŭ Fan, and Tzŭ Ch'in Chang, were conversing together, when it was asked, "Who can be, and yet not be?

Implying the absence of all consciousness.

Who can do, and yet not do?

By virtue of inaction.

Who can mount to heaven, and roaming through the clouds, pass beyond the limits of space, oblivious of existence, for ever and ever without end?"

The three looked at each other and smiled; and as neither had any misgivings, they became friends accordingly.

Shortly afterwards Tzŭ Sang Hu died; whereupon Confucius sent Tzŭ Kung

One of his chief disciples.

to take part in the mourning. But Tzŭ Kung found that one had composed a song which the other was accompanying on the lute,

Strictly speaking, a kind of zitha, played with two hammers.

as follows:—

> Ah! Wilt thou come back to us, Sang Hu?
> Ah! Wilt thou come back to us, Sang Hu?
> Thou hast already returned to thy God,
> While we still remain here as men,—alas!

Tzŭ Kung hurried in and said, "How can you sing alongside of a corpse? Is this decorum?"

The two men looked at each other and laughed, saying, "What should this man know of decorum indeed?"

Not the outward decorum of the body, but the inward decorum of the heart.

Tzŭ Kung went back and told Confucius, asking him, "What manner of men are these? Their object is nothingness and a separation from their corporeal frames.

Various commentators give various renderings of this sentence,—mostly forced.

They can sit near a corpse and yet sing, unmoved. There is no class for such. What are they?"

"These men," replied Confucius, "travel beyond the rule of life. I travel within it. Consequently, our paths do not meet; and I was wrong in sending you to mourn. They consider themselves as one with God, recognising no distinctions between human and divine. They look on life as a huge tumour from which death sets them free. All the same they know not where they were before birth, nor where they will be after death. Though admitting different elements, they take their stand upon the unity of all things. They ignore their passions. They take no count of their ears and eyes. Backwards and forwards through all eternity, they do not admit a beginning or end. They stroll beyond the dust and dirt of mortality, to wander in the realms of inaction. How should such men trouble themselves with the conventionalities of this world, or care what people may think of them?"

"But if such is the case," said Tzŭ Kung, "why should we stick to the rule?"

"Heaven has condemned me to this," replied Confucius. "Nevertheless, you and I may perhaps escape from it."

"By what method?" asked Tzŭ Kung.

"Fishes," replied Confucius, "are born in water. Man is born in Tao. If fishes get ponds to live in, they thrive. If man gets Tao to live in, he may live his life in peace.

Without reference to the outward ceremonial of this world.

Hence the saying, 'All that a fish wants is water; all that a man wants is Tao.'"

It is of course by a literary coup de main that Confucius is here and elsewhere made to stand sponsor to the Tao of the rival school.

"May I ask," said Tzŭ Kung, "about divine men?"

"Divine men," replied Confucius, "are divine to man, but ordinary to God. Hence the saying that the meanest being in heaven would be the best on earth; and the best on earth, the meanest in heaven."

"Man is a kind of very minute heaven. God is the grand man."—Swedenborg.

Yen Hui said to Confucius, "When Mêng Sun Ts'ai's mother died, he wept, but without snivelling;

Which the Chinese regard as the test of real sorrow.

he grieved but his grief was not heartfelt; he wore mourning but without howling. Yet although wanting in these three points, he is considered the best mourner in the State of Lu. Surely this is the name and not the reality. I am astonished at it."

"Mêng Sun," said Confucius, "did all that was required. He has made an advance towards wisdom.

Towards Tao, wherein there is no weeping nor gnashing of teeth.

He could not do less;

Than mourn outwardly, for fear of committing a breach of social etiquette, in harmony if not in accordance with which the true Sage passes his life.

while all the time actually doing less.

As seen from the absence of those signs which prove inward grief.

"Mêng Sun knows not whence we come nor whither we go. He knows not whether the end will come early or late. Passing into life as a man, he quietly awaits his passage into the unknown. What should the dead know of the living, or the living know of the dead? Even you and I may be in a dream from which we have not yet awaked.

"Then again, he adapts himself physically,
To the ceremonial of the body,
while avoiding injury to his higher self.
Keeping his soul free from the disturbance of passion.
He regards a dying man simply as one who is going home. He sees others weep, and he naturally weeps too.

"Besides, a man's personality is something of which he is subjectively conscious. It is impossible for him to say if he is really that which he is conscious of being. You dream you are a bird, and soar to heaven. You dream you are a fish, and dive into the ocean's depths. And you cannot tell whether the man now speaking is awake or in a dream.

"A pleasurable sensation precedes the smile it evokes. The smile itself is not dependent upon a reminding nudge.
And just so was Mêng Sun's outward expression of grief,— spontaneous, as being in harmony with his surroundings.
Resign yourself,
To your mortal environment.
unconscious of all changes,
Of life into death, etc.
and you shall enter into the pure, the divine, the One."

I Erh Tzǔ went to see Hsü Yu. The latter asked him, saying, "How has Yao benefited you?"

"He bade me," replied the former, "practise charity and do my duty, and distinguish clearly between right and wrong."

"Then what do you want here?" said Hsü Yu. "If Yao has already branded you with charity and duty, and cut off your nose with right and wrong, what do you do in this free-and-easy, care-for-nobody, topsy-turvy neighbourhood?"
Of Tao.
"Nevertheless," replied I Erh Tzǔ, "I should like to be on its confines."

"If a man has lost his eyes," retorted Hsü Yu, "it is impossible for him to join in the appreciation of beauty. A man with a film over his eyes cannot tell a blue sacrificial robe from a yellow one."

"Wu Chuang's disregard of her beauty," answered I Erh Tzǔ, "Chü Liang's disregard of his strength, the Yellow Emperor's abandonment of wisdom,—all these were brought about by a process of filing and hammering. And how do you know but that God would rid me of my brands, and give me a new nose, and make me fit to become a disciple of yourself?"

"Ah!" replied Hsü Yu, "that cannot be known. But I will just give you an outline. The Master I serve succours all things, and does not account it duty. He continues his blessings through countless generations, and does not account it charity. Dating back to the remotest antiquity, he does not account himself old. Covering heaven, supporting earth, and fashioning the various forms of things, he does not account himself skilled. He it is whom you should seek."

And he is Tao.

"I am getting on," observed Yen Hui to Confucius.

The most famous of all the disciples of Confucius, admitted by the latter to have been as near perfection as possible.

"How so?" asked the latter.

"I have got rid of charity and duty," replied the former.

"Very good," replied Confucius, "but not perfect."

Another day Yen Hui met Confucius and said, "I am getting on."

"How so?" asked Confucius.

"I have got rid of ceremonial and music," answered Yen Hui.

"Very good," said Confucius, "but not perfect."

On a third occasion Yen Hui met Confucius and said, "I am getting on."

"How so?" asked the Sage.

"I have got rid of everything," replied Yen Hui.

"Got rid of everything!" said Confucius eagerly. "What do you mean by that?"

"I have freed myself from my body," answered Yen Hui. "I have discarded my reasoning powers. And by thus getting rid of body and mind, I have become One with the Infinite. This is what I mean by getting rid of everything."

"If you have become One," cried Confucius, "there can be no room for bias. If you have passed into space, you are indeed without beginning or end. And if you have really attained to this, I trust to be allowed to follow in your steps."

Tzŭ Yü and Tzŭ Sang were friends. Once when it had rained for ten days, Tzŭ Yü said, "Tzŭ Sang is dangerously ill." So he packed up some food and went to see him.

In accordance with the exigencies of mortality. How Tzŭ Yü knew that his friend was ill is not clear. An attempt has been made by one commentator on the basis of animal magnetism, in which the Chinese have believed for centuries.

Arriving at the door, he heard something between singing and lamentation, accompanied with the sound of music, as follows:—

"O father! O mother! O Heaven! O Man!"

These words seemed to be uttered with a great effort; whereupon Tzŭ Yü went in and asked what it all meant.

"I was trying to think who could have brought me to this extreme," replied Tzŭ Sang, "but I could not guess. My father and mother would hardly wish me to be poor. Heaven covers all equally. Earth supports all equally. How can they make me in particular poor? I was seeking to know who it was, but without success. Surely then I am brought to this extreme by Destiny."

"The word Fate, or Destiny, expresses the sense of mankind in all ages—that the laws of the world do not always befriend, but often hurt and crush us."—Emerson.

CHAPTER VII

How to Govern

Argument:—Princes should reign, not rule—Rulers find their standards of right in themselves—They thus coerce their people into obeying artificial laws, instead of leaving them to obey natural laws—By action they accomplish nothing—By inaction there is nothing which they would not accomplish—Individuals think they know what the empire wants—In reality it is the empire itself which know best—Illustrations.

Yeh Ch'üeh asked Wang I
See ch. ii.
four questions, none of which he could answer. Thereat the former was greatly delighted,
For now he discovered that ignorance is true knowledge:—an explanation which I adopt only for want of a better.
and went off and told P'u I Tzŭ.
Of whom nothing definite is known.
"Have you only just found that out?" said P'u I Tzŭ. "The Emperor Shun was not equal to T'ai Huang.
A legendary ruler. For Shun, see ch. i.
Shun was all for charity in his zeal for mankind; but although he succeeded in government, he himself never rose above the level of artificiality. Now T'ai Huang was peaceful when asleep and inactive when awake. At one time he would think himself a horse; at another, an ox.
So effectually had he closed all channels leading to consciousness of self.
His wisdom was substantial and above suspicion. His virtue was genuine indeed. And yet he never sank to the level of artificiality."
He was a monarch after the pattern of Tao.
Chien Wu meeting the eccentric Chieh Yü, the latter enquired, saying, "What did Jih Chung Shih teach you?"
Of the last nothing is known. The first two have been already mentioned in chs. i. and vi.
"He taught me," replied Chien Wu, "about the laws and regulations which princes evolve, and which he said none would venture not to hear and obey."

"That is a false teaching indeed," replied Chieh Yü. "To attempt to govern mankind thus,—as well try to wade through the sea, to hew a passage through a river, or make a mosquito fly away with a mountain!

"The government of the truly wise man has no concern with externals. He first perfects himself, and then by virtue thereof he is enabled to accomplish what he wants.

Passively, without effort of any kind.

"The bird flies high to avoid snare and dart. The mouse burrows down below the hill to avoid being smoked or cut out of its nest. Is your wit below that of these two creatures?"

That you should be unable to devise means of avoiding the artificial restraints of princes. Better than coercing into goodness is letting men be good of their own accord.

T'ien Kên

Of whom nothing is known.

was travelling on the south of the Yin mountain. He had reached the river Liao when he met a certain Sage to whom he said, "I beg to ask about the government of the empire."

"Begone!" cried the Sage. "You are a low fellow, and your question is ill timed. God has just turned me out a man. That is enough for me. Borne on light pinions I can soar beyond the cardinal points, to the land of nowhere, in the domain of nothingness. And you come to worry me with government of the empire!"

But T'ien Kên enquired a second time, and the Sage replied, "Resolve your mental energy into abstraction, your physical energy into inaction. Allow yourself to fall in with the natural order of phenomena, without admitting the element of self,—and the empire will be governed."

By virtue of natural laws which lead, without man's interference, to the end desired.

Yang Tzŭ Chü went to see Lao Tzŭ, and said, "Suppose a man were ardent and courageous, acquainted with the order and principles of things, and untiring in the pursuit of Tao—would he be accounted a wise ruler?"

"From the point of view of a truly wise man," replied Lao Tzŭ, "such a one would be a mere handicraftsman, wearing out body and mind alike. The tiger and the pard suffer from the beauty of their skins. The cleverness of the monkey, the tractability of the ox, bring them both to the tether. It is not on such grounds that a ruler may be accounted wise."

"But in what, then," cried Yang Tzŭ Chü, "does the government of a wise man consist?"

"The goodness of a wise ruler," answered Lao Tzŭ, "covers the whole empire, yet he himself seems to know it not. It influences all creation, yet none is conscious thereof. It appears under countless forms, bringing joy to all things. It is based upon the baseless, and travels through the realms of Nowhere."

The operation of true government is invisible to the eye of man.

In the State of Chêng there was a wonderful magician, named Chi Han. He knew all about birth and death, gain and loss, misfortune and happiness, long life and short life,—predicting events to a day with supernatural accuracy. The people of Chêng used to flee at his approach; but Lieh Tzŭ

See ch. i.

went to see him, and became so infatuated that on his return he said to Hu Tzŭ,

Who appears to have been his tutor.

"I used to look upon your Tao as perfect. Now I know something more perfect still."

"So far," replied Hu Tzŭ, "I have only taught you the ornamentals, not the essentials, of Tao; and yet you think you know all about it. Without cocks in your poultry-yard, what sort of eggs do the hens lay? If you go about trying to force Tao down people's throats, you will be simply exposing yourself. Bring your friend with you, and let me show myself to him."

So next day Lieh Tzŭ went with Chi Han to see Hu Tzŭ, and when they came out Chi Han said, "Alas! your teacher is doomed. He cannot live. I hardly give him ten days. I am astonished at him. He is but wet ashes."

And cannot burn much longer.

Lieh Tzŭ went in and wept bitterly, and told Hu Tzŭ; but the latter said, "I showed myself to him just now as the earth shows us its outward form, motionless and still, while production is all the time going on. I merely prevented him from seeing my pent-up energy

Of Tao.

within. Bring him again."

Next day the interview took place as before; but as they were leaving Chi Han said to Lieh Tzŭ, "It is lucky for your teacher that he met me. He is better. He will recover. I saw he had recuperative power."

Lieh Tzŭ went in and told Hu Tzŭ; whereupon the latter replied, "I showed myself to him just now as heaven shows itself in all its dispassionate grandeur, letting a little energy run out of my heels. He was thus able to detect that I had some. Bring him here again."

Next day a third interview took place, and as they were leaving, Chi Han said to Lieh Tzŭ, "Your teacher is never one day like another. I can tell nothing from his physiognomy. Get him to be regular, and I will then examine him again."

This being repeated to Hu Tzŭ as before, the latter said, "I showed myself to him just now in a state of harmonious equilibrium. Where the whale disports itself,—is the abyss. Where water is at rest,—is the abyss. Where water is in motion,—is the abyss. The abyss has nine names. These are three of them."

Alluding to three phases of Tao as manifested at the three interviews above described, Tao being the abyss.

Next day the two went once more to see Hu Tzŭ; but Chi Han was unable to stand still, and in his confusion turned and fled.

"Pursue him!" cried Hu Tzŭ; whereupon Lieh Tzŭ ran after him, but could not overtake him, so he returned and told Hu Tzŭ that the fugitive had disappeared.

"I showed myself to him just now," said Hu Tzŭ, "as Tao appeared before time was. I was to him as a great blank, existing of itself. He knew not who I was. His face fell. He became confused. And so he fled."

Upon this Lieh Tzǔ stood convinced that he had not yet acquired any real knowledge, and at once set to work in earnest, passing three years without leaving the house. He helped his wife to cook the family dinner, and fed his pigs just like human beings. He discarded the artificial and reverted to the natural. He became merely a shape. Amidst confusion,

Of this material world.
he was unconfounded. And so he continued to the end.

By Inaction, fame comes as the spirits of the dead come to the boy who impersonates the corpse.

See ch. i. In the old funeral rites of China, a boy was made to sit speechless and motionless as a corpse, for the reason assigned in the text.

By Inaction, one can become the centre of thought, the focus of responsibility, the arbiter of wisdom. Full allowance must be made for others, while remaining unmoved oneself. There must be a thorough compliance with divine principles, without any manifestation thereof.

Non mihi res, sed me rebus, subjungere conar.

All of which may be summed up in the one word passivity. For the perfect man employs his mind as a mirror. It grasps nothing: it refuses nothing. It receives, but does not keep. And thus he can triumph over matter, without injury to himself.

Without the wear and tear suffered by those who allow their activities free play.

The ruler of the southern sea was called Shu. The ruler of the northern sea was called Hu. The ruler of the central zone was called Hun Tun.

This term is generally used to denote the condition of matter before separation and subdivision into the phenomena of the visible universe.

Shu and Hu often met on Hun Tun's territory, and being always well treated by him, determined to repay his kindness.

They said, "All men have seven holes,—for seeing, hearing, eating, and breathing. Hun Tun alone has none. We will bore some for him."

So every day they bored one hole; but on the seventh day Hun Tun died.

Illustrating the perils of action. "The empire," says Lao Tzǔ, "is a divine trust, and may not be ruled. He who rules, ruins. He who holds by force, loses."

"Men's actions," says Emerson, "are too strong for them."

With this chapter Chuang Tzǔ completes the outline of his system. The remaining chapters are either supplementary to the preceding seven, or independent essays upon cognate subjects.

CHAPTER VIII

Joined Toes

Argument:—Virtues should be natural, not artificial; passive not active. [Chs. viii to xiii inclusive are illustrative of, or supplementary to, ch. vii.]

Joined toes and extra fingers are an addition to nature, though, functionally speaking, superfluous. Wens and tumours are an addition to the bodily form, though, as far as nature is concerned, superfluous. And similarly, to include charity and duty to one's neighbour among the functions of man's organism, is not true Tao.

The whole of this chapter is a violent tirade against the leading doctrines of Confucianism.

For just as joined toes are but useless lumps of flesh, and extra fingers but useless excrescences, so are any artificial additions to our internal economy but harmful adjuncts to real charity and duty to one's neighbour,

Which are the outcome of Tao.

and are moreover prejudicial to the right use of intelligence.

People with extra keenness of vision muddle themselves over the five colours, exaggerate the value of shades, and of distinctions of greens and yellows for sacrificial robes. Of such was Li Chu.

Who could see a pin's point at a distance of 1,000 li. He is mentioned by Mencius.

People with extra keenness of hearing muddle themselves over the five notes, exaggerate the tonic differences of the six pitch-pipes, and the various timbres of metal, stone, silk, and bamboo, of the Huang-chung, and of the Ta-lü. Of such was Shih K'uang.

The blind musician mentioned in ch. ii. The Huang-chung and the Ta-lü were two of the twelve bamboo tubes, or pitch-pipes, on which ancient Chinese music was based. Six were male or positive, and six female or negative. Hence they are spoken of collectively as six.

People who graft on charity, force themselves to display this virtue in order to gain reputation and to enjoy the applause of the world for that which is of no account. Of such were Tsêng and Shih.

Tsêng Shên, a famous disciple of Confucius, and Shih Yu, both noted for their high moral characters.

People who refine in argument do but pile up tiles or knot ropes in their maunderings over the hard and white, the like and the unlike, wearing themselves out over mere useless terms. Of such were Yang and Mih.

Yang Chu, a philosopher of the fourth century B.C., whose "selfish" system was condemned by Mencius; and Mih Tzŭ, already mentioned in ch. ii.

Therefore every addition to or deviation from nature belongs not to the ultimate perfection of all.

Which is in Tao.

He who would attain to such perfection never loses sight of the natural conditions of his existence. With him the joined is not united, nor the separated apart, nor the long in excess, nor the short wanting. For just as a duck's legs, though short, cannot be lengthened without pain to the duck, and a crane's legs, though long, cannot be shortened without misery to the crane, so that which is long in man's moral nature cannot be cut off, nor that which is short be lengthened. All sorrow is thus avoided.

Intentional charity and intentional duty to one's neighbour are surely not included in our moral nature. Yet what sorrow these have involved. Divide your joined toes and you will howl: bite off your extra finger and you will scream. In one case there is too much, in the other too little; but the sorrow is the same. And the charitable of the age go about sorrowing over the ills of the age, while the non-charitable cut through the natural conditions of things in their greed after place and wealth. Surely then intentional charity and duty to one's neighbour are not included in our moral nature. Yet from the time of the Three Dynasties downwards what a fuss has been made about them!

Those who cannot make perfect without arc, line, compasses, and square, injure the natural constitution of things. Those who require cords to bind and glue to stick, interfere with the natural functions of things. And those who seek to satisfy the mind of man by hampering with ceremonies and music and preaching charity and duty to one's neighbour, thereby destroy the intrinsicality of things.

For such intrinsicality does exist, in this sense:—Things which are curved require no arcs; things which are straight require no lines; things which are round require no compasses; things which are rectangular require no squares; things which stick require no glue; things which hold together require no cords. And just as all things are produced, and none can tell how they are produced, so do all things possess their own intrinsic qualities and none can tell how they possess them. From time immemorial this has always been so, without variation. Why then should charity and duty to one's neighbour be as it were glued or corded on, and introduced into the domain of Tao, to give rise to doubt among mankind?

Lesser doubts change the rule of life; greater doubts change man's nature.

How do we know this? By the fact that ever since the time when Shun bid for charity and duty to one's neighbour in order to secure the empire, men have devoted their lives to the pursuit thereof. Is it not then charity and duty to one's neighbour which change the nature of man?

Therefore I have tried to show that from the time of the Three Dynasties it has always been the external which has changed the nature of man. If a mean man, he will die for gain. If a superior man, he will die for fame. If a man of rank, he will die for his ancestral honours. If a Sage, he will die for the world. The pursuits and ambitions of these men differ, but the injury to their natures involved in the sacrifice of their lives is the same.

Tsang and Ku were shepherds, both of whom lost their flocks. On inquiry, it appeared that Tsang had been engaged in reading, while Ku had gone to take part in some trials of strength. Their occupations had been different, but the result was in each case loss of the sheep.

Poh I died for fame at the foot of Mount Shou-yang.

See ch. vi.

Robber Chê died for gain on Mount T'ai.

Robber Chê has a chapter to himself, from which, though spurious, it may be gathered that he was a very remarkable personage in his day.

Mount T'ai has been mentioned in ch. i.

Their deaths were not the same, but the injury to their lives and natures was in each case the same. How then can we applaud the former and blame the latter?

And so, if a man dies for charity and duty to his neighbour the world calls him a noble fellow; but if he dies for gain, the world calls him a low fellow. The dying being the same, one is nevertheless called noble and the other low. But in point of injury to life and nature, the robber Chê and Poh I are one. Where then does the distinction of noble and low come in?

Were a man to apply himself to charity and duty towards his neighbour until he were the equal of Tsêng or Shih, this would not be what I mean by perfection. Or to flavours, until he were the equal of Yü Erh.

Probably identical with I Ya, the Soyer of China.

Or to sounds, until he were the equal of Shih K'uang. Or to colours, until he were the equal of Li Chu. What I mean by perfection is not what is meant by charity and duty to one's neighbour. It is found in the cultivation of Tao. And those whom I regard as cultivators of Tao are not those who cultivate charity and duty to one's neighbour. They are those who yield to the natural conditions of things. What I call perfection of hearing is not hearing others but oneself. What I call perfection of vision is not seeing others but oneself.

A saying attributed by Han Fei Tzǔ to Lao Tzǔ:—"To see oneself is to be clear of sight." See The Remains of Lao Tzǔ, p. 18.

For a man who sees not himself but others, takes not possession of himself but of others, thus taking what others should take and not what he himself should take.

Multi sunt, qui urbes, qui populos habuere in potestate, paucissimi, qui se.

Instead of being himself, he in fact becomes some one else. And if a man thus becomes some one else instead of himself, this is a fatal error of which both the robber Chê and Poh I can be equally guilty.

And so, conscious of my own deficiency in regard to Tao, I do not venture at my best to practise the principles of charity and duty to my neighbour, nor at my worst to fall into the fatal error above-mentioned.

CHAPTER IX

Horses' Hoofs

Argument:—Superiority of the natural over the artificial—Application of this principle to government.

Horses have hoofs to carry them over frost and snow; hair, to protect them from wind and cold. They eat grass and drink water, and fling up their heels over the champaign. Such is the real nature of horses. Palatial dwellings are of no use to them.

One day Poh Loh
A Chinese Rarey, of somewhat legendary character.
appeared, saying, "I understand the management of horses."

So he branded them, and clipped them, and pared their hoofs, and put halters on them, tying them up by the head and shackling them by the feet, and disposing them in stables, with the result that two or three in every ten died. Then he kept them hungry and thirsty, trotting them and galloping them, and grooming, and trimming, with the misery of the tasselled bridle before and the fear of the knotted whip behind, until more than half of them were dead.

The potter says, "I can do what I will with clay. If I want it round, I use compasses; if rectangular, a square."

The carpenter says, "I can do what I will with wood. If I want it curved, I use an arc; if straight, a line."

But on what grounds can we think that the natures of clay and wood desire this application of compasses and square, of arc and line? Nevertheless, every age extols Poh Loh for his skill in managing horses, and potters and carpenters for their skill with clay and wood. Those who govern the empire make the same mistake.

Now I regard government of the empire from quite a different point of view.

The people have certain natural instincts;—to weave and clothe themselves, to till and feed themselves. These are common to all humanity, and all are agreed thereon. Such instincts are called "Heaven-sent."

And so in the days when natural instincts prevailed, men moved quietly and gazed steadily. At that time, there were no roads over mountains, nor boats, nor bridges over water. All things were produced, each for its own proper sphere. Birds and beasts multiplied; trees and shrubs grew up. The former might be led by the hand; you could climb up and peep into the raven's nest. For then man dwelt with birds and beasts, and all creation was one. There were no distinctions of good and bad men. Being all equally without knowledge, their virtue could not go astray. Being all equally without evil desires, they were in a state of natural integrity, the perfection of human existence.

But when Sages appeared, tripping people over charity and fettering with duty to one's neighbour, doubt found its way into the world. And then with their gushing over music and fussing over ceremony, the empire became divided against itself.

Music and ceremonies are important factors in the Confucian system of government.

Were the natural integrity of things left unharmed, who could make sacrificial vessels? Were white jade left unbroken, who could make the regalia of courts? Were Tao not abandoned, who could introduce charity and duty to one's neighbour? Were man's natural instincts his guide, what need would there be for music and ceremonies? Were the five colours not confused, who would practise decoration? Were the five notes not confused, who would adopt the six pitch-pipes?

See chs. viii and x.

Destruction of the natural integrity of things, in order to produce articles of various kinds,—this is the fault of the artisan. Annihilation of Tao in order to practise charity and duty to one's neighbour,—this is the error of the Sage.

Horses live on dry land, eat grass and drink water. When pleased, they rub their necks together. When angry, they turn around and kick up their heels at each other. Thus far only do their natural dispositions carry them. But bridled and bitted, with a plate of metal on their foreheads, they learn to cast vicious looks, to turn the head to bite, to resist, to get the bit out of the mouth or the bridle into it. And thus their natures become depraved,—the fault of Poh Loh.

In the days of Ho Hsü

A legendary ruler of old.

the people did nothing in particular when at rest, and went nowhere in particular when they moved. Having food, they rejoiced; having full bellies, they strolled about. Such were the capacities of the people. But when the Sages came to worry them with ceremonies and music in order to rectify the form of government, and dangled charity and duty to one's neighbour before them in order to satisfy their hearts,—then the people began to develop a taste for knowledge and to struggle one with the other in their desire for gain. This was the error of the Sages.

The simplicity of style, and general intelligibility of this chapter have raised doubts as to its genuineness. But as Lin Hsi Chung justly observes, its sympathetic tone in relation to dumb animals, stamps it, in spite of an undue proportion of word to thought, as beyond reach of the forger's art.

CHAPTER X

Opening Trunks

Argument:—All restrictions artificial, and therefore deceptive—Only by shaking off such fetters, and reverting to the natural, can man hope to attain.

The precautions taken against thieves who open trunks, search bags, or ransack tills, consist of securing with cords and fastening with bolts and locks. This is what the world calls wit.

But a strong thief comes who carries off the till on his shoulders, with box and bag to boot. And his only fear is that the cords and locks should not be strong enough!

Therefore, what the world calls wit, simply amounts to assistance given to the strong thief.

And I venture to state that nothing of that which the world calls wit, is otherwise than serviceable to strong thieves; and that nothing of that which the world calls wisdom is other than a protection to strong thieves.

How can this be shown?—In the State of Ch'i a man used to be able to see from one town to the next, and hear the barking and crowing of its dogs and cocks.

So near were they. This sentence has been incorporated in ch. LXXX of the Tao-Tê-Ching. See The Remains of Lao Tzŭ, p. 50.

The area covered by the nets of fishermen and fowlers, and pricked by the plough, was a square of two thousand and odd li.

Of which three go to a mile, roughly. This statement is intended to convey an idea of prosperity.

And within its four boundaries not a temple or shrine was dedicated, nor a district or hamlet governed, but in accordance with the rules laid down by the Sages.

Yet one morning

B.C. 481.

T'ien Ch'êng Tzŭ slew the Prince of Ch'i, and stole his kingdom. And not his kingdom only, but the wisdom-tricks which he had got from the Sages as well; so that although T'ien Ch'êng Tzŭ acquired the reputation of a thief, he lived as comfortably as ever did either Yao or Shun. The small States did not venture to blame, nor the great States to punish him; and so for twelve generations his descendants ruled over Ch'i.

Commentators have failed to explain away this last sentence. On the strength of an obvious anachronism, some have written off the whole chapter as a forgery; but the general style of argument is against this view.

Was not this stealing the State of Ch'i and the wisdom-tricks of the Sages as well in order to secure himself from the consequences of such theft?

This amounts to what I have already said, namely that nothing of what the world esteems great wit is otherwise than serviceable to strong thieves, and that nothing of what the world calls great wisdom is other than a protection to strong thieves.

Let us take another example. Of old, Lung Fêng was beheaded, Pi Kan was disembowelled, Chang Hung was sliced to death, Tzǔ Hsü was chopped to mince-meat.

The first two have been already mentioned in ch. iv. Chang Hung was minister to Prince Ling of the Chou dynasty. Tzǔ Hsü was a name of the famous Wu Yüan, prime minister of the Ch'u State, whose corpse is said to have been sewn up in a sack and thrown into the river near Soochow.

All these four were Sages, but their wisdom could not preserve them from death.

In fact, it rather hastened their ends.

An apprentice to Robber Chê asked him saying, "Is there then Tao in thieving?"

"Pray tell me of something in which there is not Tao," Chê replied. "There is the wisdom by which booty is located. The courage to go in first, and the heroism of coming out last. There is the shrewdness of calculating success, and justice in the equal division of the spoil. There has never yet been, a great robber who was not possessed of these five."

Thus the doctrine of the Sages is equally indispensable to good men and to Chê. But good men are scarce and bad men plentiful, so that the good the Sages do to the world is little and the evil great.

Therefore it has been said, "If the lips are gone, the teeth will be cold." It was the thinness of the wine of Lu which caused the siege of Han Tan.

The prince of Ch'u held an assembly, to which the princes of Lu and Chao brought presents of wine. That of Lu was poor stuff, while the wine of Chao was rich and generous. Because, however, the Master of the Cellar to the prince of Ch'u failed to get a bribe of wine from the prince of Chao, he maliciously changed the presents; and the prince of Ch'u, displeased at what he regarded as an insult, shortly after laid siege to Han Tan, the chief city of Chao.

It was the appearance of Sages which caused the appearance of great robbers.

Drive out the Sages and leave the robbers alone,—then only will the empire be governed. As when the stream ceases the gully dries up, and when the hill is levelled the chasm is filled; so when Sages are extinct, there will be no more robbers, but the empire will rest in peace.

On the other hand, unless Sages disappear, neither will great robbers disappear; nor if you double the number of Sages wherewithal to govern the empire will you do more than double the profits of Robber Chê.

If pecks and bushels are used for measurement, they will also be stolen.

There will simply be something more to steal.

If scales and steelyards are used for weighing, they will also be stolen. If tallies and signets are used for good faith, they will also be stolen. If charity and duty to one's neighbour are used for rectification, they will also be stolen.

How is this so?—One man steals a purse, and is punished. Another steals a State, and becomes a Prince. But charity and duty to one's neighbour are integral parts of princedom. Does he not then steal charity and duty to one's neighbour together with the wisdom of the Sages?

So it is that to attempt to drive out great robbers

Who steal States.

is simply to help them to steal principalities, charity, duty to one's neighbour, together with measures, scales, tallies, and signets. No reward of official regalia and uniform will dissuade, nor dread of sharp instruments of punishment will deter such men from their course. These do but double the profits of robbers like Chê, and make it impossible to get rid of them,—for which the Sages are responsible.

Therefore it has been said, "Fishes cannot be taken away from water: the instruments of government cannot be delegated to others."

These words were uttered by Lao Tzŭ. So say Han Fei Tzŭ and Huai Nan Tzŭ. They have been incorporated in ch. xxxvi of the Tao-Tê-Ching.

In the wisdom of Sages the instruments of government are found. This wisdom is not fit for enlightening the world.

Away then with wisdom and knowledge, and great robbers will disappear! Discard jade and destroy pearls, and petty thieves will cease to exist. Burn tallies and break signets, and the people will revert to their natural integrity. Split measures and smash scales, and the people will not fight over quantities. Utterly abolish all the restrictions of Sages, and the people will begin to be fit for the reception of Tao.

Confuse the six pitch-pipes, break up organs and flutes, stuff up the ears of Shih K'uang,—and each man will keep his own sense of hearing to himself.

Put an end to decoration, disperse the five categories of colour, glue up the eyes of Li Chu,—and each man will keep his own sense of sight to himself.

Destroy arcs and lines, fling away square and compasses, snap off the fingers of Kung Ch'ui,—

A famous artisan who could draw an exact circle with his unaided hand.

and each man will use his own natural skill.

Wherefore the saying, "Great skill is as clumsiness."

Extremes meet. These words are attributed to Lao Tzŭ by Huai Nan Tzŭ, and are incorporated in ch. xlv of the Tao-Tê-Ching.

Restrain the actions of Tsêng and Shih, stop the mouths of Yang and Mih, get rid of charity and duty to one's neighbour,—and the virtue of the people will become one with God.

If each man keeps to himself his own sense of sight, the world will escape confusion. If each man keeps to himself his own sense of hearing, the world will escape entanglements. If each man keeps his knowledge to himself, the world will escape doubt. If each man keeps his own virtue to himself, the world will avoid deviation from the true path.

Tsêng, Shih, Yang, Mih, Shih K'uang, Kung Ch'ui, and Li Chu, all set up their virtue outside themselves and involve the world in such angry discussions that nothing definite is accomplished.

Have you never heard of the Golden Age,—

This question must be addressed to the reader.

the days of Yung Ch'êng, Ta T'ing, Poh Huang, Chung Yang, Li Lu, Li Hsü, Hsien Yüan, Hê Hsü, Tsun Lu, Chu Yung, Fu Hsi, and Shên Nung?

Ancient rulers, several of whom have already been mentioned.

Then the people used knotted cords.

As a means of intercommunication. The details of the system have not, however, come down to us.

They were contented with what food and raiment they could get. They lived simple and peaceful lives. Neighbouring districts were within sight, and the cocks and dogs of one could be heard in the other, yet the people grew old and died without ever interchanging visits.

In those days, government was indeed perfect. But nowadays any one can excite the people by saying, "In such and such a place there is a Sage."

Immediately they put together a few provisions and hurry off, neglecting their parents at home and their master's business abroad, filing in unbroken line through territories of Princes, with a string of carts and carriages a thousand li in length. Such is the evil effect of an exaggerated desire for knowledge among our rulers. And if rulers aim at knowledge and neglect Tao, the empire will be overwhelmed in confusion.

How can it be shown that this is so?—Bows and cross-bows and hand-nets and harpoon-arrows, involve much knowledge in their use; but they carry confusion among the birds of the air. Hooks and bait and nets and traps, involve much knowledge in their use; but they carry confusion among the fishes of the deep. Fences and nets and snares, involve much knowledge in their use; but they carry confusion among the beasts of the field. In the same way the sophistical fallacies of the hard and white and the like and the unlike of schoolmen involve much knowledge of argument; but they overwhelm the world in doubt.

Therefore it is that whenever there is great confusion, love of knowledge is ever at the bottom of it. For all men strive to grasp what they do not know, while none strive to grasp what they already know; and all strive to discredit what they do not excel in, while none strive to discredit what they do excel in. The result is overwhelming confusion.

Thus, above, the splendour of the heavenly bodies is dimmed; below, the energy of land and water is disturbed; while midway the influence of the four seasons is destroyed. There is not one tiny creature which moves on earth or flies in air but becomes other than by nature it should be. So overwhelming is the confusion which desire for knowledge has brought upon the world ever since the time of the Three Dynasties downwards! The simple and the guileless have been set aside; the specious and the false have been exalted. Tranquil inaction has given place to a love of disputation; and by disputation has confusion come upon the world.

CHAPTER XI

On Letting Alone

Argument:—The natural conditions of our existence require no artificial aids—The evils of government—Failure of coercion—Tao the refuge—Inaction the secret—The action of Inaction—Illustrations.

There has been such a thing as letting mankind alone; there has never been such a thing as governing mankind.

With success.

Letting alone springs from fear lest men's natural dispositions be perverted and their virtue laid aside. But if their natural dispositions be not perverted nor their virtue laid aside, what room is there left for government?

Of old, when Yao governed the empire, he caused happiness to prevail to excess in man's nature; and consequently the people were not satisfied. When Chieh

See p. 18.

governed the empire he caused sorrow to prevail to excess in man's nature; and consequently the people were not contented. Dissatisfaction and discontent are subversive of virtue; and without virtue there is no such thing for an empire as stability.

Virtue, here in its ordinary sense.

When man rejoices greatly he gravitates towards the positive pole. When he sorrows deeply he gravitates towards the negative pole.

These "poles" are the male and female principles already alluded to on p. 37. Originally developed from the Great Monad, they became the progenitors of all creation.

If the equilibrium of positive and negative

In nature.

is disturbed, the four seasons are interrupted, the balance of heat and cold is destroyed, and man himself suffers physically thereby.

Because men are made to rejoice and to sorrow and to displace their centre of gravity, they lose their steadiness, and are unsuccessful in thought and action. And thus it is that the idea of surpassing others first came into the world, followed by the appearance of such men as Robber Chê, Tsêng, and Shih, the result being that the whole world could not furnish enough rewards for the good nor distribute punishments enough for the evil among mankind. And as this great world is not equal to the demand for rewards and punishments; and as, ever since the time of the Three Dynasties

The legendary emperors Fu Hsi, Shên Nung, and Huang Ti, or the Yellow Emperor, already mentioned.

downwards, men have done nothing but struggle over rewards and punishments,—what possible leisure can they have had for adapting themselves to the natural conditions of their existence?

Besides, over-refinement of vision leads to debauchery in colour; over-refinement of hearing leads to debauchery in sound; over-refinement of charity leads to confusion in virtue;

Here again the manifestation of Tao. See p. 21.

over-refinement of duty towards one's neighbour leads to perversion of principle;

The eternal principles which are of Tao and not of man.

over-refinement of ceremonial leads to divergence from the true object; over-refinement of music leads to lewdness of thought; over-refinement of wisdom leads to an extension of mechanical art; and over-refinement of shrewdness leads to an extension of vice.

As shown in the preceding chapter.

If people adapt themselves to the natural conditions of existence, the above eight

Vision, hearing, charity, duty to one's neighbour, ceremonial, music, wisdom, and shrewdness.

may be or may not be; it matters not. But if people do not adapt themselves to the natural conditions of existence, then these eight become hindrances and spoilers, and throw the world into confusion.

In spite of this, the world reverences and cherishes them, thereby greatly increasing the sum of human error. And not as a passing fashion, but with admonitions in words, with humility in prostrations, and with the stimulus of music and song. What then is left for me?

Therefore, for the perfect man who is unavoidably summoned to power over his fellows, there is naught like Inaction.

It is not according to the spirit of Tao that a man should shirk his mortal responsibilities. On the contrary, Tao teaches him how to meet them.

By means of inaction he will be able to adapt himself to the natural conditions of existence. And so it is that he who respects the State as his own body is fit to support it, and he who loves the State as his own body, is fit to govern it.

This last sentence is attributed by Huai Nan Tzǔ to Lao Tzǔ, and has been incorporated in the Tao-Tê-Ching, ch. xiii. It is curious that Chuang Tzǔ should say nothing about its authorship, and perhaps even more curious that Kuo Hsiang, his editor and commentator of the fourth century A.D., should say nothing either about the claims of Lao Tzǔ or the Tao-Tê-Ching.

And if I can refrain from injuring my internal economy, and from taxing my powers of sight and hearing, sitting like a corpse while my dragon-power is manifested around, in profound silence while my thunder-voice resounds, the powers of heaven responding to every phase of my will, as under the yielding influence of inaction all things are brought to maturity and thrive,—what leisure then have I to set about governing the world?

Some of this passage is repeated in ch. xiv.
Ts'ui Chü
A casual personage.

asked Lao Tzŭ, saying, "If the empire is not to be governed, how are men's hearts to be kept in order?"

"Be careful," replied Lao Tzŭ, "not to interfere with the natural goodness of the heart of man. Man's heart may be forced down or stirred up. In each case the issue is fatal.

"By gentleness, the hardest heart may be softened. But try to cut and polish it,—'twill glow like fire or freeze like ice. In the twinkling of an eye it will pass beyond the limits of the Four Seas. In repose, profoundly still; in motion, far away in the sky. No bolt can bar, no bond can bind,—such is the human heart."

"Of old, the Yellow Emperor first caused charity and duty to one's neighbour to interfere with the natural goodness of the heart of man. In consequence of which, Yao and Shun wore the hair off their legs in endeavouring to feed their people. They disturbed their internal economy in order to find room for charity and duty to one's neighbour. They exhausted their energies in framing laws and statutes. Still they did not succeed.

"Thereupon, Yao confined Huan Tou on Mount Tsung; drove the chief of San-miao and his people into San-wei, and kept them there; and banished the Minister of Works to Yu Island.

These words are quoted (with variants) from the Shu Ching or Canon of History. They refer to individuals who had misconducted themselves in carrying out the new régime.

But they were not equal to their task, and through the times of the Three Princes

The Great Yü, T'ang, and Wên Wang, founder of the Chou dynasty.
the empire was in a state of great unrest. Among the bad men were Chieh and Chê; among the good were Tsêng and Shih. By and by, the Confucianists and the Mihists arose; and then came exultation and anger of rivals, fraud between the simple and the cunning, recrimination between the virtuous and the evil, slander between the honest and the dishonest,— until decadence set in, men fell away from their original virtue, their natures became corrupt, and there was a general rush for knowledge.

"The next thing was to coerce by all kinds of physical torture, thus bringing utter confusion into the empire, the blame for which rests upon those who would interfere with the natural goodness of the heart of man.

"In consequence, virtuous men sought refuge in mountain caves, while rulers of States sat trembling in their ancestral halls. Then, when dead men lay about pillowed on each others' corpses, when cangued prisoners and condemned criminals jostled each other in crowds,—then the Confucianists and the Mihists, in the midst of gyves and fetters, stood forth to preach!

Salvation from the ills of which they and their systems had been the cause.

Alas, they know not shame, nor what it is to blush!

"Until I can say that the wisdom of Sages is not a fastener of cangues, and that charity and duty to one's neighbour are not bolts for gyves, how should I know that Tsêng and Shih are not the forerunners

> *Lit. "sounding arrows," used by bandits as a signal for beginning the attack.*

of Chieh and Chê?

> *The meaning intended is that good cannot exist without its correlative evil.*

"Therefore I said, 'Abandon wisdom and discard knowledge, and the empire will be at peace.'"

> *These words have been incorporated in ch. xix of the Tao-Tê-Ching. The present rendering somewhat modifies the view I expressed on p. 16 of The Remains of Lao Tzǔ.*

The Yellow Emperor sat on the throne for nineteen years, and his laws obtained all over the empire.

Hearing that Kuang Ch'êng Tzǔ

> *Said by some commentators to be another name for Lao Tzǔ, but if so, then it must have been Lao Tzǔ as he existed, an incarnation of Tao, before his appearance in the Confucian age.*

was living on Mount K'ung-t'ung, he went thither to see him, and said, "I am told, Sir, that you are in possession of perfect Tao. May I ask in what perfect Tao consists? I desire to avail myself of the good influence of heaven and earth in order to secure harvests and feed my people. I should also like to control the Two Powers of nature

> *The Yin and the Yang. See pp. 37, 55.*

in order to the protection of all living things. How can I accomplish this?"

"What you desire to avail yourself of," replied Kuang Ch'êng Tzǔ, "is the primordial integrity of matter. What you wish to control are the disintegrators thereof. Ever since the empire has been governed by you, the clouds have rained without waiting to thicken, the foliage of trees has fallen without waiting to grow yellow, the brightness of the sun and moon has paled, and the voice of the flatterer is heard on every side. How then speak of perfect Tao?"

The Yellow Emperor withdrew. He resigned the Throne. He built himself a solitary hut. He lay upon straw. For three months he remained in seclusion, and then went again to see Kuang Ch'êng Tzǔ.

The latter was lying down with his face to the south. The Yellow Emperor approached after the manner of an inferior, upon his knees. Prostrating himself upon the ground he said, "I am told, Sir, that you are in possession of perfect Tao. May I ask how my self may be preserved so as to last?"

Kuang Ch'êng Tzǔ jumped up with a start. "A good question indeed!" cried he. "Come, and I will speak to you of perfect Tao.

"The essence of perfect Tao is profoundly mysterious; its extent is lost in obscurity.

"See nothing; hear nothing; let your soul be wrapped in quiet; and your body will begin to take proper form. Let there be absolute repose and absolute purity; do not weary your body nor disturb your vitality,—and you will live for ever. For if the eye sees nothing, and the ear hears nothing, and the mind

> *Lit. the heart.*

thinks nothing, the soul will preserve the body, and the body will live for ever.

Not in the grosser worldly sense, but as a sublimated unit in eternity.

"Cherish that which is within you, and shut off that which is without; for much knowledge is a curse. Then I will place you upon that abode of Great Light which is the source of the positive Power, and escort you through the gate of Profound Mystery which is the source of the negative Power. These Powers are the controllers of heaven and earth, and each contains the other.

Knowledge thereof is knowledge of the great mystery of human existence.

"Cherish and preserve your own self,

In accordance with the above.

and all the rest will prosper of itself.

The welfare of the people, the success of their harvests, etc.

I preserve the original One, while resting in harmony with externals. It is because I have thus cared for my self now for twelve hundred years that my body has not decayed."

The Yellow Emperor prostrated himself and said, "Kuang Ch'êng Tzŭ is surely God...."

Whereupon the latter continued, "Come, I will tell you. That self is eternal; yet all men think it mortal. That self is infinite; yet all men think it finite. Those who possess Tao are princes in this life and rulers in the hereafter. Those who do not possess Tao, behold the light of day in this life and become clods of earth in the hereafter.

"Nowadays, all living things spring from the dust and to the dust return. But I will lead you through the portals of Eternity into the domain of Infinity. My light is the light of sun and moon. My life is the life of heaven and earth. I know not who comes nor who goes. Men may all die, but I endure for ever."

"*A mighty drama, enacted on the theatre of Infinitude, with suns for lamps, and Eternity as a background; whose author is God, and whose purport and thousandfold moral lead us up to the 'dark with excess of light' of the throne of God."—Carlyle.*

The Spirit of the Clouds when passing eastwards through the expanse of Air

The term here used has also been explained to mean some supernatural kind of tree, over which we may imagine the Cloud-Spirit to be passing.

happened to fall in with the Vital Principle. The latter was slapping his ribs and hopping about; whereupon the Spirit of the Clouds said, "Who are you, old man, and what are you doing here?"

"Strolling!" replied the Vital Principle, without stopping.

Activities ceaseless in their imperceptible operation.

"I want to know something," continued the Spirit of the Clouds.

"Ah!" uttered the Vital Principle, in a tone of disapprobation.

"The relationship of heaven and earth is out of harmony," said the Spirit of the Clouds; "the six influences do not combine,

The positive and negative principles, wind, rain, darkness, and light.
and the four seasons are no longer regular. I desire to blend the six influences so as to nourish all living beings. What am I to do?"

"I do not know!" cried the Vital Principle, shaking his head, while still slapping his ribs and hopping about; "I do not know!"

So the Spirit of the Clouds did not press his question; but three years later, when passing eastwards through the Yu-sung territory, he again fell in with the Vital Principle. The former was overjoyed, and hurrying up, said, "Has your Holiness forgotten me?"

He then prostrated himself, and desired to be allowed to interrogate the Vital Principle; but the latter said, "I wander on without knowing what I want. I roam about without knowing where I am going. I stroll in this ecstatic manner, simply awaiting events. What should I know?"

"I too roam about," answered the Spirit of the Clouds; "but the people depend upon my movements. I am thus unavoidably summoned to power; and under these circumstances I would gladly receive some advice."

"That the scheme of empire is in confusion," said the Vital Principle, "that the conditions of life are violated, that the will of God does not triumph, that the beasts of the field are disorganised, that the birds of the air cry at night, that blight reaches the trees and herbs, that destruction spreads among creeping things,—this, alas! is the fault of government."

"True," replied the Spirit of the Clouds, "but what am I to do?"

"It is here," cried the Vital Principle, "that the poison lurks! Go back!"

To the root, to that natural state in which by inaction all things are accomplished.

"It is not often," urged the Spirit of the Clouds, "that I meet with your Holiness. I would gladly receive some advice."

"Feed then your people," said the Vital Principle, "with your heart.

By the influence of your own perfection.

Rest in inaction, and the world will be good of itself. Cast your slough. Spit forth intelligence. Ignore all differences. Become one with the infinite. Release your mind. Free your soul. Be vacuous. Be Nothing!

"Let all things revert to their original constitution. If they do this, without knowledge, the result will be a simple purity which they will never lose; but knowledge will bring with it a divergence therefrom. Seek not the names nor the relations of things, and all things will flourish of themselves."

"*Knowledge is the knowing that we cannot know.*" Emerson.

"Your Holiness," said the Spirit of the Clouds, as he prostrated himself and took leave, "has informed me with power and filled me with mysteries. What I had long sought, I have now found."

The men of this world all rejoice in others being like themselves, and object to others not being like themselves.

"The man, and still more the woman, who can be accused either of doing 'what nobody does,' or of not doing 'what everybody does,' is the subject of as much depreciatory remark as if he or she had committed some grave moral delinquency." Mill's Essay on Liberty, ch. iii.

Those who make friends with their likes and do not make friends with their unlikes, are influenced by a desire to differentiate themselves from others. But those who are thus influenced by a desire to differentiate themselves from others,—how will they find it possible to do so?

As all have similar ambitions, they will only be on the same footing as the rest.

To subordinate oneself to the majority in order to gratify personal ambition, is not so good as to let that majority look each one after his own affairs. Those who desire to govern kingdoms, clutch at the advantages of the Three Princes without seeing the troubles involved. In fact, they trust to luck. But in thus trusting to luck not to destroy the kingdom, their chances of preserving it do not amount to one in ten thousand, while their chances of destroying it are ten thousand to nothing and even more. Such, alas! is the ignorance of rulers.

The above somewhat unsatisfactory paragraph condemns those who strive to distinguish themselves from, and set themselves up as governors of, their fellow-men.

For, given territory, there is the great thing—Man. Given man, he must not be managed as if he were a mere thing; though by not managing him at all he may actually be managed as if he were a mere thing. And for those who understand that the management of man as if he were a mere thing is not the way to manage him, the issue is not confined to mere government of the empire. Such men may wander at will between the six limits of space or travel over the continent of earth, unrestrained in coming and in going. This is to be distinguished from one's fellows, and this distinction is the highest attainable by man.

The doctrine of the perfect man is to him as shadow to form, as echo to sound. Ask and it responds, fulfilling its mission as the help-mate of humanity. Noiseless in repose, objectless in motion, it guides you to the goal, free to come and free to go for ever without end. Alone in its exits and its entrances, it rivals the eternity of the sun.

As for his body, that is in accordance with the usual standard. Being in accordance with the usual standard it is not distinguished in any way. But if not distinguished in any way, what becomes of the distinction by which he is distinguished?

Those who see what is to be seen,—of such were the perfect men of old. Those who see what is not to be seen,—they are the chosen of the universe.

Spiritual sight carries them beyond the horizon where natural vision stops short.

Low in the scale, but still to be allowed for,—matter. Humble, but still to be followed,—

Rather than guided.

mankind. Of others, but still to be attended to,—affairs. Harsh, but still necessary to be set forth,—the law. Far off, but still claiming our presence,—duty to one's neighbour. Near, but still claiming extension,—charity. Of sparing use, but still to be of bounteous store,—ceremony. Of middle course, but still to be of lofty scope,—virtue. One, but not to be without modification,—Tao. Spiritual, yet not to be devoid of action,—God.

In inaction there is action.

Therefore the true Sage looks up to God, but does not offer to aid. He perfects his virtue, but does not involve himself. He guides himself by Tao, but makes no plans. He identifies himself with charity, but does not rely on it. He extends to duty towards his neighbour, but does not store it up. He responds to ceremony, without tabooing it.

Although really recognising only the ceremony of the heart which requires no outward sign.

He undertakes affairs without declining them. He metes out law without confusion. He relies on his fellow-men and does not make light of them. He accommodates himself to matter and does not ignore it.

Thus the action of the Sage is after all inaction.

While there should be no action, there should be also no inaction.

Of a positive, premeditated character.

He who is not divinely enlightened will not be sublimely pure. He who has not clear apprehension of Tao will find this beyond his reach. And he who is not enlightened by Tao,—alas indeed for him!

What then is Tao?—There is the Tao of God, and the Tao of man. Inaction and compliance make the Tao of God: action and entanglement the Tao of man. The Tao of God is fundamental: the Tao of man is accidental. The distance which separates them is great. Let us all take heed thereto!

CHAPTER XII

The Universe

Argument:—The prëeminence of Tao—All things informed thereby—The true Sage illumined thereby—His attributes—His perfection—Man's senses his bane—Illustrations.

Vast as is the universe, its phenomena are regular. Countless though its contents, the laws which govern these are uniform. Many though its inhabitants, that which dominates them is sovereignty. Sovereignty begins in virtue and ends in God. Therefore it is called divine.

The term here used has been elsewhere rendered "infinite."

Of old, the empire was under the sovereignty of inaction. There was the virtue of God,—nothing more.

Meaning, of course, Tao. In other words, all things existed under their own natural conditions.

Words being in accordance with Tao, the sovereignty of the empire was correct. Delimitations being in accordance with Tao, the duties of prince and subject were clear. Abilities being in accordance with Tao, the officials of the empire governed. The point of view being always in accordance with Tao, all things responded thereto.

Under the reign of inaction, the natural prevailed over the artificial. (1) The sovereign could utter no cruel mandate. (2) Sovereign and subject each played his allotted part. (3) The right men were in the right place. (4) All things were as they were, and not as man would have them.

Thus, virtue was the connecting link between God and man, while Tao spread throughout all creation. Men were controlled by outward circumstances, applying their in-born skill to the development of civilised life. This skill was bound up with the circumstances of life, and these with duty, and duty with virtue, and virtue with Tao, and Tao with God.

Therefore it has been said, "As for those who nourished the empire of old, having no desires for themselves, the empire was not in want. They did nothing, and all things proceeded on their course. They preserved a dignified repose, and the people rested in peace."

We are not told who said these words. They are not in the Tao-Tê-Ching; and yet if Lao Tzŭ did not utter them, it is difficult to say who did.

The Record says, "By converging to One, all things may be accomplished. By the virtue which is without intention, even the supernatural may be subdued."

How much more man? Kuo Hsiang says the Record was the name of a work ascribed to Lao Tzŭ.

The Master said, "Tao covers and supports all things,"—so vast is its extent. Each man should prepare his heart accordingly.

This "Master" has been identified with both Chuang Tzŭ and Lao Tzŭ.

"To act by means of inaction is God. To speak by means of inaction is Virtue. To love men and care for things is Charity. To recognise the unlike as the like is breadth of view. To make no distinctions is liberal. To possess variety is wealth. And so, to hold fast to virtue is strength. To complete virtue is establishment. To follow Tao is to be prepared. And not to run counter to the natural bias of things is to be perfect.

"He who fully realises these ten points, by storing them within enlarges his heart, and with this enlargement brings all creation to himself. Such a man will bury gold on the hillside and cast pearls into the sea. He will not struggle for wealth, nor strive for fame. He will not rejoice at old age, nor grieve over early death. He will find no pleasure in success, no chagrin in failure. He will not account a throne as his own private gain, nor the empire of the world as glory personal to himself. His glory is to know that all things are One, and that life and death are but phases of the same existence!"

"Let man learn that he is here, not to work, but to be worked upon; and that, though abyss open under abyss, and opinion displace opinion, all are at last contained in the Eternal Cause." Emerson.

The Master said, "How profound in its repose, how infinite in its purity, is Tao!

"If metal and stone were without Tao, they would not be capable of emitting sound. And just as they possess the property of sound but will not emit sound unless struck, so surely is the same principle applicable to all creation.

Meaning that all creation is responsive to proper influences, in accordance with Tao, if we only knew where to seek them.

"The man of complete virtue remains blankly passive as regards what goes on around him. He is as originally by nature, and his knowledge extends to the supernatural. Thus, his virtue expands his heart, which goes forth to all who come to take refuge therein.

His heart does not initiate the movement, but simply responds to an influence brought to bear.

"Without Tao, form cannot be endued with life. Without virtue, life cannot be endued with intelligence. To preserve one's form, live out one's life, establish one's virtue, and realise Tao,—is not this complete virtue?

"Issuing forth spontaneously, moving without premeditation, all things following in his wake,—such is the man of complete virtue!

"He can see where all is dark. He can hear where all is still. In the darkness he alone can see light. In the stillness he alone can detect harmony. He can sink to the lowest depths of materialism. To the highest heights of spirituality he can soar. This because he stands in due relation to all things. Though a mere abstraction, he can minister to their wants, and ever and anon receive them into rest,—the great, the small, the long, the short, for ever without end."

He is, as it were, a law of compensation to all things.

The Yellow Emperor travelled to the north of the Red Lake and ascended the K'un-lun Mountains. Returning south he lost his magic pearl.

His spiritual part, his soul.

He employed Intelligence to find it, but without success. He employed Sight to find it, but without success. He employed Speech

Also explained as "Strength."

to find it, but without success. Finally, he employed Nothing, and Nothing got it.

He did not employ Nothing to find it. He only employed Nothing.

"Strange indeed," quoth the Emperor, "that Nothing should have been able to get it!"

Knowledge, sight, and speech, tend to obscure rather than illuminate the spiritual nature of man. Only in a state of negation can true spirituality be found.

Yao's tutor was Hsü Yu. The latter's tutor was Yeh Ch'üeh, and Yeh Ch'üeh's tutor was Wang I, whose tutor was Pei I.

Yao enquired of Hsü Yu, saying, "Would Yeh Ch'üeh do to be emperor? I am going to get Wang I to ask him."

"Alas!" cried Hsü Yu, "that would be bad indeed for the empire. Yeh Ch'üeh is a clever and capable man. He is by nature better than most men, but he seeks by means of the human to reach the divine. He strives to do no wrong; but he is ignorant of the source from which wrong springs. Emperor forsooth! He avails himself of the artificial and neglects the natural. He lacks unity in himself. He worships intelligence and is always in a state of ferment. He is a slave to circumstances and to things. Wherever he looks, his surroundings respond. He himself responds to his surroundings.

He is not yet an abstraction, informed by Tao.

He is always undergoing modifications and is wanting in fixity. How should such a one be fit for emperor? Still every clan has its elder. He may be leader of a clan, but not a leader of leaders. A captain who has been successful in suppressing rebellion, as minister is a bane, as sovereign, a thief."

Yao went to visit Hua. The border-warden of Hua said "Ha! a Sage. My best respects to you, Sir. I wish you a long life."

"Don't!" replied Yao.

"I wish you plenty of money," continued the border-warden.

"Don't!" replied Yao.

"And many sons," added he.

"Don't!" replied Yao.

"Long life, plenty of money, and many sons," cried the warden, "these are what all men desire. How is it you alone do not want them?"

"Many sons," answered Yao, "are many anxieties. Plenty of money means plenty of trouble. Long life involves much that is not pleasant to put up with. These three gifts do not advance virtue; therefore I declined them."

"At first I took you for a Sage," said the warden, "but now I find you are a mere man. God, in sending man into the world, gives to each his proper function. If you have many sons and give to each his proper function, what cause have you for anxiety?

"And similarly, if you have wealth and allow others to share it, what troubles will you have?"

"The true Sage dwells like the quail
 At random.
and feeds like a fledgeling.
 Which is dependent on its parents.
He travels like the bird, leaving no trace behind. If there be Tao in the empire, he and all things are in harmony. If there be not Tao, he cultivates virtue in retirement. After a thousand years of this weary world, he mounts aloft, and riding upon the white clouds passes into the kingdom of God, whither the three evils do not reach, and where he rests secure in eternity. What is there to put up with in that?"

Thereupon the border-warden went off, and Yao followed him; saying, "May I ask——," to which the warden only replied "Begone!"

The style of the above episode varies enough from Chuang Tzŭ's standard to make its authorship doubtful.

When Yao was Emperor, Poh Ch'êng Tzŭ Kao

Lao Tzŭ under a previous incarnation. See the Kuang Ch'êng Tzŭ of p. 125.

was one of his vassals. But when Yao handed over the empire to Shun, and Shun to the Great Yü, Poh Ch'êng Tzŭ Kao resigned his fief and betook himself to agriculture.

The Great Yü going to visit him, found him working in the fields; whereupon he approached humbly, saying, "When Yao was emperor, you, Sir, were a vassal; but when Yao handed over the empire to Shun, and Shun to me, you resigned your fief and betook yourself to agriculture. May I enquire the reason of this?"

"When Yao ruled the empire," said Tzŭ Kao, "the people exerted themselves without reward and behaved themselves without punishment. But now you reward and punish them, and yet they are not good. From this point virtue will decline, the reign of force will begin, and the troubles of after ages will date their rise. Away with you! Do not interrupt my work." And he quietly went on ploughing as before.

The above episode is unmistakably spurious.

At the beginning of the beginning, even Nothing did not exist. Then came the period of the Nameless.

"The Nameless," says the Tao-Tê-Ching, ch. i, "was the beginning of heaven and earth." See also ch. ii, ante.

When One came into existence, there was One, but it was formless. When things got that by which they came into existence, it was called their virtue.

Sc. that, by virtue of which they are what they are. See p. 21.

That which was formless, but divided,

I.e. allotted.

though without interstice,

Unbroken in continuity.

was called destiny.

Then came the movement which gave life, and things produced in accordance with the principles of life had what is called form. When form encloses the spiritual part, each with its own characteristics, that is its nature. By cultivating this nature, we are carried back to virtue; and if this is perfected, we become as all things were in the beginning. We become unconditioned, and the unconditioned is great. As birds join their beaks in chirping,

Unconsciously.

and beaks to chirp must be joined,—to be thus joined with the universe without being more conscious of it than an idiot, this is divine virtue, this is accordance with the eternal fitness of things.

Confucius asked Lao Tzŭ, saying, "There are persons who cultivate Tao according to fixed rules of possible and impossible, fit and unfit, just as the schoolmen speak of separating hardness from whiteness as though these could be hung up on different pegs.

See p. 10.

Could such persons be termed sages?"

"That," replied Lao Tzŭ, "is but the skill of the handicraftsman, wearing out body and soul alike. The powers of the hunting-dog involve it in trouble;

It is kept by man instead of being free.

the cleverness of the monkey brings it down from the mountain.

Into the hands of man.

Ch'iu, what I mean you cannot understand, neither can you put it into words.

Ch'iu was the personal name of Confucius. It is never uttered by the Confucianist, the term "a certain one" being usually substituted. Neither is it ever written down, except with the omission of some stroke, by which its form is changed.

Those who have a head and feet, but no mind nor ears, are many. Those who have a body without a body or appearance of one, and yet there they are,—are none. Movement and rest, life and death, rise and fall, are not at the beck and call of man. Cultivation of self is in his own hands. To be unconscious of objective existences and of God, this is to be unconscious of one's own personality. And he who is unconscious of his own personality, combines in himself the human and the divine."

Chiang Lü Mien went to see Chi Ch'ê,

Two obscure personages.

and said, "The Prince of Lu begged me to instruct him, but I declined. However, he would take no refusal, so I was obliged to do so. I don't know if I was correct in my doctrine or not. Please note what I said. I told him to be decorous and thrifty; to advance the public-spirited and loyal, and to have no partialities. Then, I said, no one would venture to oppose him."

Chi Ch'ê sniggered and said, "Your remarks on the virtues of Princes may be compared with the mantis stretching out its feelers and trying to stop a carriage,—not likely to effect the object proposed.

See ch. iv, where the same figure is used.

Besides, he would be placing himself in the position of a man who builds a lofty tower and makes a display of his valuables where all his neighbours will come and gaze at them."

Attracting people by means not in accordance with Tao.

"Alas! I fear I am but a fool," replied Chiang Lü Mien. "Nevertheless, I should be glad to be instructed by you in the proper course to pursue."

"The government of the perfect Sage," explained Chi Ch'ê, "consists in influencing the hearts of the people so as to cause them to complete their education, to reform their manners, to subdue the rebel mind, and to exert themselves one and all for the common good. This influence operates in accordance with the natural disposition of the people, who are thus unconscious of its operation. He who can so act has no need to humble himself before the teachings of Yao and Shun. He makes the desires of the people coincident with virtue, and their hearts rest therein."

When Tzŭ Kung

See ch. vi.

went south to the Ch'u State on his way back to the Chin State, he passed through Han-yin. There he saw an old man engaged in making a ditch to connect his vegetable garden with a well. He had a pitcher in his hand, with which he was bringing up water and pouring it into the ditch,—great labour with very little result.

"If you had a machine here," cried Tzŭ Kung, "in a day you could irrigate a hundred times your present area. The labour required is trifling as compared with the work done. Would you not like to have one?"

"What is it?" asked the gardener.

"It is a contrivance made of wood," replied Tzŭ Kung, "heavy behind and light in front. It draws up water as you do with your hands, but in a constantly overflowing stream. It is called a well-sweep."

Still used all over China.

Thereupon the gardener flushed up and said, "I have heard from my teacher that those who have cunning implements are cunning in their dealings, and that those who are cunning in their dealings have cunning in their hearts, and that those who have cunning in their hearts cannot be pure and incorrupt, and that those who are not pure and incorrupt are restless in spirit, and that those who are restless in spirit are not fit vehicles for Tao. It is not that I do not know of these things. I should be ashamed to use them."

At this Tzŭ Kung was much abashed, and said nothing. Then the gardener asked him who he was, to which Tzŭ Kung replied that he was a disciple of Confucius.

"Are you not one who extends his learning with a view to being a Sage; who talks big in order to put himself above the rest of mankind; who plays in a key to which no one can sing so as to spread his reputation abroad? Rather become unconscious of self and shake off the trammels of the flesh,—and you will be near. But if you cannot govern your own self, what leisure have you for governing the empire? Begone! Do not interrupt my work."

Tzŭ Kung changed colour and slunk away, being not at all pleased with this rebuff; and it was not before he had travelled some thirty li that he recovered his usual appearance.

"What did the man we met do," asked a disciple, "that you should change colour and not recover for such a long time?"

"I used to think there was only one man in all the world," replied Tzŭ Kung.

Meaning Confucius.

"I did not know that there was also this man. I have heard the Master say that the test of a scheme is its practicability, and that success must be certain. The minimum of effort with the maximum of success,— such is the way of the Sage.

The absurdity of attributing such doctrines to Confucius will be apparent to every student of the Sage's remains.

"Not so this manner of man. Aiming at Tao, he perfects his virtue. By perfecting his virtue he perfects his body, and by perfecting his body he perfects his spiritual part. And the perfection of the spiritual part is the Tao of the Sage. Coming into life he is as one of the people, knowing not whither he is bound. How complete is his purity? Success, profit, skill,— these have no place in his heart. Such a man, if he does not will it, he does not stir; if he does not wish it, he does not act. If all the world praises him, he does not heed. If all the world blames him, he does not repine.

Reminding us of the philosopher Yung of ch. i.

The praise and the blame of the world neither advantage him nor otherwise. He may be called a man of perfect virtue. As for me, I am but a mere creature of impulse."

So he went back to Lu to tell Confucius. But Confucius said, "That fellow pretends to a knowledge of the science of the ante-mundane. He knows something, but not much. His government is of the internal, not of the external. What is there wonderful in a man by clearness of intelligence becoming pure, by inaction reverting to his original integrity, and with his nature and his spiritual part wrapped up in a body, passing through this common world of ours? Besides, to you and to me the science of the ante-mundane is not worth knowing."

It is only the present which concerns man.

This last is an utterance which might well have fallen from the lips of Confucius. But the whole episode is clearly an interpolation of later times.

As Chun Mang was starting eastwards to the ocean, he fell in with Yüan Fêng on the shore of the eastern sea.

These names are probably allegorical, but it is difficult to say in exactly what sense.

"Whither bound?" cried the latter.

"I am going to the ocean," replied Chun Mang.

"What are you going to do there?" asked Yüan Fêng.

"The ocean," said Chun Mang, "is a thing you cannot fill by pouring in, nor empty by taking out. I am simply on a trip."

You cannot do anything to the infinite.

"But surely you have intentions with regard to the straight-browed people?... Come, tell me how the Sage governs."

The straight-browed, lit. horizontal-eyed, people, are said by one commentator to have been "savages."

"Oh, the government of the Sage," answered Chun Mang. "The officials confine themselves to their functions. Ability is secure of employment. The voice of the people is heard, and action is taken accordingly. Men's words and deeds are their own affairs, and so the empire is at peace. A beck or a call, and the people flock together from all sides. This is how the Sage governs."

"Tell me about the man of perfect virtue," said Yüan Fêng.

"The man of perfect virtue," replied Chun Mang, "in repose has no thoughts, in action no anxiety. He recognises no right, nor wrong, nor good, nor bad. Within the Four Seas, when all profit—that is his pleasure; when all share—that is his repose. Men cling to him as children who have lost their mothers; they rally round him as wayfarers who have missed their road. He has wealth and to spare, but he knows not whence it comes. He has food and drink more than sufficient, but knows not who provides it. Such is a man of virtue."

"And now," said Yüan Fêng, "tell me about the divine man."

"The divine man," replied Chun Mang, "rides upon the glory of the sky where his form can no longer be discerned. This is called absorption into light. He fulfils his destiny. He acts in accordance with his nature. He is at one with God and man. For him all affairs cease to exist, and all things revert to their original state. This is called envelopment in darkness."

Mên Wu Kuei and Ch'ih Chang Man Chi were looking at Wu Wang's troops.

The famous founder of the Chou dynasty, B.C. 1169-1116.

"He is not equal to the Great Yü," said the latter; and consequently "we are involved in all these troubles."

"May I ask," replied Mên Wu Kuei, "if the empire was under proper government when the Great Yü began to govern it, or had he first to quell disorder and then to proceed to government?"

"If the empire had all been under proper government," said the other, "what would there have been for the Great Yü to do? He was as ointment to a sore. Only bald men use wigs; only sick people want doctors. And the Sage blushes when a filial son, with anxious look, administers medicine to cure his loving father.

Because to need drugs, the father must first have been sick; and this, from a Chinese point of view, is clearly the fault of the son.

"In the Golden Age, good men were not appreciated; ability was not conspicuous. Rulers were mere beacons, while the people were free as the wild deer. They were upright without being conscious of duty to their neighbours. They loved one another without being conscious of charity. They were true without being conscious of loyalty. They were honest without being conscious of good faith. They acted freely in all things without recognising obligations to any one. Thus, their deeds left no trace; their affairs were not handed down to posterity.

Rousseau, in Du Contrat Social, thus describes society as it would be if every man was a true Christian:—"Chacun remplirait son devoir; le peuple serait soumis aux lois, les chefs seraient justes et modérés, les magistrats intègres, incorruptibles, les soldats mépriseraient la mort, il n'y aurait ni vanité ni luxe."

"A filial son does not humour his parents. A loyal minister does not flatter his prince. This is the acme of filial piety and loyalty. To assent to whatever a parent or a prince says, and to praise whatever a parent or a prince does, this is what the world calls unfilial and disloyal conduct, though apparently unaware that the principle is of universal application. For though a man assents to whatever the world says, and praises whatever the world does, he is not dubbed a toady; from which one might infer that the world is severer than a father and more to be respected than a prince!

"If you tell a man he is a wheedler, he will not like it. If you tell him he is a flatterer, he will be angry. Yet he is everlastingly both. But all such sham and pretence is what the world likes, and consequently people do not punish each other for doing what they do themselves. For a man to arrange his dress, or make a display, or suit his expression so as to get into the good graces of the world, and yet not to call himself a flatterer; to identify himself in every way with the yeas and nays of his fellows, and yet not call himself one of them;—this is the height of folly.

"A man who knows that he is a fool is not a great fool. A man who knows his error is not greatly in error. Great error can never be shaken off; a great fool never becomes clear-headed. If three men are travelling and one man makes a mistake, they may still arrive at their destination, error being in the minority. But if two of them make a mistake, then they will not succeed, error being in the majority. And now, as all the world is in error, I, though I know the true path, am alas! unable to guide.

"Grand music does not appeal to vulgar ears. Give them the Chê-yang or the Huang-hua,

The "Not for Joseph" and "Sally Come Up" of ancient China.

and they will roar with laughter. And likewise great truths do not take hold of the hearts of the masses. And great truths not finding utterance, common-places carry the day. Two earthen instruments will drown the sound of one metal one; and the result will not be melodious.

"And now, as all the world is in error, I, though I know the true path,—how shall I guide? If I know that I cannot succeed and yet try to force success, this would be but another source of error. Better, then, to desist and strive no more. But if I strive not, who will?

"An ugly man who has a son born to him in the middle of the night will hurry up with a light, in dread lest the child should be like himself.

"An old tree is cut down to make sacrificial vessels, which are then ornamented with colour. The stump remains in a ditch. The sacrificial vessels and the stump in the ditch are very differently treated as regards honour and dishonour; equally, as far as destruction of the woods original nature is concerned. Similarly, the acts of Robber Chê and of Tsêng and Shih are very different; but the loss of original nature is in each case the same.

"The causes of this loss are five in number; viz.—The five colours confuse the eye, and the eyes fail to see clearly. The five sounds confuse the ear, and the ear fails to hear accurately. The five scents confuse the nose, and obstruct the sense of smell. The five tastes cloy the palate, and vitiate the sense of taste. Finally, likes and dislikes cloud the understanding, and cause dispersion of the original nature.

"These five are the banes of life; yet Yang and Mih regarded them as the summum bonum.

As attainment of Tao. For Yang Chu and Mih Tzŭ, see chs. ii and viii.

They are not my summum bonum. For if men who are thus fettered can be said to have attained the summum bonum, then pigeons and owls in a cage may also be said to have attained the summum bonum!

"Besides, to stuff one's inside with likes and dislikes and sounds and colours; to encompass one's outside with fur caps, feather hats, the carrying of tablets, or girding of sashes—full of rubbish inside while swathed in magnificence without—and still to talk of having attained the summum bonum;—then the prisoner with arms tied behind him and fingers in the squeezer, the tiger or the leopard which has just been put in a cage, may justly consider that they too have attained the summum bonum!"

"L'homme," says Rousseau (op. cit.), "est né libre, et partout il est dans les fers."

This chapter, as it stands, is clearly not from the hand of Chuang Tzŭ. One critic justly points out the want of logical sequence in arrangement of argument and illustrations. Another, while admitting general refinement of style, calls attention to a superficiality of thought noticeable in certain portions. "Yet only those," he adds, "who eat and sleep with their Chuang Tzŭs would be able to detect this."

CHAPTER XIII

The Tao of God

Argument:—Tao is repose—Repose the secret of the universe—Cultivation of essentials—Neglect of accidentals—The sequence of Tao—Spontaneity of true virtue—Tao is unconditioned—Tao cannot be conveyed—Illustrations.

The Tao of God operates ceaselessly; and all things are produced. The Tao of the sovereign operates ceaselessly; and the empire rallies around him. The Tao of the Sage operates ceaselessly; and all within the limit of surrounding ocean acknowledge his sway. He who apprehends God, who is in relation with the Sage, and who recognises the radiating virtue of the sovereign,—his actions will be to him unconscious, the actions of repose.

With him all will be inaction, by which all things will be accomplished.

The repose of the Sage is not what the world calls repose. His repose is the result of his mental attitude. All creation could not disturb his equilibrium: hence his repose.

When water is still, it is like a mirror, reflecting the beard and the eyebrows. It gives the accuracy of the water-level, and the philosopher makes it his model. And if water thus derives lucidity from stillness, how much more the faculties of the mind? The mind of the Sage being in repose becomes the mirror of the universe, the speculum of all creation.

Repose, tranquillity, stillness, inaction,—these were the levels of the universe, the ultimate perfection of Tao.

In the early days of Time, ere matter had assumed shape, it was by such levels that the spiritual was adjusted.

Therefore wise rulers and Sages rest therein. Resting therein they reach the unconditioned, from which springs the conditioned; and with the conditioned comes order.

Meaning those laws which are inseparable from concrete existences.

Again, from the unconditioned comes repose, and from repose comes movement,

When once inner repose has been established, outer movement results as a matter of necessity, without injury to the organism.
and from movement comes attainment. Further, from repose comes inaction, and from inaction comes potentiality of action.

When inaction has been achieved, action results spontaneously and unconsciously to the organism.

And inaction is happiness; and where there is happiness no cares can abide, and life is long.

Repose, tranquillity, stillness, inaction,—these were the source of all things. Due perception of this was the secret of Yao's success as a ruler, and of Shun's success as his minister. Due perception of this constitutes the virtue of sovereigns on the throne, the Tao of the inspired Sage and of the uncrowned King below. Keep to this in retirement, and the lettered denizens of sea and dale will recognise your power. Keep to this when coming forward to pacify a troubled world, and your merit shall be great and your name illustrious, and the empire united into one. In your repose you will be wise; in your movements, powerful. By inaction you will gain honour; and by confining yourself to the pure and simple, you will hinder the whole world from struggling with you for show.

To fully apprehend the scheme of the universe,

Lit.: "the virtue of heaven and earth," meaning their inaction by which all things are brought to maturity.
this is called the great secret of being in accord with God, whereby the empire is so administered that the result is accord with man. To be in accord with man is human happiness; to be in accord with God is the happiness of God.

Chuang Tzŭ said, "O my exemplar! Thou who destroyest all things, and dost not account it cruelty; thou who benefitest all time, and dost not account it charity; thou who art older than antiquity and dost not account it age; thou who supportest the universe, shaping the many forms therein, and dost not account it skill;—this is the happiness of God!"

Therefore it has been said, "Those who enjoy the happiness of God, when born into the world, are but fulfilling their divine functions; when they die, they do but undergo a physical change. In repose, they exert the influence of the Negative; in motion, they wield the power of the Positive."

See ante, chs. vi and xi.

Thus, those who enjoy the happiness of God have no grievance against God, no grudge against man. Nothing material injures them; nothing spiritual punishes them. Accordingly it has been said, "Their motion is that of heaven;

One of ceaseless revolution, without beginning or end.
their repose is that of earth. Mental equilibrium gives them the empire of the world. Evil spirits do not harass them without; demons do not trouble them within. Mental equilibrium gives them sovereignty over all creation." Which signifies that in repose to extend to the whole universe and to be in relation with all creation,—this is the happiness of God. This enables the mind of the Sage to cherish the whole empire.

For the virtue of the wise ruler is modelled upon the universe, is guided by Tao, and is ever occupied in inaction. By inaction, he administers the empire, and has energy to spare; but by action he finds his energy inadequate to the administration of the empire. Therefore the men of old set great store by inaction.

But if rulers practise inaction and the ruled also practise inaction, the ruled will equal the rulers, and will not be as their subjects. On the other hand, if the ruled practise action and rulers also practise action, rulers will assimilate themselves to the ruled, and will not be as their masters. Rulers must practise inaction in order to administer the empire. The ruled must practise action in order to subserve the interests of the empire. This is an unchangeable law.

And one over which the commentators have exhausted not a little wit. At the end of the chapter, the reader will be able to draw his own conclusions.

Thus, the men of old, although their knowledge did not extend throughout the universe, were not troubled in mind. Although their intellectual powers beautified all creation, they did not rejoice. Although their abilities exhausted all things within the limits of ocean, they did not act.

Heaven has no parturitions, yet all things are evolved. Earth knows no increment, yet all things are nourished. The wise ruler practises inaction, and the empire applauds him. Therefore it has been said, "There is nothing more mysterious

In its action.

than heaven, nothing richer than earth, nothing greater than the wise ruler." Wherefore also it has been said, "The virtue of the wise ruler makes him the peer of heaven and earth." Charioted upon the universe, with all creation for his team, he passes along the highway of mortality.

The essential is in the ruler; the accidental in the ruled.

Lit. the "root," and the "tip" of the branch, respectively.

The ultima ratio lies with the prince; representation is the duty of the minister.

Appeal to arms is the lowest form of virtue. Rewards and punishments are the lowest form of education. Ceremonies and laws are the lowest form of government. Music and fine clothes are the lowest form of happiness. Weeping and mourning are the lowest form of grief. These five should follow the movements of the mind.

The ancients indeed cultivated the study of accidentals, but they did not allow it to precede that of essentials. The prince precedes, the minister follows. The father precedes, the son follows. The elder brother precedes, the younger follows. Seniors precede, juniors follow. Men precede, women follow. Husbands precede, wives follow. Distinctions of rank and precedence are part of the scheme of the universe, and the Sage adopts them accordingly. In point of spirituality, heaven is honourable, earth is lowly. Spring and summer precede autumn and winter: such is the order of the seasons. In the constant production of all things, there are phases of existence. There are the extremes of maturity and decay, the perpetual tide of change. And if heaven and earth, divinest of all, admit of rank and precedence, how much more man?

In the ancestral temple, parents rank before all; at court, the most honourable; in the village, the elders; in matters to be accomplished, the most trustworthy. Such is the order which appertains to Tao. He who in considering Tao disregards this order, thereby disregards Tao; and he who in considering Tao disregards Tao,—whence will he secure Tao?

Therefore, those of old who apprehended Tao, first apprehended God. Tao came next, and then charity and duty to one's neighbour, and then the functions of public life, and then forms and names, and then employment according to capacity, and then distinctions of good and bad, and then discrimination between right and wrong, and then rewards and punishments. Thus wise men and fools met with their dues; the exalted and the humble occupied their proper places. And the virtuous and the worthless being each guided by their own natural instincts, it was necessary to distinguish capabilities, and to adopt a corresponding nomenclature, in order to serve the ruler, nourish the ruled, administer things generally, and elevate self. Where knowledge and plans are of no avail, one must fall back upon the natural. This is perfect peace, the acme of good government. Therefore it has been written, "Wherever there is form, there is also its name." Forms and names indeed the ancients had, but did not give precedence to them.

Thus, those of old who considered Tao, passed through five phases before forms and names were reached, and nine before rewards and punishments could be discussed.

As given in the preceding paragraph.

To rise per saltum to forms and names is to be ignorant of their source; to rise per saltum to rewards and punishments is to be ignorant of their beginning. Those who invert the process of discussing Tao, arguing in a directly contrary sense, are rather to be governed by others than able to govern others themselves.

To rise per saltum to forms and names and rewards and punishments, this is to understand the instrumental part of government, but not to understand the great principle of government.

Which is Tao.

This is to be of use in the administration of the empire, but not to be able to administer the empire. This is to be a sciolist, a man of narrow views.

Ceremonies and laws were indeed cultivated by the ancients; but they were employed in the service of the rulers by the ruled. Rulers did not employ them as a means of nourishing the ruled.

From the beginning of this chapter, the argument has been eminently unsatisfactory.

Of old, Shun asked Yao, saying, "How does your Majesty employ your faculties?"

"I am not arrogant towards the defenceless," replied Yao. "I do not neglect the poor. I grieve for those who die. I pity the orphan. I sympathise with the widow. Beyond this, nothing."

"Good indeed!" cried Shun, "but yet not great."

"How so?" inquired Yao.

"Be passive," said Shun, "like the virtue of God. The sun and moon shine; the four seasons revolve; day and night alternate; clouds come and rain falls."

"Alas!" cried Yao, "what a muddle I have been making. You are in accord with God; I am in accord with man."

Of old, heaven and earth were considered great; and the Yellow Emperor and Yao and Shun all thought them perfection. Consequently, what did those do who ruled the empire of old? They did what heaven and earth do; no more.

When Confucius was going west to place his works in the Imperial library of the House of Chou, Tzŭ Lu

The most popular of all the disciples of Confucius. In the striking words of Mr. Watters, "He was equally ready to argue, fight, be silent, pray for his master, and die with him. So it is very unfair in Dr. Legge to call him a kind of Peter, meaning of course Simon Peter, a man who lacked faith, courage, and fidelity, and who moreover cursed and swore."—Guide to the Tablets in a Confucian Temple.

counselled him, saying, "I have heard that a certain librarian of the Chêng department, by name Lao Tan,

Or, as usually named in this work, Lao Tzŭ. "Chêng" appears to have been merely a distinctive name.

has resigned and retired into private life. Now as you, Sir, wish to deposit your works, it would be advisable to go and interview him."

"Certainly," said Confucius; and he thereupon went to see Lao Tzŭ. The latter would not hear of the proposal; so Confucius began to expound the doctrines of his twelve canons, in order to convince Lao Tzŭ.

These twelve have been variously enumerated as (1) the Book of Changes, Parts i and ii, with the ten Wings. (2) The twelve Dukes of the Spring and Autumn, etc.

"This is all nonsense," cried Lao Tzŭ, interrupting him. "Tell me what are your criteria."

"Charity," replied Confucius, "and duty towards one's neighbour."

"Tell me, please," asked Lao Tzŭ, "are these part of man's original nature?"

The question of an innate moral sense early occupied the attention of Chinese thinkers.

"They are," answered Confucius. "Without charity, the superior man could not become what he is. Without duty to one's neighbour, he would be of no effect. These two belong to the original nature of a pure man. What further would you have?"

"Tell me," said Lao Tzŭ, "in what consist charity and duty to one's neighbour?"

"They consist," answered Confucius, "in a capacity for rejoicing in all things; in universal love, without the element of self. These are the characteristics of charity and duty to one's neighbour."

"What stuff!" cried Lao Tzŭ. "Does not universal love contradict itself?

If every one loves every one, there can be no such thing as love, just as absolute altruism only achieves the same result as absolute egoism.

Is not your elimination of self a positive manifestation of self?

On the "Don't nail his ear to the pump" principle.

Sir, if you would cause the empire not to lose its source of nourishment,—there is the universe, its regularity is unceasing; there are the sun and moon, their brightness is unceasing; there are the stars, their groupings never change; there are birds and beasts, they flock together without varying; there are trees and shrubs, they grow upwards without exception, Be like these; follow Tao; and you will be perfect. Why then these vain struggles after charity and duty to one's neighbour, as though beating a drum in search of a fugitive. Alas! Sir, you have brought much confusion into the mind of man."

The drum similitude occurs again in ch. xiv.

Shih Ch'êng Ch'i

Of whom nothing is known.

visited Lao Tzŭ, and addressed him, saying, "Having heard, Sir, that you were a Sage, I put aside all thought of distance to come and visit you. Travelling many stages, the soles of my feet thickened, but I did not venture to rest. And now I see you are not a Sage. While rats feasted off your leavings, you turned your sister out of doors. This is not charity. Though you have no lack of food, raw and cooked, you are stingy beyond all bounds."

At this Lao Tzŭ was silent and made no reply; and the next day Shih Ch'êng Ch'i came again and said, "Before, I was rude to you; now, I am sorry. How is this?"

"I have no pretension," replied Lao Tzŭ, "to be possessed of cunning knowledge nor of divine wisdom. Had you yesterday called me an ox, I should have considered myself an ox. Had you called me a horse, I should have considered myself a horse.

"For if men class you in accordance with truth, and you reject the classification, you only double the reproach. My humility is natural humility. It is not humility for humility's sake."

Shih Ch'êng Ch'i moved respectfully away.

Without allowing his shadow to fall on Lao Tzŭ. Bringing one foot up to the other only. Not venturing to let it pass as in ordinary walking.

Then he advanced again, also respectfully, and said, "May I ask you about personal cultivation?"

Lao Tzŭ said, "Your countenance is a strange one. Your eyes protrude. Your jaws are heavy. Your lips are parted. Your demeanour is self-satisfied. You look like a man on a tethered horse.

His body there, his mind elsewhere.

You are too confident. You are too hasty. You think too much of your own powers. Such men are not trusted. Those who are found on the wrong side of a boundary line are called thieves."

Lao Tzŭ said, "Tao is not too small for the greatest, nor too great for the smallest. Thus all things are embosomed therein; wide indeed its boundless capacity, unfathomable its depth.

"Form, and virtue, and charity, and duty to one's neighbour, these are the accidentals of the spiritual. Except he be a perfect man, who shall determine their place? The world of the perfect man, is not that vast? And yet it is not able to involve him in trouble. All struggle for power, but he does not join. Though discovering nothing false, he is not tempted astray. In spite of the utmost genuineness, he still confines himself to essentials.

To the root, not to the branch.

"He thus places himself outside the universe, beyond all creation, where his soul is free from care. Apprehending Tao, he is in accord with virtue. He leaves charity and duty to one's neighbour alone. He treats ceremonies and music as adventitious. And so the mind of the perfect man is at peace.

"Books are what the world values as representing Tao. But books are only words, and the valuable part of words is the thought therein contained. That thought has a certain bias which cannot be conveyed in words, yet the world values words as being the essence of books. But though the world values them, they are not of value; as that sense in which the world values them is not the sense in which they are valuable.

"That which can be seen with the eye is form and colour; that which can be heard with the ear is sound and noise. But alas! the people of this generation think that form, and colour, and sound, and noise, are means by which they can come to understand the essence of Tao. This is not so. And as those who know, do not speak, while those who speak do not know, whence should the world derive its knowledge?"

The first half of this last sentence has been pitchforked à propos de bottes into ch. lvi of the Tao-Tê-Ching. See The Remains of Lao Tzǔ, pp. 7 and 38.

Duke Huan.
The famous ruler of the Ch'i State. Flourished 7th century B.C.
was one day reading in his hall, when a wheelwright who was working below,

Below the covered dais, termed "hall," which has an open frontage, in full view of which such work might be carried on.
flung down his hammer and chisel, and mounting the steps said, "What words may your Highness be studying?"

"I am studying the words of the Sages," replied the Duke.

"Are the Sages alive?" asked the wheelwright.

"No," answered the Duke; "they are dead."

"Then the words your Highness is studying," rejoined the wheelwright, "are only the dregs of the ancients."

"What do you mean, sirrah!" cried the Duke, "by interfering with what I read? Explain yourself, or you shall die."

"Let me take an illustration," said the wheelwright, "from my own trade. In making a wheel, if you work too slowly, you can't make it firm; if you work too fast, the spokes won't fit in. You must go neither too slowly nor too fast. There must be co-ordination of mind and hand. Words cannot explain what it is, but there is some mysterious art herein. I cannot teach it to my son; nor can he learn it from me. Consequently, though seventy years of age, I am still making wheels in my old age. If the ancients, together with what they could not impart, are dead and gone, then what your Highness is studying must be the dregs."

This episode of the wheelwright is to be found in the works of Huai Nan Tzǔ, of the 2nd century B.C. He used it to illustrate the opening words of the Tao-Tê-Ching; and in The Remains of Lao Tzŭ, p. 6, it is stated that he stole it from Chuang Tzŭ without acknowledgment.

When that statement was made I had not come to the conclusion, now forced upon me, that the above chapter is not from the hand of Chuang Tzŭ. As one critic remarks, the style is generally admirable; but it is not the style of Chuang Tzŭ.

CHAPTER XIV

The Circling Sky

Argument:—The Ultimate Cause—Integrity of Tao—Music and Tao—Failure of Confucianism—Confucius and Lao Tzŭ—Confucius attains to Tao—Illustrations.

[This chapter is supplementary to ch. v.]
"The sky turns round; the earth stands still; sun and moon pursue one another. Who causes this? Who directs this? Who has leisure enough to see that such movements continue?

"Some think there is a mechanical arrangement which makes these bodies move as they do. Others think that they revolve without being able to stop.

"The clouds cause rain; rain causes clouds. Whose kindly bounty is this? Who has leisure enough to see that such, result is achieved?

"Wind comes from the north. It blows now east, now west; and now it whirls aloft. Who puffs it forth? Who has leisure enough to be flapping it this way or that? I should like to know the cause of all this."
We are not told the name of this questioner.
Wu Han Chao
An ancient worthy.
said, "Come here, and I will tell you. Above there are the Six Influences
The Yin and Yang principles, wind, rain, darkness, and light; as in ch. xi.
Some commentators read, the "Six Cardinal Points," viz.: N., E., S., W., above, and below.
and the Five Virtues.
Charity, duty to one's neighbour, order, wisdom, and truth.
If a ruler keeps in harmony with these, his rule is good; if not, it is bad. By following the nine chapters of the Lo book,
Containing a mystic revelation of knowledge in the form of a diagram, supposed to have been delivered to one of the legendary rulers of China more than 2,000 years before the Christian era.

his rule will be a success and his virtue complete; he will watch over the interests of his people, and all the empire will owe him gratitude. This is to be an eminent ruler."

"A very round answer," says Lin Hsi Chung, "to a very square question."

Tang, a high official of Sung, asked Chuang Tzŭ about charity. Chuang Tzŭ said, "Tigers and wolves have it."

"How so?" asked Tang.

"The natural love between parents and offspring," replied Chuang Tzŭ,—"is not that charity?"

Tang then inquired about perfect charity.

"Perfect charity," said Chuang Tzŭ, "does not admit of love for the individual."

It embraces all men equally. To love one person would imply at least the possibility of hating another. See also p.76, where Lao Tzŭ refutes the doctrine of universal love.

"Without such love," replied Tang, "it appears to me there would be no such thing as affection, and without affection no filial piety. Does perfect charity not admit of filial piety?"

"Not so," said Chuang Tzŭ. "Perfect charity is the more extensive term. Consequently, it was unnecessary to mention filial piety. It was not that filial piety was omitted. It was merely not particularised.

"A man who travels southwards to Ying,

Capital of the Ch'u State.

cannot see Mount Ming in the north. Why? Because he is too far off.

"Therefore it has been said that it is easy to be respectfully filial, but difficult to be affectionately filial.

The artificial is easier than the natural.

But even that is easier than to become unconscious of one's natural obligations, which is in turn easier than to cause others to be unconscious of the operations thereof.

I.e. to be filial without letting others be conscious of the fact.

Similarly, this is easier than to become altogether unconscious of the world, which again is easier than to cause the world to be unconscious of one's influence upon it.

Such is perfect charity, which operates without letting its operation be known.

"True virtue does nothing, yet it leaves Yao and Shun far behind. Its good influence extends to ten thousand generations, yet no man knoweth it to exist. What boots it then to sigh after charity and duty to one's neighbour?

"Filial piety, fraternal love, charity, duty to one's neighbour, loyalty, truth, chastity, and honesty,—these are all studied efforts, designed to aid the development of virtue. They are only parts of a whole.

"Therefore it has been said, 'Perfect honour includes all the honour a country can give. Perfect wealth includes all the wealth a country can give. Perfect ambition includes all the reputation one can desire.' And by parity of reasoning, Tao does not admit of sub-division."

Pei Mên Ch'êng
Of whom nothing is recorded.
said to the Yellow Emperor, "When your Majesty played the Han-ch'ih
Name of a piece of music, the meaning of which is not known.
in the wilds of Tung-t'ing, the first time I heard it I was afraid, the second time I was amazed, and the last time I was confused, speechless, overwhelmed."

"You are not far from the truth," replied the Yellow Emperor. "I played as a man, drawing inspiration from God. The execution was punctilious, the expression sublime.

"Perfect music first shapes itself according to a human standard; then it follows the lines of the divine; then it proceeds in harmony with the five virtues; then it passes into spontaneity. The four seasons are then blended, and all creation is brought into accord. As the seasons come forth in turn, so are all things produced. Now fulness, now decay, now soft and loud in turn, now clear, now muffled, the harmony of Yin and Yang. Like a flash was the sound which roused you as the insect world is roused,
By the warm breath of spring.
followed by a thundering peal, without end and without beginning, now dying, now living, now sinking, now rising, on and on without a moment's break. And so you were afraid.

"When I played again, it was the harmony of the Yin and Yang, lighted by the glory of sun and moon; now broken, now prolonged, now gentle, now severe, in one unbroken, unfathomable volume of sound. Filling valley and gorge, stopping the ears and dominating the senses, adapting itself to the capacities of things,—the sound whirled around on all sides, with shrill note and clear. The spirits of darkness kept to their domain. Sun, moon, and stars, pursued their appointed course. When the melody was exhausted I stopped; if the melody did not stop, I went on.
The music was naturally what it was, independently of the player.
You would have sympathised, but you could not understand. You would have looked, but you could not see. You would have pursued, but you could not overtake. You stood dazed in the middle of the wilderness, leaning against a tree and crooning, your eye conscious of exhausted vision, your strength failing for the pursuit, and so unable to overtake me. Your frame was but an empty shell. You were completely at a loss, and so you were amazed.

"Then I played in sounds which produce no amazement, the melodious law of spontaneity, springing forth like nature's countless buds, in manifold but formless joy, as though poured forth to the dregs, in deep but soundless bass. Beginning nowhere, the melody rested in void; some would say dead, others alive, others real, others ornamental, as it scattered itself on all sides in never to be anticipated chords.

"The wondering world enquires of the Sage. He is in relation with its variations and follows the same eternal law.

"When no machinery is set in motion, and yet the instrumentation is complete, this is the music of God. The mind awakes to its enjoyment without waiting to be called. Accordingly, Yu Piao praised it, saying, 'Listening you cannot hear its sound; gazing you cannot see its form.

Yu Piao is said to have been one of the pre-historic rulers of China. Readers of the Tao-Tê-Ching (ch. xiv) will here find another nail for the coffin of that egregious fraud. See The Remains of Lao Tzŭ, p. 14. Also ch. xxii of this work.

It fills heaven and earth. It embraces the six cardinal points.' Now you desired to listen to it, but you were not able to grasp its existence. And so you were confused.

"My music first induced fear; and as a consequence, respect. I then added amazement, by which you were isolated.

From consciousness of your surroundings.

And lastly, confusion; for confusion means absence of sense, and absence of sense means Tao, and Tao means absorption therein."

When Confucius travelled west to the Wei State, Yen Yüan

The "John" among the disciples of Confucius. He closed a pure and gentle life at the early age of 32, to the inexpressible grief of the Sage.

asked Shih Chin,

Chief musician of the Lu State.

saying, "What think you of my Master?"

"Alas!" replied Shih Chin, "he is not a success."

"How so?" enquired Yen Yüan.

"Before the straw dog has been offered in sacrifice," replied Shih Chin, "it is kept in a box, wrapped up in an embroidered cloth, and the augur fasts before using it. But when it has once been offered up, passers-by trample over its body, and fuel-gatherers pick it up for burning. Then, if any one should take it, and again putting it in a box and wrapping it up in an embroidered cloth, watch and sleep alongside, he would not only dream, but have nightmare into the bargain.

The thing being uncanny. From which it would appear that the use of the straw dog was to induce dreams of future events.

"Now your Master has been thus treating the ancients, who are like the dog which has already been offered in sacrifice. He causes his disciples to watch and sleep alongside of them. Consequently, his tree

Beneath which he used to teach.

has been cut down in Sung; they will have none of him in Wei; in fact, his chances among the Shangs and the Chous are exhausted. Is not this the dream? And then to be surrounded by the Ch'êns and the Ts'ais, seven days without food, death staring him in the face,—is not this the nightmare?

"For travelling by water there is nothing like a boat. For travelling by land there is nothing like a cart. This because a boat moves readily in water; but were you to try to push it on land you would never succeed in making it go.

Be in harmony with your surroundings.

Now ancient and modern times may be likened unto water and land; Chou and Lu to the boat and the cart. To try to make the customs of Chou succeed in Lu, is like pushing a boat on land: great trouble and no result, except certain injury to oneself. Your Master has not yet learnt the doctrine of non-angularity, of self-adaptation to externals.

"Have you never seen a well-sweep? You pull it, and down it comes. You release it, and up it goes. It is the man who pulls the well-sweep, and not the well-sweep which pulls the man; so that both in coming down and going up, it does not run counter to the wishes of the man. And so it was that the ceremonial and obligations and laws of the Three Emperors and Five Rulers did not aim at uniformity of application but at good government of the empire. Their ceremonial, obligations, laws, etc., were like the cherry-apple, the pear, the orange, and the pumelo,—all differing in flavour but each palatable. They changed with the changing season.

"Dress up a monkey in the robes of Chou Kung,

See ch. iv.

and it will not be happy until they are torn to shreds. And the difference between past and present is much the same as the difference between Chou Kung and a monkey.

"When Hsi Shih

A famous beauty of old.

was distressed in mind, she knitted her brows. An ugly woman of the village, seeing how beautiful she looked, went home, and having worked herself into a fit frame of mind, knitted her brows. The result was that the rich people of the place barred up their doors and would not come out, while the poor people took their wives and children and departed elsewhere. That woman saw the beauty of knitted brows, but she did not see wherein the beauty of knitted brows lay.

In suitability to the individual.

Alas! your Master is emphatically not a success."

Confucius had lived to the age of fifty-one without hearing Tao, when he went south to P'ei, to see Lao Tzŭ.

Lao Tzŭ said, "So you have come, Sir, have you? I hear you are considered a wise man up north. Have you got Tao?"

"Not yet," answered Confucius.

"In what direction," asked Lao Tzŭ, "have you sought for it?"

"I sought it for five years," replied Confucius, "in the science of numbers, but did not succeed."

"And then?..." continued Lao Tzŭ.

"Then," said Confucius, "I spent twelve years seeking for it in the doctrine of the Yin and Yang, also without success."

"Just so," rejoined Lao Tzŭ. "Were Tao something which could be presented, there is no man but would present it to his sovereign, or to his parents. Could it be imparted or given, there is no man but would impart it to his brother or give it to his child. But this is impossible, for the following reason. Unless there is a suitable endowment within, Tao will not abide. Unless there is outward correctness, Tao will not operate. The external being unfitted for the impression of the internal, the true Sage does not seek to imprint. The internal being unfitted for the reception of the external, the true Sage does not seek to receive.

Attempting neither to teach nor to learn.

"Reputation is public property; you may not appropriate it in excess. Charity and duty to one's neighbour are as caravanserais established by wise rulers of old; you may stop there one night, but not for long, or you will incur reproach.

"The perfect men of old took their road through charity, stopping a night with duty to their neighbour, on their way to ramble in transcendental space. Feeding on the produce of non-cultivation, and establishing themselves in the domain of no obligations, they enjoyed their transcendental inaction. Their food was ready to hand; and being under no obligations to others, they did not put any one under obligation to themselves. The ancients called this the outward visible sign of an inward and spiritual grace.

"Those who make wealth their all in all, cannot bear loss of money. Those who make distinction their all in all, cannot bear loss of fame. Those who affect power will not place authority in the hands of others. Anxious while holding, distressed if losing, yet never taking warning from the past and seeing the folly of their pursuit,—such men are the accursed of God.

"Resentment, gratitude, taking, giving, censure of self, instruction of others, power of life and death,—these eight are the instruments of right; but only he who can adapt himself to the vicissitudes of fortune, without being carried away, is fit to use them. Such a one is an upright man among the upright. And he whose heart is not so constituted,—the door of divine intelligence is not yet opened for him."

Confucius visited Lao Tzŭ, and spoke of charity and duty to one's neighbour.

Lao Tzŭ said, "The chaff from winnowing will blind a man's eyes so that he cannot tell the points of the compass. Mosquitoes will keep a man awake all night with their biting. And just in the same way this talk of charity and duty to one's neighbour drives me nearly crazy. Sir! strive to keep the world to its own original simplicity. And as the wind bloweth where it listeth, so let Virtue establish itself. Wherefore such undue energy, as though searching for a fugitive with a big drum?

See p. 167.

"The snow-goose is white without a daily bath. The raven is black without daily colouring itself. The original simplicity of black and of white is beyond the reach of argument. The vista of fame and reputation is not worthy of enlargement. When the pond dries up and the fishes are left upon dry ground, to moisten them with the breath or to damp them with a little spittle is not to be compared with leaving them in the first instance in their native rivers and lakes."

Repeated from ch. vi.

On returning from this visit to Lao Tzŭ, Confucius did not speak for three days. A disciple asked him, saying, "Master, when you saw Lao Tzŭ, in what direction did you admonish him?"

"I saw a Dragon," replied Confucius, "—a Dragon which by convergence showed a body, by radiation became colour, and riding upon the clouds of heaven, nourished the two Principles of Creation. My mouth was agape: I could not shut it. How then do you think I was going to admonish Lao Tzŭ?"

Upon this Tzŭ Kung remarked, "Ha! then a man can sit corpse-like manifesting his dragon-power around, his thunder-voice heard though profound silence reigns, his movements like those of the universe? I too would go and see him."

More repetition, this time from ch. xi.

So on the strength of his connection with Confucius, Tzŭ Kung obtained an interview. Lao Tzŭ received him distantly and with dignity, saying in a low voice, "I am old, Sir. What injunctions may you have to give me?"

"The administration of the Three Kings and of the Five Rulers," replied Tzŭ Kung, "was not uniform; but their reputation has been identical. How then, Sir, is it that you do not regard them as Sages?"

"Come nearer, my son," said Lao Tzŭ. "What mean you by not uniform?"

"Yao handed over the empire to Shun," replied Tzŭ Kung; "and Shun to Yü. Yü employed labour, and T'ang employed troops. Wên Wang followed Chou Hsin and did not venture to oppose him. Wu Wang opposed him and would not follow. Therefore I said not uniform."

"Come nearer, my son," said Lao Tzŭ, "and I will tell you about the Three Kings and the Five Rulers.

"The Yellow Emperor's administration caused the affections of the people to be catholic. Nobody wept for the death of his parents, and nobody found fault.

All loved each other equally.

"The administration of Yao diverted the affections of the people into particular channels. If a man slew the slayer of his parents, nobody blamed him.

Filial affection began to predominate.

"The administration of Shun brought a spirit of rivalry among the people. Children were born after ten months' gestation; when five months old, they could speak; and ere they were three years of age,

Including gestation.

could already tell one person from another. And so early death came into the world.

A veritable anti-climax, hopelessly unworthy of either Lao Tzŭ or Chuang Tzŭ.

"The administration of Yü wrought a change in the hearts of the people. Individuality prevailed, and force was called into play. Killing robbers was not accounted murder; and throughout the empire people became sub-divided into classes. There was great alarm on all sides, and the Confucianists and the Mihists arose. At first the relationships were duly observed; but what about the women of to-day?

Meaning that in the olden days men could not marry before thirty, women before twenty, whereas now the State is cursed with early marriages. Or, according to Dr. Legge's view of a famous passage in the Book of Rites, that formerly it was shameful in men and women not to be married at the age of thirty and twenty, respectively, whereas now the State is cursed with late marriages.

"Let me tell you. The government of the Three Kings and Five Rulers was so only in name. In reality, it was utter confusion. The wisdom of the Three Kings was opposed to the brilliancy of the sun and moon above, destructive of the energy of land and water below, and subversive of the influence of the four seasons between.

More repetition. See ch. x. ad fin.

That wisdom is more harmful than a hornet's tail, preventing the very animals from putting themselves into due relation with the conditions of their existence—and yet they call themselves Sages! Is not their shamelessness shameful indeed?"

At this Tzŭ Kung became ill at ease.

The whole of the above episode may without hesitation be written off as a feeble forgery.

Confucius said to Lao Tzŭ, "I arranged the Six Canons of Poetry, History, Rites, Music, Changes, and Spring and Autumn. I spent much time over them, and I am well acquainted with their purport. I used them in admonishing seventy-two rulers, by discourses on the wisdom of ancient sovereigns and illustrations from the lives of Chou and Shao. Yet not one ruler has in any way adopted my suggestions. Alas that man should be so difficult to persuade, and wisdom so difficult to illustrate."

"It is well for you, Sir," replied Lao Tzŭ, "that you did not come across any real ruler of mankind. Your Six Canons are but the worn-out foot-prints of ancient Sages. And what are foot-prints? Why, the words you now utter are as it were foot-prints. Foot-prints are made by the shoe: they are not the shoe itself.

"Fish-hawks gaze at each other with motionless eyes,—and their young are produced. The male of a certain insect chirps with the wind while the female chirps against it,—and their offspring is produced. There is another animal which, being an hermaphrodite, produces its own offspring. Nature cannot be changed. Destiny cannot be altered. Time cannot stop. Tao cannot be obstructed. Once attain to Tao, and there is nothing which you cannot accomplish. Without it, there is nothing which you can accomplish."

For three months after this Confucius did not leave his house. Then he again visited Lao Tzŭ and said, "I have attained. Birds lay eggs, fish spawn, insects undergo metamorphosis, and mammals suckle their young.

Lit. "when a younger brother comes, the elder cries,"—from which may be inferred the meaning in the translation.

The whole sentence signifies that every development proceeds according to fixed laws. It is useless to try to do anything. Nature is always self-similar.

For a long time I have not been enlightened. And he who is not enlightened himself,—how should he enlighten others?"

Lao Tzŭ said, "Ch'iu, you have attained!"

"The style of this chapter," says Lin Hsi Chung, "gives it a foremost place among the 'outside' essays of Chuang Tzŭ. But the insertion of that dialogue between Confucius and Lao Tzŭ on charity and duty towards one's neighbour is like eking out a sable robe with a dog's tail."

CHAPTER XV

Self-Conceit

Argument:—Would-be sages—The vanity of effort—Method of the true Sage—Passivity the key—The soul and mortality—Re-absorption into the immortal.

Self-conceit and assurance, which lead men to quit society, and be different from their fellows, to indulge in tall talk and abuse of others,—these are nothing more than personal over-estimation, the affectation of recluses and those who have done with the world and have closed their hearts to mundane influences.

Preaching of charity and duty to one's neighbour, of loyalty and truth, of respect, of economy, and of humility,—this is but moral culture, affected by would-be pacificators and teachers of mankind, and by scholars at home or abroad.

Preaching of meritorious services, of fame, of ceremonial between sovereign and minister, of due relationship between upper and lower classes,—this is mere government, affected by courtiers or patriots who strive to extend the boundaries of their own State and to swallow up the territory of others.

Living in marshes or in wildernesses, and passing one's days in fishing—this is mere inaction, affected by wanderers who have turned their backs upon the world and have nothing better to do.

Exhaling and inhaling,

The "breathing" theory. See ch. vi., ad init.

getting rid of the old and assimilating the new, stretching like a bear and craning like a bird,—

As these creatures are supposed to do in order to get good air into their systems.

—this is but valetudinarianism, affected by professors of hygiene and those who try to preserve the body to the age of P'êng Tsu.

See ch. i.

But in self-esteem without self-conceit, in moral culture without charity and duty to one's neighbour, in government without rank and fame, in retirement without solitude, in health without hygiene,—there we have oblivion absolute coupled with possession of all things; an infinite calm which becomes an object to be attained by all.

Such is the Tao of the universe, such is the virtue of the Sage. Wherefore it has been said, "In tranquillity, in stillness, in the unconditioned, in inaction, we find the levels of the universe, the very constitution of Tao."

Almost verbatim from ch. xiii, p. 72, where the passage appears as part of Chuang Tzŭ's own text, and not as a quotation from any other author.

Wherefore it has been said, "The Sage is a negative quantity, and is consequently in a state of passivity. Being passive he is in a state of repose. And where passivity and repose are, there sorrow and anxiety do not enter, and foul influences do not collect. And thus his virtue is complete and his spirituality unimpaired."

Wherefore it has been said, "The birth of the Sage is the will of God; his death is but a modification of existence. In repose, he shares the passivity of the Yin; in action, the energy of the Yang. He will have nothing to do with happiness, and so has nothing to do with misfortune.

Each of which proceeds from the other in an endless chain.

He must be influenced ere he will respond. He must be urged ere he will move. He must be compelled ere he will arise. Ignoring the future and the past, he resigns himself to the laws of God.

"And therefore no calamity comes upon him, nothing injures him, no man is against him, no spirit punishes him. He floats through life to rest in death. He has no anxieties; he makes no plans. His honour does not make him illustrious. His good faith reflects no credit upon himself.

It is all God's, as part of the great scheme.

His sleep is dreamless, his awaking without pain. His spirituality is pure,

Without desires.

and his soul vigorous. Thus unconditioned and in repose, he is a partaker of the virtue of God."

Wherefore it has been said, "Sorrow and happiness are the heresies

Evil influences.

of virtue; joy and anger lead astray from Tao; love and hate cause the loss of virtue. The heart unconscious of sorrow and happiness,—that is perfect virtue. One, without change,—that is perfect repose. Without any obstruction,—that is the perfection of the unconditioned. Holding no relations with the external world,—that is perfection of the negative state. Without blemish of any kind,—that is the perfection of purity."

Wherefore it has been said, "If the body toils without rest, it dies. If the mind is employed without ceasing, it becomes wearied; and being wearied, its power is gone."

Pure water is by nature clear. If untouched, it is smooth. If dammed, it will not flow, neither will it be clear. It is an emblem of the virtue of God. Wherefore it has been said, "Pure, without admixture; uniform, without change; negative, without action; moved, only at the will of God;—such would be the spirituality nourished according to Tao."

Those who possess blades from Kan

The Wu State.

or Yüeh, keep them carefully in their scabbards, and do not venture to use them. For they are precious in the extreme. The spirit spreads forth on all sides: there is no point to which it does not reach, attaining heaven above, embracing earth beneath. Influencing all creation, its form cannot be portrayed. Its name is then Of-God.

Such is man's spiritual existence before he is born into the world of mortals.

The Tao of the pure and simple consists in preserving spirituality. He who preserves his spirituality and loses it not, becomes one with that spirituality. And through that unity the spirit operates freely, and comes into due relationship with God.

Returning after its brief career on earth, to the eternity whence it came.

A vulgar saying has it, "The masses value money; honest men, fame; virtuous men, resolution; and Sages, the soul."

Thus, the pure is that in which there is nothing mixed; the simple is that which implies no injury to the spirituality. And he who can keep the pure and simple within himself,—he is a divine man.

It requires but scant acumen to relegate this chapter to the limbo of forgeries. Lin Hsi Chung thinks it is probably from the hand of the unknown artist who is responsible for ch. xiii.

CHAPTER XVI

Exercise of Faculties

Argument:—Tao unattainable by mundane arts—To be reached through repose—The world's infancy—The reign of peace—Government sets in—Tao declines—The true Sages of old—Their purity of aim.

Those who exercise their faculties in mere worldly studies, hoping thereby to revert to their original condition; and those who sink their aspirations in mundane thoughts, hoping thereby to reach enlightenment;—these are the dullards of the earth.

The ancients, in cultivating Tao, begat knowledge out of repose. When born, this knowledge was not applied to any purpose; and so it may be said that out of knowledge they begat repose. Knowledge and repose thus mutually producing each other, harmony and order were developed. Virtue is harmony; Tao is order.

Virtue all-embracing,—hence charity. Tao all-influencing,—hence duty to one's neighbour. From the establishment of these two springs loyalty. Then comes music, an expression of inward purity and truth; followed by ceremonial, or sincerity expressed in ornamental guise. If music and ceremonial are ill regulated, the empire is plunged into confusion. And to attempt to correct others while one's own virtue is clouded, is to set one's own virtue a task for which it is inadequate, the result being that the natural constitution of the object will suffer.

Primeval man enjoyed perfect tranquillity throughout life. In his day, the Positive and Negative principles were peacefully united; spiritual beings gave no trouble; the four seasons followed in due order; nothing suffered any injury; death was unknown; men had knowledge, but no occasion to use it. This may be called perfection of unity.

All things, all conditions, were One.

At that period, nothing was ever made so; but everything was so.

By and by, virtue declined. Sui Jen

The Prometheus of China.

and Fu Hsi

See ch. vi.

ruled the empire. There was still natural adaptation,

Of man to his surroundings.

but the unity was gone.

The tide of coercion had set in.

A further decline in virtue. Shên Nung

The inventor of agriculture.

and Huang Ti

The Yellow Emperor. See ch. vi.

ruled the empire. There was peace, but the natural adaptation was gone.

Again virtue declined. Yao and Shun ruled the empire. Systems of government and moral reform were introduced. Man's original integrity was scattered. Goodness led him astray from Tao;

But for goodness, evil could not exist.

his actions imperilled his virtue.

As opposed to inaction.

Then he discarded natural instinct and took up with the intellectual. Mind was pitted against mind, but it was impossible thus to settle the empire. So art and learning were added. But art obliterated the original constitution, and learning overwhelmed mind; upon which confusion set in, and man was unable to revert to his natural instincts, to the condition in which he at first existed.

Thus it may be said that the world destroys Tao, and that Tao destroys the world. And the world and Tao thus mutually destroying each other, how can the men of Tao elevate the world, and how can the world elevate Tao? Tao cannot elevate the world; neither can the world elevate Tao. Though the Sages were not to dwell on mountain and in forest, their virtue would still be hidden;—hidden, but not by themselves.

Those of old who were called retired scholars, were not men who hid their bodies, or kept back their words, or concealed their wisdom. It was that the age was not suitable for their mission. If the age was suitable and their mission a success over the empire, they simply effaced themselves in the unity which prevailed. If the age was unsuitable and their mission at failure, they fell back upon their own resources and waited. Such is the way to preserve oneself.

Those of old who preserved themselves, did not ornament their knowledge with rhetoric. They did not exhaust the empire with their knowledge. They did not exhaust virtue. They kept quietly to their own spheres, and reverted to their natural instincts. What then was left for them to do?

Tao does not deal with detail. Virtue does not take cognizance of trifles. Trifles injure virtue; detail injures Tao. Wherefore it has been said, "Self-reformation is enough." He whose happiness is complete has attained his desire.

Of old, attainment of desire did not mean office. It meant that nothing could be added to the sum of happiness. But now it does mean office, though office is external and is not a part of oneself. That which is adventitious, comes. Coming, you cannot prevent it; going, you cannot arrest it. Therefore, not to look on office as the attainment of desire, and not because of poverty to become a toady, but to be equally happy under all conditions,—this is to be without sorrow.

But now-a-days, both having and not having
Office.
are causes of unhappiness. From which we may infer that even happiness is not exempt from sorrow.

A reductio ad absurdum.

Wherefore it has been said, "Those who over-estimate the external and lose their natural instincts in worldliness,—these are the people of topsy-turvydom."

We are left in the dark as to the authorship of the numerous quotations in this and the preceding chapter. It is, however, a point of minor importance, neither chapter having the slightest claim to be regarded as the genuine work of Chuang Tzŭ.

CHAPTER XVII

Autumn Floods

Argument:—Greatness and smallness always relative—Time and space infinite—Abstract dimensions do not exist—Their expression is concrete—Terms are not absolute—Like causes produce unlike effects—In the unconditioned alone can the absolute exist—The only absolute is Tao—Illustrations.

[*This chapter is supplementary to chapter ii. It is the most popular of all, and has earned for its author the sobriquet of "Autumn Floods."*]

It was the time of autumn floods. Every stream poured into the river, which swelled in its turbid course. The banks receded so far from one another that it was impossible to tell a cow from a horse.

Then the Spirit of the River laughed for joy that all the beauty of the earth was gathered to himself. Down with the stream he journeyed east, until he reached the ocean. There, looking eastwards and seeing no limit to its waves, his countenance changed. And as he gazed over the expanse, he sighed and said to the Spirit of the Ocean, "A vulgar proverb says that he who has heard but part of the truth thinks no one equal to himself. And such a one am I.

"When formerly I heard people detracting from the learning of Confucius or underrating the heroism of Poh I,

See ch. vi.

I did not believe. But now that I have looked upon your inexhaustibility—alas for me had I not reached your abode, I should have been for ever a laughing-stock to those of comprehensive enlightenment!"

The Spirit of a paltry river learns that the ripple of his rustic stream is scarcely the murmur of the world.

To which the Spirit of the Ocean replied, "You cannot speak of ocean to a well-frog,—the creature of a narrower sphere. You cannot speak of ice to a summer insect,—the creature of a season. You cannot speak of Tao to a pedagogue: his scope is too restricted. But now that you have emerged from your narrow sphere and have seen the great ocean, you know your own insignificance, and I can speak to you of great principles.

"There is no body of water beneath the canopy of heaven which is greater than ocean. All streams pour into it without cease, yet it does not overflow. It is constantly being drained off, yet it is never empty. Spring and autumn bring no change; floods and droughts are equally unknown. And thus it is immeasurably superior to mere rivers and brooks,—though I would not venture to boast on this account, for I get my shape from the universe, my vital power from the Yin and Yang. In the universe I am but as a small stone or a small tree on a vast mountain. And conscious thus of my own insignificance, what is there of which I can boast?

"The Four Seas,—are they not to the universe but like puddles in a marsh? The Middle Kingdom,—is it not to the surrounding ocean like a tare-seed in a granary? Of all the myriad created things, man is but one. And of all those who inhabit the land, live on the fruit of the earth, and move about in cart and boat, an individual man is but one. Is not he, as compared with all creation, but as the tip of a hair upon a horse's skin?

"The succession of the Five Rulers, the contentions of the Three Kings, the griefs of the philanthropist, the labours of the administrator, are but this and nothing more.

Sc. ambition.

Poh I refused the throne for fame's sake. Confucius discoursed to get a reputation for learning. This over-estimation of self on their part, was it not very much your own in reference to water?"

"Very well," replied the Spirit of the River, "am I then to regard the universe as great and the tip of a hair as small?"

"Not at all," said the Spirit of the Ocean. "Dimensions are limitless; time is endless. Conditions are not invariable; terms are not final. Thus, the wise man looks into space, and does not regard the small as too little, nor the great as too much; for he knows that there is no limit to dimension. He looks back into the past, and does not grieve over what is far off, nor rejoice over what is near; for he knows that time is without end.

Space infinite has been illustrated by Locke by a centre from which you can proceed for ever in all directions. Time infinite, by a point in a line from which you can proceed backwards and forwards for ever.

He investigates fulness and decay, and does not rejoice if he succeeds, nor lament if he fails; for he knows that conditions are not invariable.

Fulness and decay are the inevitable precursors of each other.

He who clearly apprehends the scheme of existence, does not rejoice over life, nor repine at death; for he knows that terms are not final.

Life and death are but links in an endless chain.

"What man knows is not to be compared with what he does not know. The span of his existence is not to be compared with the span of his non-existence. With the small to strive to exhaust the great, necessarily lands him in confusion, and he does not attain his object. How then should one be able to say that the tip of a hair is the ne plus ultra of smallness, or that the universe is the ne plus ultra of greatness?"

These predicates are abstract terms, which are not names of real existences but of relations, states, or conditions of existences; not things, but conditions of things.

"Dialecticians of the day," replied the Spirit of the River, "all say that the infinitesimally small has no form, and that the infinitesimally great is beyond all measurement. Is that so?"

"If we regard greatness as compared with that which is small," said the Spirit of the Ocean, "there is no limit to it; and if we regard smallness as compared with that which is great, it eludes our sight.

That is, if we proceed from the concrete to the abstract. Given a large or a small thing, there is no limit to the smallness or greatness with which each may be respectively compared.

The infinitesimal is a subdivision of the small; the colossal is an extension of the great. In this sense the two fall into different categories.

"Both small and great things must equally possess form. The mind cannot picture to itself a thing without form, nor conceive a form of unlimited dimensions. The greatness of anything may be a topic of discussion, or the smallness of anything may be mentally realized. But that which can be neither a topic of discussion nor be realized mentally, can be neither great nor small.

"Therefore, the truly great man, although he does not injure others, does not credit himself with charity and mercy.

These are natural to him.

He seeks not gain, but does not despise his followers who do. He struggles not for wealth, but does not take credit for letting it alone. He asks help from no man, but takes no credit for his self-reliance, neither does he despise those who seek preferment through friends. He acts differently from the vulgar crowd, but takes no credit for his exceptionality; nor because others act with the majority does he despise them as hypocrites. The ranks and emoluments of the world are to him no cause for joy; its punishments and shame no cause for disgrace. He knows that positive and negative cannot be distinguished,

What is positive under certain conditions will be negative under others. These terms are in fact identical. See ch. ii.
that great and small cannot be defined.

They are infinite.

"I have heard say, the man of Tao has no reputation; perfect virtue acquires nothing; the truly great man ignores self;—this is the height of self-discipline."

Clause 2 of the above quotation appears with variations in ch. xxxviii of the Tao-Te-Ching. The variations settle the correctness of the rendering already given in The Remains of Lao Tzŭ, p. 26.

"But how then," asked the Spirit of the River, "are the internal and external extremes of value and worthlessness, of greatness and smallness, to be determined?"

With no standard of measurement.

"From the point of view of Tao," replied the Spirit of the Ocean, "there are no such extremes of value or worthlessness. Men individually value themselves and hold others cheap. The world collectively withholds from the individual the right of appraising himself.

"If we say that a thing is great or small because it is relatively great or small, then there is nothing in all creation which is not great, nothing which is not small. To know that the universe is but as a tare-seed, and that the tip of a hair is a mountain,—this is the expression of relativity.

"If we say that something exists or does not exist, in deference to the function it fulfils or does not fulfil, then there is nothing which does not exist, nothing which does exist. To know that east and west are convertible and yet necessary terms,—this is the due adjustment of functions.

Any given point is of course east in relation to west, west in relation to east. Absolutely, it may be said that its westness does not exclude its eastness; or, that it is neither east nor west.

"If we say that anything is good or evil because it is either good or evil in our eyes, then there is nothing which is not good, nothing which is not evil. To know that Yao and Chieh were both good and both evil from their opposite points of view,—this is the expression of a standard.

"Of old Yao abdicated in favour of Shun, and the latter ruled. Kuei abdicated in favour of Chih, and the latter failed.

Kuei was a prince of the Yen State, who was humbugged into imitating the glorious example of Yao and abdicating in favour of his minister Chih. Three short years of power landed the latter in all the horrors of a general revolution.

T'ang and Wu

See ch. xii.

got the empire by fighting. By fighting, Poh Kung lost it.

A revolutionary leader who, on the failure of his scheme, ended his life by strangulation. See the Tso Chuan, 16th year of Duke Ai.

From which it may be seen that the rationale of abdicating or fighting, of acting like Yao or like Chieh, must be determined according to the opportunity, and may not be regarded as a constant quantity.

"A battering-ram can knock down a wall, but it cannot repair the breach.

This sentence has sorely puzzled all commentators.
Different things are differently applied.

"Ch'ih-Chi and Hua Liu could travel 1,000 li in one day, but for catching rats they were not equal to a wild cat.

Two of the eight famous steeds of Muh Wang, a semi-historical ruler of old.

Different animals possess different aptitudes.

"An owl can catch fleas at night, and see the tip of a hair, but if it comes out in the daytime its eyes are so dazzled it cannot see a mountain. Different creatures are differently constituted.

"Thus, as has been said, those who would have right without its correlative, wrong; or good government without its correlative, misrule,—they do not apprehend the great principles of the universe nor the conditions to which all creation is subject. One might as well talk of the existence of heaven without that of earth, or of the negative principle without the positive, which is clearly absurd. Such people, if they do not yield to argument, must be either fools or knaves.

"Rulers have abdicated under different conditions, dynasties have been continued under different conditions. Those who did not hit off a favourable time and were in opposition to their age,—they were called usurpers. Those who did hit off the right time and were in harmony with their age,—they were called patriots. Fair and softly, my River friend; what should you know of value and worthlessness, of great and small?"

It is therefore quite unnecessary to teach you where to fix the limits of that of which you know nothing.

"In this case," replied the Spirit of the River, "what am I to do and what am I not to do? How am I to arrange my declinings and receivings, my takings-hold and my lettings-go?"

"From the point of view of Tao," said the Spirit of the Ocean, "value and worthlessness are like slopes and plains.

A slope to-day may be a plain to-morrow.

To consider either as absolutely such would involve great injury to Tao. Few and many are like giving and receiving presents. These must not be regarded from one side, or there will be great confusion to Tao.

It would be unfair only to regard, from the receiver's standpoint, the amount given. The intention of the giver must also be taken into the calculation.

Be discriminating, as the ruler of a State whose administration is impartial. Be dispassionate, as the worshipped deity whose dispensation is impartial. Be expansive, like the points of the compass, to whose boundlessness no limit is set. Embrace all creation, and none shall be more sheltered than another. This is the unconditioned. And where all things are equal, how can we have the long and the short?

"Tao is without beginning, without end. Other things are born and die. They are impermanent; and now for better, now for worse, they are ceaselessly changing form. Past years cannot be recalled: time cannot be arrested. The succession of states is endless; and every end is followed by a new beginning. Thus it may be said that man's duty to his neighbour is embodied in the eternal principles of the universe.

All he has to do is to be.

"The life of man passes by like a galloping horse, changing at every turn, at every hour. What should he do, or what should he not do, other than let his decomposition go on?"

"If this is the case," retorted the Spirit of the River, "pray what is the value of Tao?"

"Those who understand Tao," answered the Spirit of the Ocean, "must necessarily apprehend the eternal principles above mentioned and be clear as to their application. Consequently, they do not suffer any injury from without.

They never oppose, but let all things take their course.

"The man of perfect virtue cannot be burnt by fire, nor drowned in water, nor hurt by frost or sun, nor torn by wild bird or beast. Not that he makes light of these; but that he discriminates between safety and danger. Happy under prosperous and adverse circumstances alike, cautious as to what he discards and what he accepts;—nothing can harm him.

Plato taught that it was impossible to make a slave of a wise man, meaning that the latter by virtue of his mental endowment would rise superior to mere physical thrall. "A wise and just man," said he, "could be as happy in a state of slavery as in a state of freedom."

"Therefore it has been said that the natural abides within, the artificial without. Virtue abides in the natural. Knowledge of the action of the natural and of the artificial has its root in the natural, its development in virtue. And thus, whether in motion or at rest, whether in expansion or in contraction, there is always a reversion to the essential and to the ultimate."

Those eternal principles which embody all human obligations.

"What do you mean," enquired the Spirit of the River, "by the natural and the artificial?"

"Horses and oxen," answered the Spirit of the Ocean, "have four feet. That is the natural. Put a halter on a horse's head, a string through a bullock's nose,—that is the artificial.

"Therefore it has been said, do not let the artificial obliterate the natural; do not let will obliterate destiny; do not let virtue be sacrificed to fame. Diligently observe these precepts without fail, and thus you will revert to the divine."

If man does not set himself in opposition to God, the result will be Tao.

The walrus envies the centipede;
Its many legs and nimble gait.
the centipede envies the snake;
Which moves without legs.
the snake envies the wind;
Which moves far more quickly even without body.
the Wind envies the eye;
Which travels even without moving.
the eye envies the mind;
Which can comprehend the whole universe, past and present alike.

The walrus said to the centipede, "I hop about on one leg, but not very successfully. How do you manage all these legs you have?"

"Walrus" is of course an analogue. But for the one leg, the description given by a commentator of the creature mentioned in the text applies with significant exactitude.

"I don't manage them," replied the centipede. "Have you never seen saliva? When it is ejected, the big drops are the size of pearls, the small ones like mist. They fall promiscuously on the ground and cannot be counted. And so it is that my mechanism works naturally, without my being conscious of the fact."

The centipede said to the snake, "With all my legs I do not move as fast as you with none. How is that?"

"One's natural mechanism," replied the snake, "is not a thing to be changed. What need have I for legs?"

The snake said to the wind, "I can manage to wriggle along, but I have a form. Now you come blustering down from the north sea to bluster away to the south sea, and you seem to be without form. How is that?"

"'Tis true," replied the wind, "that I bluster as you say; but any one who can point at me or kick at me, excels me.

As I cannot do as much to them.

On the other hand, I can break huge trees and destroy large buildings. That is my strong point. Out of all the small things in which I do not excel I make one great one in which I do excel. And to excel in great things is given only to the Sages."

Everything has its own natural qualifications. What is difficult to one is easy to another.

No illustration is given of the "eye" and "mind." "'Tis the half-length portrait," says Lin Hsi Chung, "of a beautiful girl;"—which is ingenious if not sound.

When Confucius visited K'uang, the men of Sung surrounded him closely.

This is a mistake. "K'uang" was in the Wei State, and it was by the men of Wei that Confucius was surrounded.

Yet he went on playing and singing to his guitar without ceasing.

"How is it, Sir," enquired Tzŭ Lu, "that you are so cheerful?"

See p. 75. Tzŭ Lu would have been the first to be cheerful himself.

"Come here," replied Confucius, "and I will tell you. For a long time I have been struggling against failure, but in vain. Fate is against me. For a long time I have been seeking success, but in vain. The hour has not come.

"In the days of Yao and Shun, no man throughout the empire was a failure, though no one was conscious of the gain. In the days of Chieh and Chou, no man throughout the empire was a success, though no one was conscious of the loss. The times and circumstances were adapted accordingly.

"To travel by water and not avoid sea-serpents and dragons,—this is the courage of the fisherman. To travel by land and not avoid the rhinoceros and the tiger,—this is the courage of hunters. When bright blades cross, to look on death as on life,—this is the courage of the hero. To know that failure is fate and that success is opportunity, and to remain fearless in great danger,—this is the courage of the Sage. Yu! rest in this. My destiny is cut out for me."

Shortly afterwards, the captain of the troops came in and apologised, saying, "We thought you were Yang Hu; consequently we surrounded you. We find we have made a mistake." Whereupon he again apologised and retired.

Yang Hu was "wanted" by the people of Wei, and it appears that Confucius was unfortunately like him in feature. But the whole episode is clearly the interpolation of a forger.

Kung Sun Lung

A philosopher of the Chao State, whose treatise on the "hard and white" etc. is said to be still extant. See ch. ii.

said to Mou of Wei, "When young I studied the Tao of the ancient Sages. When I grew up I knew all about the practice of charity and duty to one's neighbour, the identification of like and unlike, the separation of hardness and whiteness, and about making the not-so so, and the impossible possible. I vanquished the wisdom of all the philosophies. I exhausted all the arguments that were brought against me. I thought that I had indeed reached the goal. But now that I have heard Chuang Tzŭ, I am lost in astonishment at his grandeur. I know not whether it is in arguing or in knowledge that I am not equal to him. I can no longer open my mouth. May I ask you to impart to me the secret?"

Kung Tzŭ Mou leant over the table and sighed. Then he looked up to heaven, and smiling replied, saying, "Have you never heard of the frog in the old well?—The frog said to the turtle of the eastern sea, 'Happy indeed am I! I hop on to the rail around the well. I rest in the hollow of some broken brick. Swimming, I gather the water under my arms and shut my mouth. I plunge into the mud, burying my feet and toes; and not one of the cockles, crabs, or tadpoles I see around me are my match. [Fancy pitting the happiness of an old well against all the water of Ocean!] Why do you not come, Sir, and pay me a visit?'

"Now the turtle of the eastern sea had not got its left leg down ere its right had already stuck fast, so it shrank back and begged to be excused. It then described the sea, saying, 'A thousand li would not measure its breadth, nor a thousand fathoms its depth. In the days of the Great Yü, there were nine years of flood out of ten; but this did not add to its bulk. In the days of T'ang, there were seven years out of eight of drought; but this did not narrow its span. Not to be affected by duration of time, not to be affected by volume of water,—such is the great happiness of the eastern sea.'

To be impervious to external influences.

"At this the well-frog was considerably astonished, and knew not what to say next. And for one whose knowledge does not reach to the positive-negative domain,

Where contraries are identical.

to attempt to understand Chuang Tzŭ, is like a mosquito trying to carry a mountain, or an ant to swim a river,—they cannot succeed. And for one whose knowledge does not reach to the abstrusest of the abstruse, but is based only upon such victories as you have enumerated,—is not he like the frog in the well?

"Chuang Tzŭ moves in the realms below while soaring to heaven above. For him north and south do not exist; the four points are gone; he is engulphed in the unfathomable. For him east and west do not exist. Beginning with chaos, he has gone back to Tao; and yet you think you are going to examine his doctrines and meet them with argument! This is like looking at the sky through a tube, or pointing at the earth with an awl,—a small result.

The area covered by an awl's point being infinitesimal.

"Have you never heard how the youth of Shou-ling went to study at Han-tan? They did not learn what they wanted at Han-tan, and forgot all they knew before into the bargain, so that they returned home in disgrace. And you, if you do not go away, you will forget all you know, and waste your time into the bargain."

Kung Sun Lung's jaw dropped; his tongue clave to his palate; and he slunk away.

Another spurious episode, as is evident from its general weakness, not to mention repetitions of figures and allusions taken from other chapters.

Chuang Tzŭ was fishing in the P'u when the prince of Ch'u sent two high officials to ask him to take charge of the administration of the Ch'u State.

Chuang Tzŭ went on fishing, and without turning his head said, "I have heard that in Ch'u there is a sacred tortoise which has been dead now some three thousand years. And that the prince keeps this tortoise carefully enclosed in a chest on the altar of his ancestral temple. Now would this tortoise rather be dead and have its remains venerated, or be alive and wagging its tail in the mud?"

"It would rather be alive," replied the two officials, "and wagging its tail in the mud."

"Begone!" cried Chuang Tzŭ. "I too will wag my tail in the mud."

Hui Tzŭ was prime minister in the Liang State. Chuang Tzŭ went thither to visit him.

Some one remarked, "Chuang Tzŭ has come. He wants to be minister in your place."

Thereupon Hui Tzŭ was afraid, and searched all over the State

With warrants.

for three days and three nights to find him.

Then Chuang Tzŭ went to see Hui Tzŭ, and said, "In the south there is a bird. It is a kind of phœnix. Do you know it? It started from the south sea to fly to the north sea. Except on the wu-t'ung tree,

Eleococca verrucosa. Williams.

it would not alight. It would eat nothing but the fruit of the bamboo, drink nothing but the purest spring water. An owl which had got the rotten carcass of a rat, looked up as the phœnix flew by, and screeched.

To warn it off.

Are you not screeching at me over your kingdom of Liang?"

Chuang Tzŭ and Hui Tzŭ had strolled on to the bridge over the Hao, when the former observed, "See how the minnows are darting about! That is the pleasure of fishes."

"You not being a fish yourself," said Hui Tzŭ, "how can you possibly know in what consists the pleasure of fishes?"

"And you not being I," retorted Chuang Tzŭ, "how can you know that I do not know?"

"If I, not being you, cannot know what you know," urged Hui Tzŭ, "it follows that you, not being a fish, cannot know in what consists the pleasure of fishes."

"Let us go back," said Chuang Tzŭ, "to your original question. You asked me how I knew in what consists the pleasure of fishes. Your very question shows that you knew I knew.

For you asked me how I knew.

I knew it from my own feelings on this bridge."

From my own feelings above the bridge I infer those of the fishes below.

CHAPTER XVIII

Perfect Happiness

Argument:—The uncertainty of human happiness—What the world aims at is physical well-being—This is not profitable even to the body—In inaction alone is true happiness to be found—Inaction the rule of the material universe—Acquiescence in whatever our destiny may bring forth—Illustrations.

[This chapter is supplementary to chapter vi.]

Is perfect happiness to be found on earth, or not? Are there those who can enjoy life, or not? If so, what do they do, what do they affect, what do they avoid, what do they rest in, accept, reject, like, and dislike?

What the world esteems comprises wealth, rank, old age, and goodness of heart. What it enjoys comprises comfort, rich food, fine clothes, beauty, and music. What it does not esteem comprises poverty, want of position, early death, and evil behaviour. What it does not enjoy comprises lack of comfort for the body, lack of rich food for the palate, lack of fine clothes for the back, lack of beauty for the eye, and lack of music for the ear. If men do not get these, they are greatly miserable. Yet from the point of view of our physical frame, this is folly.

Physically we can, and most of us do, get along very well without these extras.

Wealthy people who toil and moil, putting together more money than they can possibly use,—from the point of view of our physical frame, is not this going beyond the mark?

Officials of rank who turn night into day in their endeavours to compass the best ends;—from the point of view of our physical frame, is not this a divergence?

Man is born to sorrow, and what misery is theirs whose old age with dulled faculties only means prolonged sorrow! From the point of view of our physical frame, this is going far astray.

Patriots are in the world's opinion admittedly good. Yet their goodness does not enable them to enjoy life;

Patriotism has been illustrated in China by countless heroic deeds, associated always with the death of the hero concerned.

and so I know not whether theirs is veritable goodness or not. If the former, it does not enable them to enjoy life; if the latter, it at any rate enables them to cause others to enjoy theirs.

It has been said, "If your loyal counsels are not attended to, depart quietly without resistance." Thus, when Tzŭ Hsü

The famous Wu Yüan, 6th century B.C., whose opposition to his sovereign led to his own disgrace and death.

resisted, his physical frame perished; yet had he not resisted, he would not have made his name. Is there then really such a thing as this goodness, or not?

As to what the world does and the way in which people are happy now, I know not whether such happiness be real happiness or not. The happiness of ordinary persons seems to me to consist in slavishly following the majority, as if they could not help it. Yet they all say they are happy.

"The general average of mankind are not only moderate in intellect, but also in inclinations: they have no tastes or wishes strong enough to incline them to do anything unusual." Mill's Essay on Liberty.

But I cannot say that this is happiness or that it is not happiness. Is there then, after all, such a thing as happiness?

I make true pleasure to consist in inaction, which the world regards as great pain. Thus it has been said, "Perfect happiness is the absence of happiness;

The non-existence of any state or condition necessarily includes the non-existence of its correlate. If we do not have happiness, we are at once exempt from misery; and such a negative state is a state of "perfect happiness."

perfect renown is the absence of renown."

Now in this sublunary world of ours it is impossible to assign positive and negative absolutely. Nevertheless, in inaction they can be so assigned. Perfect happiness and preservation of life are to be sought for only in inaction.

Let us consider. Heaven does nothing; yet it is clear. Earth does nothing; yet it enjoys repose. From the inaction of these two proceed all the modifications of things. How vast, how infinite is inaction, yet without source! How infinite, how vast, yet without form!

The endless varieties of things around us all spring from inaction. Therefore it has been said, "Heaven and earth do nothing, yet there is nothing which they do not accomplish." But among men, who can attain to inaction?

Lin Hsi Chung condemns the whole of the above exordium as too closely reasoned for Chuang Tzŭ, with his rugged, elliptical style.

When Chuang Tzŭ's wife died, Hui Tzŭ went to condole. He found the widower sitting on the ground, singing, with his legs spread out at a right angle, and beating time on a bowl.

"To live with your wife," exclaimed Hui Tzŭ, "and see your eldest son grow up to be a man, and then not to shed a tear over her corpse,—this would be bad enough. But to drum on a bowl, and sing; surely this is going too far."

"Not at all," replied Chuang Tzŭ. "When she died, I could not help being affected by her death. Soon, however, I remembered that she had already existed in a previous state before birth, without form, or even substance; that while in that unconditioned condition, substance was added to spirit; that this substance then assumed form; and that the next stage was birth. And now, by virtue of a further change, she is dead, passing from one phase to another like the sequence of spring, summer, autumn, and winter. And while she is thus lying asleep in Eternity, for me to go about weeping and wailing would be to proclaim myself ignorant of these natural laws. Therefore I refrain."

A hunchback and a one-legged man were looking at the tombs of departed heroes, on the K'un-lun Mountains, where the Yellow Emperor rests. Suddenly, ulcers broke out upon their left elbows, of a very loathsome description.

"Do you loathe this?" asked the hunchback.

"Not I," replied the other, "why should I? Life is a loan with which the borrower does but add more dust and dirt to the sum total of existence. Life and death are as day and night; and while you and I stand gazing at the evidences of mortality around us, if the same mortality overtakes me, why should I loathe it?"

Chuang Tzŭ one day saw an empty skull, bleached, but still preserving its shape. Striking it with his riding whip, he said, "Wert thou once some ambitious citizen whose inordinate yearnings brought him to this pass?—some statesman who plunged his country in ruin and perished in the fray?—some wretch who left behind him a legacy of shame?—some beggar who died in the pangs of hunger and cold? Or didst thou reach this state by the natural course of old age?"

When he had finished speaking, he took the skull, and placing it under his head as a pillow, went to sleep. In the night, he dreamt that the skull appeared to him and said, "You speak well, Sir; but all you say has reference to the life of mortals, and to mortal troubles. In death there are none of these. Would you like to hear about death?"

Chuang Tzŭ having replied in the affirmative, the skull began:—"In death, there is no sovereign above, and no subject below. The workings of the four seasons are unknown. Our existences are bounded only by eternity. The happiness of a king among men cannot exceed that which we enjoy."

Chuang Tzŭ, however, was not convinced, and said, "Were I to prevail upon God to allow your body to be born again, and your bones and flesh to be renewed, so that you could return to your parents, to your wife, and to the friends of your youth,—would you be willing?"

At this, the skull opened its eyes wide and knitted its brows and said, "How should I cast aside happiness greater than that of a king, and mingle once again in the toils and troubles of mortality?"

Reminding us strangely of Hamlet.

When Yen Yüan

See p. 81.

went eastwards to the Ch'i State, Confucius was sad. Tzŭ Kung arose and said, "Is it, Sir, because Hui

Yen Yüan's personal name.

has gone east to Ch'i that you are sad?"

"A good question," replied Confucius. "There is a saying by Kuan Chung

Prime Minister to Duke Huan of the Ch'i State, 7th century B.C.

of old which I highly esteem: 'Small bags won't hold big things; short ropes won't reach down deep wells.' Thus, destiny is a pre-arrangement, just as form has its limitations. From neither, to neither, can you either take away or add. And I fear lest Hui, on his visit to the prince of Ch'i, should preach the Tao of Yao and Shun, and dwell on the words of Sui Jen and Shên Nung. The prince will then search within himself, but will not find. And not finding, he will doubt. And when a man doubts, he will kill.

Lit. "he will die." But the verb "to die" is often used in the sense of "to make to die;" and this seems to be the only available sense here.

"Besides, have you not heard that of old when a sea-bird alighted outside the capital of Lu, the prince went out to receive it, and gave it wine in the temple, and had the Chiu Shao

Music composed by the legendary Emperor Shun.

played to amuse it, and a bullock slaughtered to feed it? But the bird was dazed and too timid to eat or drink anything; and in three days it was dead. This was treating the bird like oneself, and not as a bird would treat a bird. Had he treated it as a bird would have treated a bird, he would have put it to roost in a deep forest, to wander over a plain, to swim in a river or lake, to feed upon fish, to fly in order, and to settle leisurely. When the bird was already terrified at human voices, fancy adding music! Play the Hsien Ch'ih

Music of the Yellow Emperor.

or the Chiu Shao in the wilds of Tung-t'ing, and birds will fly away, beasts will take themselves off, and fishes will dive down below. But men will collect to hear.

See p. 111.

"Water, which is life to fishes, is death to man. Being differently constituted, their likes and dislikes are different. Therefore the Sages of the past favoured not uniformity of skill or of occupation. Reputation was commensurate with reality; means were adapted to the end. This was called a due relationship with others coupled with advantage to oneself."

Several sentences of the above are clearly in imitation of parts of ch. ii. The whole episode is beyond doubt a forgery.

Lieh Tzŭ, being on a journey, was eating by the roadside, when he saw an old skull. Plucking a blade of grass, he pointed at it and said, "Only you and I know that there is no such thing as life and no such thing as death.

Lit. "that you have never died nor lived."

Are you really at peace? Or am I really happy?

Who can say whether what we call death may not after all be life, and life death?

"Certain germs, falling upon water, become duckweed. When they reach the junction of the land and the water, they become lichen. Spreading up the bank, they become the dog-tooth violet. Reaching rich soil, they become wu-tsu, the root of which becomes grubs, while the leaves comes from butterflies, or hsü. These are changed into insects, born in the chimney corner, which look like skeletons. Their name is ch'ü-to. After a thousand days, the ch'ü-to becomes a bird, called Kan-yü-ku, the spittle of which becomes the ssŭ-mi. The ssŭ-mi becomes a wine fly, and that comes from an i-lu. The huang-k'uang produces the chiu-yu and the mou-jui produces the glow-worm. The yang-ch'i grafted to an old bamboo which has for a long time put forth no shoots, produces the ch'ing-ning, which produces the leopard, which produces the horse, which produces man.

"Then man goes back into the great Scheme, from which all things come and to which all things return."

Such is the eternal round, marked by the stages which we call life and death.

Many of the names in the above paragraph have not been identified even by Chinese commentators. On all counts then they may safely be left where they are.

CHAPTER XIX

The Secret of Life

Argument:—The soul is from God—Man's body its vehicle—The soul quickening the body is life—Care of the internal and of the external must be simultaneous—In due nourishment of both is Tao.

[This chapter is supplementary to chapter iii.]

Those who understand the conditions of life devote no attention to things which life cannot accomplish. Those who understand the conditions of destiny devote no attention to things over which knowledge has no control.

For the due nourishment of our physical frames, certain things are needful. Yet where such things abound, the physical frame is not always nourished. For the preservation of life it is necessary that there should be no abandonment of the physical frame. Yet where the physical frame is not abandoned, life does not always remain.

Life comes, and cannot be declined. It goes, and cannot be stopped. But alas! the world thinks that to nourish the frame is enough to keep life. And if indeed it is not enough, what then is the world to do?

Although not enough, it must still be done. It cannot be neglected. For if one is to neglect the physical frame, better far to retire at once from the world. By renouncing the world, one gets rid of the cares of the world. The result is a natural level, which is equivalent to a re-birth. And he who is re-born is near.

To Tao.

But what inducement is there to renounce the affairs of men, to become indifferent to life?—In the first case, the physical body suffers no wear and tear; in the second, the vitality is left unharmed. And he whose physical frame is perfect and whose vitality is in its original purity,—he is one with God.

Mens sana in corpore sano.

Heaven and earth are the father and mother of all things. When they unite, the result is shape. When they disperse, the original condition is renewed.

As in the case of ordinary mortals.

But if body and vitality are both perfect, this state is called fit for translation.

In the Biblical sense, as applied to Enoch.

Such perfection of vitality goes back to the minister of God.

"Vitality" is the subtle essence, the immaterial informing principle which, united with matter, exhibits the phenomenon of life. The term has already occurred in ch. xi.

Lieh Tzŭ asked Kuan Yin,

A sage who by some is said to have flourished five or six hundred years before Lieh Tzŭ; by others, to have been an immediate disciple of Lao Tzŭ, and to have been entrusted by him with the publication of the Tao-Tê-Ching.

saying, "The perfect man can walk through solid bodies without obstruction. He can pass through fire without being burnt. He can scale the highest heights without fear. How does he bring himself to this?"

"It is because he is in a condition of absolute purity," replied Kuan Yin. "It is not cunning which enables him to dare such feats. Be seated, and I will tell you.

"All that has form, sound, and colour, may be classed under the head thing. Man differs so much from the rest, and stands at the head of all things, simply because the latter are but what they appear and nothing more. But man can attain to formlessness and vanquish death. And with that which is in possession of the eternal, how can mere things compare?

"Man may rest in the eternal fitness; he may abide in the everlasting; and roam from the beginning to the end of all creation. He may bring his nature to a condition of ONE; he may nourish his strength; he may harmonize his virtue, and so put himself into partnership with God. Then, when his divinity is thus assured, and his spirit closed in on all sides, how can anything find a passage within?

He is beyond the reach of objective existences.

"A drunken man who falls out of a cart, though he may suffer, does not die. His bones are the same as other people's; but he meets his accident in a different way. His spirit is in a condition of security. He is not conscious of riding in the cart; neither is he conscious of falling out of it. Ideas of life, death, fear, etc., cannot penetrate his breast; and so he does not suffer from contact with objective existences. And if such security is to be got from wine, how much more is it to be got from God. It is in God that the Sage seeks his refuge, and so he is free from harm.

"An avenger does not snap in twain the murderous weapon; neither does the most spiteful man carry his resentment to a tile which may have hit him on the head. And by the extension of this principle, the empire would be at peace; no more confusion of war, no more punishment of death.

"Do not develop your artificial intelligence, but develop that intelligence which is from God. From the latter, results virtue; from the former, cunning. And those who do not shrink from the natural, nor wallow in the artificial,—they are near to perfection."

When Confucius was on his way to the Ch'u State, he came to a forest where he saw a hunchback catching cicadas as though with his hand.

It is still the delight of the Chinese gamin to capture the noisy "scissor-grinder" with the aid of a long bamboo tipped with bird-lime.

"How clever you are!" cried Confucius. "Have you any way of doing this?"

"Way," i.e. road, is the primary meaning of Tao.

"I have a way," replied the hunchback. "In the fifth and sixth moons I practise balancing two balls one on top of the other.

At the top of his pole.

If they do not fall, I do not miss many cicadas. When I can balance three balls, I only miss one in ten; and when five, then it is as though I caught the cicadas with my hand. My body is as motionless as the stump of a tree; my arms like dead branches. Heaven and earth and all creation may be around me, but I am conscious only of my cicada's wings. How should I not succeed?"

Confucius looked round at his disciples and said, "Singleness of purpose induces concentration of the faculties. Of such is the success of this hunchback."

Yen Yüan said to Confucius, "When I crossed over the Shang-shên rapid, the boatman managed his craft with marvellous skill. I asked him if handling a boat could be learnt. 'It can,' replied he. 'The way of those who know how to keep you afloat is more like sinking you. They row as if the boat wasn't there.'

"I enquired what this meant, but he would not tell me. May I ask its signification."

"It means," answered Confucius, "that such a man is oblivious of the water around him. He regards the rapid as though dry land. He looks upon an upset as an ordinary cart accident. And if a man can but be impervious to capsizings and accidents in general, whither should he not be able comfortably to go?

"A man who plays for counters will play well. If he stakes his girdle,
In which he keeps his loose cash.
he will be nervous; if yellow gold, he will lose his wits. His skill is the same in each case, but he is distracted by the value of his stake. And every one who attaches importance to the external, becomes internally without resource."

T'ien K'ai Chih had an audience of Duke Wei of Chou. The Duke asked him, saying, "I have heard that Chu Hsien is studying the art of life. As you are a companion of his, pray tell me anything you know about it."

"I do but ply the broom at his outer gate," replied T'ien K'ai Chih; "what should I know about my Master's researches?"

"Don't be so modest," said the Duke. "I am very anxious to hear about it."

"Well," replied T'ien, "I have heard my master say that keeping life is like keeping a flock of sheep. You look out for the laggards, and whip them up."

"What does that mean?" asked the Duke.

"In the State of Lu," said T'ien, "there was a man named Shan Pao. He lived on the mountains and drank water. All worldly interests he had put aside. And at the age of seventy, his complexion was like that of a child. Unluckily, he one day fell in with a hungry tiger who killed and ate him.

"There was also a man named Chang I, who frequented the houses of rich and poor alike. At the age of forty he was attacked by some internal disease and died.

"Shan Pao took care of his inner self, and a tiger ate his external man. Chang I took care of himself externally, but disease attacked him internally. These two individuals both omitted to whip up the laggards."

There is no particular record of the worthies mentioned above.

Confucius said, "Neither affecting obscurity, nor courting prominence, but unconsciously occupying the happy mean,—he who can attain to these three will enjoy a surpassing fame.

"In dangerous parts, where one wayfarer out of ten meets his death, fathers and sons and brothers will counsel each other not to travel without a sufficient escort. Is not this wisdom? And there where men are also greatly in danger, in the lists of passion, in the banquet hour, not to warn them is error indeed."

Physical precautions are not alone sufficient. Man's moral nature equally requires constant watchfulness and care.

The Grand Augur, in his ceremonial robes, approached the shambles and thus addressed the pigs:—

"How can you object to die? I shall fatten you for three months. I shall discipline myself for ten days and fast for three. I shall strew fine grass, and place you bodily upon a carved sacrificial dish. Does not this satisfy you?"

Then speaking from the pigs' point of view, he continued, "It is better perhaps after all to live on bran and escape the shambles...."

"But then," added he, speaking from his own point of view, "to enjoy honour when alive one would readily die on a war-shield or in the headsman's basket."

So he rejected the pigs' point of view and adopted his own point of view. In what sense then was he different from the pigs?

Even as a pig thinks of nothing but eating, so was the Grand Augur ready to sacrifice everything, life itself, for paltry fame.

When Duke Huan was out hunting, with Kuan Chung as his charioteer, he saw a bogy. Catching hold of Kuan Chung's hand, he asked him, saying, "What do you see?"

"I see nothing," replied Kuan Chung. But when the Duke got home he became delirious, and for many days was unable to go out.

There came a certain Huang Tzŭ Kao Ngao of the Ch'i State

"A sage of the Ch'i State,"—as the commentators usually say when in reality they know nothing about the individual.

and said, "Your Highness is self-injured. How could a bogy injure you? When the vital strength is dissipated in anger, and is not renewed, there is a deficiency. When its tendency is in one direction upwards, the result is to incline men to wrath. When its tendency is in one direction downwards, the result is loss of memory. When it remains stagnant, in the middle of the body, the result is disease."

"Very well," said the Duke, "but are there such things as bogies?"

"There are," replied Huang. "There is the mud spirit Li; the fire spirit Kao; Lei T'ing, the spirit of the dust-bin; P'ei O and Wa Lung, sprites of the north-east; Yi Yang of the north-west; Wang Hsiang of the water; the Hsin of the hills; the K'uei of the mountain; the P'ang Huang of the moor; the Wei I of the marsh."

The garb and bearing of the above beings are very fully described by commentators.

"And what may the Wei I be like?" asked the Duke.

"The Wei I," replied Huang, "is as broad as a cart-wheel and as long as the shaft. It wears purple clothes and a red cap. It is a sentient being, and whenever it hears the rumble of thunder, it stands up in a respectful attitude. Those who see this bogy are like to be chieftains among men."

The Duke laughed exultingly and said, "The very one I saw!" Thereupon he dressed himself and sat up; and ere the day had closed, without knowing it, his sickness had left him.

The above episode teaches that the evils which appear to come upon us from without, in reality have their origin within.

Chi Hsing Tzŭ was training fighting cocks for the prince.

Of Ch'i, says a commentator.

At the end of ten days the latter asked if they were ready. "Not yet," replied Chi; "they are in the stage of seeking fiercely for a foe."

Again ten days elapsed, and the prince made a further enquiry. "Not yet," replied Chi; "they are still excited by the sounds and shadows of other cocks."

Ten days more, and the prince asked again. "Not yet," answered Chi; "the sight of an enemy is still enough to excite them to rage."

But after another ten days, when the prince again enquired, Chi said, "They will do. Other cocks may crow, but they will take no notice. To look at them one might say they were of wood. Their virtue is complete. Strange cocks will not dare meet them, but will run."

Illustrating the value of internal concentration.

Confucius was looking at the cataract at Lü-liang. It fell from a height of thirty jen,

1 jen = 7 Chinese feet. What the ancient Chinese foot measured, it is impossible to say. For the height of the cataract it will be near enough to say 200 English feet.

and its foam reached forty li away. No scaly, finny creature could enter therein.

Meaning the rapids below.

Yet Confucius saw an old man go in, and thinking that he was suffering from some trouble and desirous of ending his life, bade a disciple run along the side to try and save him. The old man emerged about a hundred paces off, and with flowing hair went carolling along the bank. Confucius followed him and said, "I had thought, Sir, you were a spirit, but now I see you are a man. Kindly tell me, is there any way to deal thus with water?"

"No," replied the old man; "I have no way. There was my original condition to begin with; then habit growing into nature; and lastly acquiescence in destiny. Plunging in with the whirl, I come out with the swirl. I accommodate myself to the water, not the water to me. And so I am able to deal with it after this fashion."

"What do you mean," enquired Confucius, "by your original condition to begin with, habit growing into nature, and acquiescence in destiny?"

"I was born," replied the old man, "upon dry land, and accommodated myself to dry land. That was my original condition. Growing up on the water, I accommodated myself to the water. That was what I meant by nature.

Habit is second nature.

And doing as I did without being conscious of any effort so to do, that was what I meant by destiny."

Objective existences cannot injure him who puts his trust in God.

[This episode occurs twice, with textual differences, in the works of Lieh Tzǔ, chs. ii. and viii.]

Ch'ing, the chief carpenter,

Of the Lu State.

was carving wood into a stand for hanging musical instruments. When finished, the work appeared to those who saw it as though of supernatural execution. And the prince of Lu asked him, saying, "What mystery is there in your art?"

"No mystery, your Highness," replied Ch'ing; "and yet there is something.

"When I am about to make such a stand, I guard against any diminution of my vital power. I first reduce my mind to absolute quiescence. Three days in this condition, and I become oblivious of any reward to be gained. Five days, and I become oblivious of any fame to be acquired. Seven days, and I become unconscious of my four limbs and my physical frame. Then, with no thought of the Court present to my mind, my skill becomes concentrated, and all disturbing elements from without are gone. I enter some mountain forest. I search for a suitable tree. It contains the form required, which is afterwards elaborated. I see the stand in my mind's eye, and then set to work. Otherwise, there is nothing. I bring my own natural capacity into relation with that of the wood. What was suspected to be of supernatural execution in my work was due solely to this."

To obliteration of self in the infinite causality of God.

Tung Yeh Chi exhibited his charioteering skill before Duke Chuang.

"Of Lu," says one commentator. But another points out that Yen Ho (infra) is mentioned in chapter iv. as tutor to the son of Duke Ling of Wei, which would involve an anachronism.

Backwards and forwards he drove in lines which might have been ruled, sweeping round at each end in curves which might have been described by compasses.

The Duke, however, said that this was nothing more than weaving; and bidding him drive round and round a hundred times, returned home.

Yen Ho came upon him, and then went in and said to the Duke, "Chi's horses are on the point of breaking down."

The Duke remained silent, making no reply; and in a short time it was announced that the horses had actually broken down, and that Chi had gone away.

"How could you tell this?" said the Duke to Yen Ho.

"Because," replied the latter, "Chi was trying to make his horses perform a task to which they were unequal. Therefore I said they would break down."

Illustrating the strain which mortality daily puts upon the bodies and minds of all men.

Ch'ui the artisan could draw circles with his hand better than with compasses. His fingers seemed to accommodate themselves so naturally to the thing he was working at, that it was unnecessary to fix his attention. His mental faculties thus remained ONE, and suffered no hindrance.

To be unconscious of one's feet implies that the shoes are easy. To be unconscious of a waist implies that the girdle is easy. The intelligence being unconscious of positive and negative implies that the heart is at ease. No modifications within, no yielding to influences without,

But always following a natural course.

—this is ease under all conditions. And he who beginning with ease, is never not at ease, is unconscious of the ease of ease.

Such is the condition of oblivion necessary to the due development of our natural spontaneity.

A certain Sun Hsiu went to the house of Pien Ch'ing Tzŭ

Both unknown to fame.

and complained, saying, "In peace I am not considered wanting in propriety. In times of trouble I am not considered wanting in courage. Yet my crops fail; and officially I am not a success. From my village an outcast, I am an outlaw from my State. How have I offended against God that he should visit me with such a fate?"

"Have you not heard," replied Pien Tzŭ, "how the perfect man conducts himself? He is oblivious of his physical organisation. He is beyond the reach of sight and hearing. He moves outside the limits of this dusty world, rambling transcendentally in the domain of no-affairs. This is called acting but not from self-confidence, influencing but not from authority.

That is, acting not in consequence of self-confidence, but without reference to it; sc. naturally. Influencing, not because of authority, but gaining authority because of natural influence.

This quotation appears, though Chuang Tzŭ or whoever may be responsible for this episode does not say so, in chs. x. and li. of the Tao-Tê-Ching.

"But you, you make a show of your knowledge in order to startle fools. You cultivate yourself in contrast to the degradation of others. And you blaze along as though the sun and moon were under your arms.

These last three sentences will be found verbatim in ch. xx.

Whereas, that you have a whole body in a whole skin, and have not perished in mid career, dumb, blind, or halt, but actually hold a place among men,—this ought to be enough for you. Why rail at God? Begone!"

Sun Hsiu went away, and Pien Tzŭ went in and sat down. Shortly afterwards, he looked up to heaven and sighed; whereupon a disciple asked him what was the matter.

"When Hsiu was here just now," answered Pien Tzŭ, "I spoke to him of the virtue of the perfect man. I fear lest he be startled and so driven on to doubt."

"No, Sir," answered the disciple. "If he was right and you were wrong, wrong will never drive right into doubt. If, on the other hand, he was wrong and you were right, he brought his doubt with him, and you are not responsible."

"Not so," said Pien Tzŭ. "Of old, when a bird alighted outside the capital of Lu, the prince was delighted, and killed an ox to feed it and had the Chiu Shao played to entertain it. The bird, however, was timid and dazed and dared not to eat or drink. This was treating the bird like oneself. But to treat a bird as a bird would treat a bird, you must put it to roost in a deep forest, let it swim in river or lake, and feed at its ease on the plain. Now Sun Hsiu is a man of small understanding; and for me to speak to him of the perfect man is like setting a mouse to ride in a coach or a band of music to play to a quail. How should he not be startled?"

The above episode has already appeared in ch. xviii., ad fin.

CHAPTER XX

Mountain Trees

Argument:—The alternatives of usefulness and uselessness—Tao a tertium quid—The human a hindrance to the divine—Altruism—Adaptation—Destiny—Illustrations.

[This chapter is supplementary to chapter iv.]

Chuang Tzŭ was travelling over a mountain when he saw a huge tree well covered with foliage. A woodsman had stopped near by, not caring to take it; and on Chuang Tzŭ enquiring the reason, he was told that it was of no use.

"This tree," cried Chuang Tzŭ, "by virtue of being good for nothing succeeds in completing its allotted span."

When Chuang Tzŭ left the mountain, he put up at the house of an old friend. The latter was delighted, and ordered a servant to kill a goose and cook it.

"Which shall I kill?" enquired the servant; "the one that cackles or the one that doesn't?"

His master told him to kill the one which did not cackle. And accordingly, the next day, a disciple asked Chuang Tzŭ, saying, "Yesterday, that tree on the mountain, because good for nothing, was to succeed in completing its allotted span. But now, our host's goose, which is good for nothing, has to die. Upon which horn of the dilemma will you rest?"

"I rest," replied Chuang Tzŭ with a smile, "halfway between the two. In that position, appearing to be what I am not, it is impossible to avoid the troubles of mortality;

The text is here doubtful, and commentators explain according to the fancy of each. When a Chinese commentator does not understand his text, he usually slurs it over. He never says "I do not understand." Chu Fu Tzŭ alone could rise to this height.

though, if charioted upon Tao and floating far above mortality, this would not be so. No praise, no blame; both great and small; changing with the change of time, but ever without special effort; both above and below; making for harmony with surroundings; reaching creation's First Cause; swaying all things and swayed by none;—how then shall such troubles come? This was the method of Shên Nung and Huang Ti.

"If another guest had happened to arrive," says Lin Hsi Chung, "I fancy the chance even of the cackling goose would have been small."

"But amidst the mundane passions and relationships of man, such would not be the case. For where there is union, there is also separation; where there is completion, there is also destruction; where there is purity, there is also oppression; where there is honour, there is also disparagement; where there is doing, there is also undoing; where there is openness, there is also underhandedness; and where there is no semblance, there is also deceit. How then can there be any fixed point? Alas indeed! Take note, my disciples, that such is to be found only in the domain of Tao."

I Liao

A sage of the Ch'u State.

of Shih-nan paid a visit to the prince of Lu. The latter wore a melancholy look; whereupon the philosopher of Shih-nan enquired what was the cause.

"I study the doctrines of the ancient Sages," replied the prince. "I carry on the work of my predecessors. I respect religion. I honour the good. Never for a moment do I relax in these points; yet I cannot avoid misfortune, and consequently I am sad."

"Your Highness' method of avoiding misfortune," said the philosopher of Shih-nan, "is but a shallow one. A handsome fox or a striped leopard will live in a mountain forest, hiding beneath some precipitous cliff. This is their repose. They come out at night and keep in by day. This is their caution. Though under the stress of hunger and thirst, they lie hidden, hardly venturing to slink secretly to the river bank in search of food. This is their resoluteness. Nevertheless, they do not escape the misfortune of the net and the trap. But what crime have they committed? 'Tis their skin which is the cause of their trouble; and is not the State of Lu your Highness' skin? I would have your Highness put away body and skin alike, and cleansing your heart and purging it of passion, betake yourself to the land where mortality is not.

Tao.

"In Nan-yüeh there is a district, called Established-Virtue. Its people are simple and honest, unselfish, and without passions. They can make, but cannot keep. They give, but look for no return. They are not conscious of fulfilling obligations. They are not conscious of subservience to etiquette.

Theirs is the natural etiquette of well-regulated minds.

Their actions are altogether uncontrolled, yet they tread in the way of the wise. Life is for enjoyment; death, for burial. And thither I would have your Highness proceed, power discarded and the world left behind, only putting trust in Tao."

"The road is long and dangerous," said the prince. "Rivers and hills to be crossed, and I without boat or chariot;—what then?"

"Unhindered by body and unfettered in mind," replied the philosopher, "your Highness will be a chariot to yourself."

"But the road is long and dreary," argued the prince, "and uninhabited.

This is a play on "where mortality is not," above.

I shall have no one to turn to for help; and how, without food, shall I ever be able to get there?"

"Decrease expenditure

Of energy.

and lessen desires," answered the philosopher, "and even though without provisions, there will be enough. And then through river and over sea your

Highness will travel into shoreless illimitable space. From the border-land, those who act as escort will return; but thence onwards your Highness will travel afar.

"It is the human in ourselves which is our hindrance; and the human in others which causes our sorrow. The great Yao had not this human element himself, nor did he perceive it in others. And I would have your Highness put off this hindrance and rid yourself of this sorrow, and roam with Tao alone through the realms of Infinite Nought.

"Suppose a boat is crossing a river, and another empty boat is about to collide with it. Even an irritable man would not lose his temper. But supposing there was some one in the second boat. Then the occupant of the first would shout to him to keep clear. And if the other did not hear the first time, nor even when called to three times, bad language would inevitably follow. In the first case there was no anger, in the second there was; because in the first case the boat was empty, and in the second it was occupied. And so it is with man. If he could only roam empty through life, who would be able to injure him?"

With his mind in a negative state, closed to all impressions conveyed within by the senses from without.

Pei Kung Shê, minister to Duke Ling of Wei, levied contributions for making bells. An altar was built outside the city gate;

For purposes of sacrifice.

and in three months the bells, upper and lower, were all hung.

The bell-chime consisted of a frame with bells swung on an upper and lower bar.

When Wang Tzŭ Ch'ing Chi

Minister to the ruling House of Chou.

saw them, he asked, saying, "How, Sir, did you manage this?"

"In the domain of ONE," replied Shê, "there may not be managing. I have heard say that which is carved and polished reverts nevertheless to its natural condition. And so I made allowances for ignorance and for suspicion. I betrayed no feeling when welcomed or dismissed. I forbade not those who came, nor detained those who went away. I showed no resentment towards the unwilling, nor gratitude towards those who gave. Every one subscribed what he liked; and thus in my daily collection of subscriptions, no injury was done.—How much more then those who have the great WAY?"

If my success was due to the simple principle above enunciated, what a success would result from Tao, which is the infinite extension of such principles into every phase of existence!

The Chinese word here used for "way," as a synonym of Tao, settles the original meaning of the latter in the sense of "road." Thus Lao Tzŭ is said to have explained that the Way he taught was not the way which could be walked upon.

When Confucius was hemmed in between Ch'ên and Ts'ai, he passed seven days without food.

The minister Jen went to condole with him, and said, "You were near, Sir, to death."

"I was indeed," replied Confucius.

"Do you fear death, Sir?" enquired Jen.

"I do," said Confucius.

"Then I will try to teach you," said Jen, "the way not to die.

"In the eastern sea there are certain birds, called the i-êrh. They behave themselves in a modest and unassuming manner, as though unpossessed of ability. They fly simultaneously: they roost in a body. In advancing, none strives to be first; in retreating, none ventures to be last. In eating, none will be the first to begin; it is considered proper to take the leavings of others. Therefore, in their own ranks they are at peace, and the outside world is unable to harm them. And thus they escape trouble.

"Straight trees are the first felled. Sweet wells are soonest exhausted. And you, you make a show of your knowledge in order to startle fools. You cultivate yourself in contrast to the degradation of others. And you blaze along as though the sun and moon were under your arms; consequently, you cannot avoid trouble.

See p. 111.

"Formerly, I heard a very wise man say, Self-praise is no recommendation. In merit achieved there is deterioration. In fame achieved there is loss. Who can discard both merit and fame and become one with the rest? Tao pervades all things but is not seen. Tê

This is "virtue," the expression of Tao.

moves through all things but its place is not known. In its purity and constancy, it may be compared with the purposeless. Remaining concealed, rejecting power, it works not for merit nor for fame. Thus, not censuring others, it is not censured by others.

"And if the perfect man cares not for fame, why, Sir, should you take pleasure in it?"

"Good indeed!" replied Confucius; and forthwith he took leave of his friends and dismissed his disciples and retired to the wilds, where he dressed himself in skins and serge and fed on acorns and chestnuts. He passed among the beasts and birds and they took no heed of him. And if so, how much more among men?

An unquestionably spurious episode.

Confucius asked Tzŭ Sang Hu,

See ch. vi.

saying, "I have been twice expelled from Lu. My tree was cut down in Sung. I have been tabooed in Wei. I am a failure in Shang and Chou. I was surrounded between Ch'ên and Ts'ai. And in addition to all these troubles, my friends have separated from me and my disciples are gone. How is this?"

See p. 82.

"Have you not heard," replied Sang Hu, "how when the men of Kuo fled, one of them, named Lin Hui, cast aside most valuable regalia and carried away his child upon his back? Some one suggested that he was influenced by the value of the child;—but the child's value was small. Or by the inconvenience of the regalia;—but the inconvenience of the child would be much greater. Why then did he leave behind the regalia and carry off the child?

"Lin Hui himself said, 'The regalia involved a mere question of money. The child was from God.'

"And so it is that in trouble and calamity mere money questions are neglected, while we ever cling nearer to that which is from God. And between neglecting and clinging to, the difference is great.

"The friendship of the superior man is negative like water. The friendship of the mean man is full-flavoured like wine. That of the superior man passes from the negative to the affectionate. That of the mean man passes from the full-flavoured to nothing. The friendship of the mean man begins without due cause, and in like manner comes to an end.

"I hear and obey," replied Confucius; and forthwith he went quietly home, put an end to his studies and cast aside his books. His disciples no longer saluted him as teacher; but his love for them deepened every day.

On another occasion, Sang Hu said to him again, "When Shun was about to die, he commanded the Great Yü as follows:—Be careful. Act in accordance with your physical body. Speak in accordance with your feelings. You will thus not get into difficulty with the former nor suffer annoyance in the latter. And as under these conditions you will not stand in need of outward embellishment of any kind, it follows that you therefore will not stand in need of anything."

Also an episode of doubtful authorship. The commentators, however, have nothing to say against its genuineness.

Chuang Tzŭ put on cotton clothes with patches in them, and arranging his girdle and tieing on his shoes,
To keep them from falling off.
went to see the prince of Wei.

"How miserable you look, Sir!" cried the prince.

"It is poverty, not misery," replied Chuang Tzŭ. "A man who has Tao cannot be miserable. Ragged clothes and old boots make poverty, not misery. Mine is what is called being out of harmony with one's age.

"Has your Highness never seen a climbing ape? Give it some large tree, and it will twist and twirl among the branches as though monarch of all it surveys. Yi and Fêng Mêng
An ancient archer and his apprentice.
can never catch a glimpse of it.

"But put it in a bramble bush, and it will move cautiously with sidelong glances, trembling all over with fear. Not that its muscles relax in the face of difficulty, but because it is at a disadvantage as regards position, and is unable to make use of its skill. And how should any one, living under foolish sovereigns and wicked ministers, help being miserable, even though he might wish not to be so?

"It was under such circumstances that Pi Kan was disembowelled."

See ch. iv. The above episode is too much even for Chinese critics, and has been condemned accordingly.

When Confucius was hemmed in between Ch'ên and Ts'ai and had gone seven days without food, then, holding in his left hand a piece of dry wood and in his right hand a dry stick, he sang a ballad of Piao Shih.

An ancient ruler.

He had an instrument, but the gamut was wanting. There was sound, but no tune. The sound of the wood accompanied by the voice of the man yielded a harsh result, but it was in keeping with the feelings of his audience.

Yen Hui, who was standing by in a respectful attitude, thereupon began to turn his eyes about him; and Confucius, fearing lest he should be driven by exaltation into bragging, or by a desire for safety into sorrow,

As a result of hearing the song.
spoke to him as follows:—

"Hui! it is easy to escape injury from God; it is difficult to avoid the benefits of man. There is no beginning and there is no end. Man and God are ONE. Who then was singing just now?"

"Pray, Sir, what do you mean," asked Yen Hui, "by saying that it is easy to escape injury from God?"

"Hunger, thirst, cold, and heat," replied Confucius, "are but as fetters in the path of life. They belong to the natural laws which govern the universe; and in obedience thereto I pass on my allotted course. The subject dares not disregard the mandates of his prince. And if this is man's duty to man, how much more shall it be his duty to God?"

"What is the meaning of difficult to avoid the benefits of man?" asked Yen Hui.

"If one begins," replied Confucius, "by adaptation to surroundings, rank and power follow without cease. Such advantages are external; they are not derived from oneself. And my life is more or less dependent upon the external. The superior man does not steal these; nor does the good man pilfer them. What then do I but take them as they come?

"Therefore it has been said that no bird is so wise as the swallow. If it sees a place unfit to dwell in, it will not bestow a glance thereon; and even though it should drop food there, it will leave the food and fly away. Now swallows fear man. Yet they dwell among men. Because there they find their natural abode."

In the same way, man should adapt himself to the conditions which surround him.

"And what is the meaning," enquired Yen Hui, "of no beginning and no end?"

"The work goes on," replied Confucius, "and no man knoweth the cause. How then shall he know the end, or the beginning? There is nothing left to us but to wait."

"And that man and God are One," said Yen Hui. "What does that mean?"

"That man is," replied Confucius, "is from God. That God is, is also from God. That man is not God, is his nature.

Sc. that which makes him man.
The Sage quietly waits for death as the end."
Which shall unite him once again with God.

When Chuang Tzŭ was wandering in the park at Tiao-ling, he saw a strange bird which came from the south. Its wings were seven feet across. Its eyes were an inch in circumference. And it flew close past Chuang Tzŭ's head to alight in a chestnut grove.

"What manner of bird is this?" cried Chuang Tzŭ. "With strong wings it does not fly away. With large eyes it does not see."

Or it would not have flown so near.

So he picked up his skirts and strode towards it with his cross-bow, anxious to get a shot. Just then he saw a cicada enjoying itself in the shade, forgetful of all else. And he saw a mantis spring and seize it, forgetting in the act its own body, which the strange bird immediately pounced upon and made its prey. And this it was which had caused the bird to forget its own nature.

And approach so close to man.

This episode has been widely popularised in Chinese every-day life. Its details have been expressed pictorially in a roughly-executed woodcut, with the addition of a tiger about to spring upon the man, and a well into which both will eventually tumble. A legend at the side reads,—"All is Destiny!"

"Alas!" cried Chuang Tzŭ with a sigh, "how creatures injure one another. Loss follows the pursuit of gain."

Those who would prey on others are preyed upon in turn themselves.

So he laid aside his bow and went home, driven away by the park-keeper who wanted to know what business he had there.

For three months after this, Chuang Tzŭ did not leave the house; and at length Lin Chü

A disciple.

asked him, saying, "Master, how is it that you have not been out for so long?"

"While keeping my physical frame," replied Chuang Tzŭ, "I lost sight of my real self. Gazing at muddy water, I lost sight of the clear abyss. Besides, I have learnt from the Master as follows:—"When you go into the world, follow its customs.""

This saying is attributed, in uncanonical works, to Confucius. But if any one was "Master" to Chuang Tzŭ, it would of course be Lao Tzŭ.

Now when I strolled into the park at Tiao-ling, I forgot my real self. That strange bird which flew close past me to the chestnut grove, forgot its nature. The keeper of the chestnut grove took me for a thief. Consequently I have not been out."

When Yang Tzŭ

Yang Chu. See ch. viii.

went to the Sung State, he passed a night at an inn.

The innkeeper had two concubines, one beautiful, the other ugly. The latter he loved; the former, he hated.

Yang Tzŭ asked how this was; whereupon one of the inn servants said, "The beautiful one is so conscious of her beauty that one does not think her beautiful. The ugly one is so conscious of her ugliness that one does not think her ugly."

"Note this, my disciples!" cried Yang Tzŭ. "Be virtuous, but without being consciously so; and wherever you go, you will be beloved."

CHAPTER XXI

T'ien Tzŭ Fang

Argument:—Tao cannot be imparted in words—It is not at man's disposal—It does not consist in formal morality—It is an inalienable element of existence—Without it the soul dies—With it man is happy and his immortality secure—Illustrations.

[This chapter is supplementary to chapter vi.]
T'ien Tzŭ Fang was in attendance upon Prince Wên of Wei.
Whose tutor he was.
He kept on praising Ch'i Kung, until at length Prince Wên said, "Is Ch'i Kung your tutor?"
"No," replied Tzŭ Fang; "he is merely a neighbour. He discourses admirably upon Tao. That is why I praise him."
"Have you then no tutor?" enquired the Prince.
"I have," replied Tzŭ Fang.
"And who may he be?" said Prince Wên.
"Tung Kuo Shun Tzŭ," answered Tzŭ Fang.
"Then how is it you do not praise him?" asked the Prince.
"He is perfect," replied Tzŭ Fang. "In appearance, a man; in reality, God. Unconditioned himself, he falls in with the conditioned, to his own greater glory. Pure himself, he can still tolerate others. If men are without Tao, by a mere look he calls them to a sense of error, and causes their intentions to melt away. How could I praise him?"
Thereupon Tzŭ Fang took his leave, and the Prince remained for the rest of the day absorbed in silence. At length he called an officer in waiting and said, "How far beyond us is the man of perfect virtue! Hitherto I have regarded the discussion of holiness and wisdom, and the practice of charity and duty to one's neighbour, as the utmost point attainable. But now that I have heard of Tzŭ Fang's tutor, my body is relaxed and desires not movement, my mouth is closed and desires not speech. All I have learnt, verily it is mere undergrowth. And the kingdom of Wei is my bane."
Tao is not to be reached by the superficial worker, or by such as value the distinctions of this world.
When Wên Po Hsüeh Tzŭ
"A sage from the south," as the commentators say, anticipating the "Middle Kingdom" below.
was on his way to Ch'i, he broke his journey in Lu. A certain man of Lu begged for an interview, but Wên Po Hsüeh Tzŭ said, "No. I have heard that the gentlemen of the Middle Kingdom are experts in ceremonies and obligations, but wanting in knowledge of the human heart. I do not wish to see him."
So he went on to Ch'i; but once more at Lu, on his way home, the same man again begged to have an interview.

"When I was last here," cried Wên Po Hsüeh Tzŭ, "he asked to see me, and now again he asks to see me. Surely he must have something to communicate."

Whereupon he went and received the stranger, and on returning gave vent to sighs. Next day he received him again, and again after the interview gave vent to sighs. Then his servant asked him, saying, "How is it that whenever you receive this stranger, you always sigh afterwards?"

"I have already told you," replied Wên Po Hsüeh Tzŭ, "that the people of the Middle Kingdom are experts in ceremonies and obligations but wanting in knowledge of the human heart. The man who visited me came in and went out as per compasses and square. His demeanour was now that of the dragon, now that of the tiger. He criticised me as though he had been my son. He admonished me as though he had been my father. Therefore I gave vent to sighs."

When Confucius saw Wên Po Hsüeh Tzŭ, the former did not utter a word. Whereupon Tzŭ Lu said, "Master, you have long wished to see Wên Po Hsüeh Tzŭ. How is it that when you do see him you do not speak?"

"With such men as these," replied Confucius, you have only to look, and Tao abides. There is no room for speech."

See ch. v, ad init., on "the Doctrine which is not expressed in words."

Yen Yüan

See p. 81.

asked Confucius, saying, "Master, when you go at a walk, I go at a walk. When you trot, I trot. When you gallop, I gallop. But when you dash beyond the bounds of mortality, I can only stand staring behind. How is this?"

"Explain yourself," said Confucius.

"I mean," continued Yen Yüan, "that as you speak, I speak. As you argue, I argue. As you preach Tao, so I preach Tao. And by 'when you dash beyond the bounds of mortality I can only stand staring behind,' I mean that without speaking you make people believe you, without striving you make people love you, without factitious attractions you gather people around you. I cannot understand how this is so."

"What is there to prevent you from finding out?" replied Confucius. "There is no sorrow to be compared with the death of the mind. The death of the body is of but secondary importance.

Cf. ch. ii, "The body decomposes, and the mind goes with it. This is our real cause for sorrow."

"The sun rises in the east and sets in the west. There is no place which he does not illuminate; and those who have eyes and feet depend upon him to use them with success. When he comes forth, that is existence; when he disappears, that is non-existence.

"And every human being has that upon which he depends for death or for life.

Mind, which rises with life and sets at death.

But if I, receiving this mind-informed body, pass without due modification to the end,

So that the mind perishes with the body.

day and night subject to ceaseless wear and tear like a mere thing, unknowing what the end will be, and in spite of this mind-informed body
Which should teach a higher lesson.
conscious only that fate cannot save me from the inevitable grave-yard,—then I am consuming life until at death it is as though you and I had but once linked arms to be finally parted for ever! Is not that indeed a cause for sorrow?

The motive of this involved paragraph is identical with that of Mr. Mallock's famous essay Is Life Worth Living?

"Now you fix your attention upon something in me which, while you look, has already passed away. Yet you seek for it as though it must be still there,—like one who seeks for a horse in a market-place.
In the interim the animal has been sold.
What I admire in you is transitory. Nevertheless, why should you grieve? Although my old self is constantly passing away, there remains that which does not pass away."

The mind, which feeds and thrives upon change.

Confucius went to see Lao Tzŭ. The latter had just washed his head, and his hair was hanging down his back to dry. He looked like a lifeless body; so Confucius waited awhile, but at length approached and said, "Do my eyes deceive me, or is this really so? Your frame, Sir, seems like dry wood, as if it had been left without that which informs it with the life of man."

Chuang Tzŭ (?) is here repeating himself.

"I was wandering," replied Lao Tzŭ, "in the unborn."
Reflecting upon the state of man before his birth into the world.
"What does that mean?" asked Confucius.

"My mind is trammelled," replied Lao Tzŭ, "and I cannot know. My mouth is closed and I cannot speak. But I will try to tell you what is probably the truth.

"The perfect Negative principle is majestically passive. The perfect Positive principle is powerfully active. Passivity emanates from heaven above; activity proceeds from earth beneath. The interaction of the two results in that harmony by which all things are produced. There may be a First Cause, but we never see his form. His report fills space. There is darkness and light. Days come and months go. Work is being constantly performed, yet we never witness the performance. Life must bring us from somewhere, and death must carry us back. Beginning and end follow ceaselessly one upon the other, and we cannot say when the series will be exhausted. If this is not the work of a First Cause, what is it?"

"Kindly explain," said Confucius, "what is to be got by wandering as you said."

"The result," answered Lao Tzŭ, "is perfect goodness and perfect happiness. And he who has these is a perfect man."

"And by what means," enquired Confucius, "can this be attained?"

"Animals," said Lao Tzŭ, "that eat grass do not mind a change of pasture. Creatures that live in water do not mind a change of pond. A slight change may be effected so long as the essential is untouched.

"Joy, anger, sorrow, happiness, find no place in that man's breast; for to him all creation is One. And all things being thus united in One, his body and limbs are but as dust of the earth, and life and death, beginning and end, are but as night and day, and cannot destroy his peace. How much less such trifles as gain or loss, misfortune or good fortune?

"He rejects rank as so much mud. For he knows that if a man is of honourable rank, the honour is in himself, and cannot be lost by change of condition, nor exhausted by countless modifications of existence. Who then can grieve his heart? Those who practise Tao understand the secret of this."

"Master," said Confucius, "your virtue equals that of Heaven and Earth; yet you still employ perfect precepts in the cultivation of your heart. Who among the sages of old could have uttered such words?"

"Not so," answered Lao Tzŭ. "The fluidity of water is not the result of any effort on the part of the water, but is its natural property. And the virtue of the perfect man is such that even without cultivation there is nothing which can withdraw from his sway. Heaven is naturally high, the earth is naturally solid, the sun and moon are naturally bright. Do they cultivate these attributes?"

Confucius went forth and said to Yen Hui,

"In point of Tao, I am but as an animalcule in vinegar. Had not the Master opened my eyes, I should not have perceived the vastness of the universe."

He who would concentrate himself upon life after death must first familiarise himself with life before birth.

When Chuang Tzŭ was at an interview with Duke Ai of Lu,

Who had then been dead 120 years.

the latter said, "We have many scholars, Sir, in Lu, but few of your school."

"In Lu," replied Chuang Tzŭ, "there are but few scholars."

"Look at the number who wear scholars' robes," said the Duke. "How can you say they are few?"

"Scholars who wear round hats," answered Chuang Tzŭ, "know the seasons of Heaven. Scholars who wear square shoes know the shape of Earth.

According to ancient Chinese cosmogony, "Heaven is round: Earth is square."

And scholars who loosely gird themselves are ready to decide whatever questions may arise. But scholars who have Tao do not necessarily wear robes; neither does the wearing of robes necessarily mean that a scholar has Tao. If your Highness does not think so, why not issue an order through the Middle Kingdom, making death the punishment for all who wear the robes without having the Tao?"

Thereupon Duke Ai circulated this mandate for five days, the result being that not a single man in Lu dared to don scholars' robes,—with the exception of one old man who, thus arrayed, took his stand at the Duke's gate.

My Ming editor (a priest) says this was Confucius himself!

The Duke summoned him to the presence, and asked him many

questions on politics, trying to entangle him, but in vain. Then Chuang Tzǔ said, "If there is only one scholar in Lu, surely that is not many."

It is unnecessary, says Lin Hsi Chung, to descend to anachronisms in reference to the genuineness of this episode.

Rank and power had no charms for Po Li Ch'i.

7th century BC. This story is alluded to by Mencius.

So he took to feeding cattle. His cattle were always fat, which caused Duke Mu of Ch'in to ignore his low condition and entrust him with the administration.

Shun cared nothing for life or death. He was therefore able to influence men's hearts.

His parents even went so far as to try to kill him.

Prince Yüan of Sung desiring to draw a map, the officials of that department presented themselves, and after making obeisance stood waiting for the order, more than half of them already licking their brushes and mixing their ink.

One of them arrived late. He sauntered in without hurrying himself; and when he had made obeisance, did not wait but went off home.

The Prince sent a man to see what he did. He took off his clothes and squatted down bare-backed.

"He will do," cried the Prince. "He is a true artist."

The commentators do not get much out of this episode. Lin Hsi Chung damns it as a forgery.

When Wên Wang was on a tour of inspection in Tsang, he saw an old man fishing. But his fishing was not real fishing, for he did not fish to catch fish, but to amuse himself.

Wherefore, from the standpoint of Tao, he was the more likely to succeed.

So Wên Wang wished to employ him in the administration of government, but feared lest his own ministers, uncles, and brothers, might object. On the other hand, if he let the old man go, he could not bear to think of the people being deprived of such an influence.

Accordingly, that very morning he informed his ministers, saying, "I once dreamt that a Sage of a black colour and with a large beard, riding upon a parti-coloured horse with red stockings on one side, appeared and instructed me to place the administration in the hands of the old gentleman of Tsang, promising that the people would benefit greatly thereby."

The ministers at once said, "It is a command from your Highness' father."

"I think so," answered Wên Wang. "But let us try by divination."

"It is a command from your Highness' late father," said the ministers, "and may not be disobeyed. What need for divination?"

So the old man of Tsang was received and entrusted with the administration. He altered none of the existing statutes. He issued no unjust regulations. And when, after three years, Wên Wang made another inspection, he found all dangerous organisations broken up, the officials doing their duty as a matter of course, while the use of measures of grain was unknown within the four boundaries of the State. There was thus unanimity in the public voice, singleness of official purpose, and identity of interests to all.

So Wên Wang appointed the old man Grand Tutor; and then, standing with his face to the north,

An attitude of respect. Facing the south was the conventional position of a ruler.

asked him, saying, "Can such government be extended over the empire?"

The old man of Tsang was silent and made no reply. He then abruptly took leave, and by the evening of that same day had disappeared, never to be heard of again.

Yen Yüan said to Confucius, "If Wên Wang was unable to do this of himself, how was he able to do it by a dream?"

"Silence!" cried Confucius: "It is not for you to criticise Wên Wang who succeeded in fulfilling his mission. The dream was merely to satisfy the vulgar mind."

The whole episode is of course spurious.

Lieh Yü K'ou

Or Lieh Tzŭ. See ch. i.

instructed Po Hun Wu Jên

See ch. v.

in archery. Drawing the bow to its full, he placed a cup of water on his elbow and began to let fly. Hardly was one arrow out of sight ere another was on the string, the archer standing all the time like a statue.

"But this is shooting under ordinary conditions," cried Po Hun Wu Jên; "it is not shooting under extraordinary conditions. Now I will ascend a high mountain with you, and stand on the edge of a precipice a thousand feet in height, and see how you can shoot then."

Thereupon Wu Jên went with Lieh Tzŭ up a high mountain, and stood on the edge of a precipice a thousand feet in height, approaching it backwards until one-fifth of his feet overhung the chasm, when he beckoned to Lieh Tzŭ to come on. But the latter had fallen prostrate on the ground, with the sweat pouring down to his heels.

"The perfect man," said Wu Jên, "soars up to the blue sky, or dives down to the yellow springs,

The infernal regions.

or flies to some extreme point of the compass, without change of countenance. But you are terrified, and your eyes are dazed. Your internal economy is defective."

You have not Tao.

Chien Wu

See ch. i.

said to Sun Shu Ao,

A famous minister of the Ch'u State.

"Sir, you have been three times called to office without showing any elation, and you have been three times dismissed without displaying any chagrin. At first, I doubted you; but now I notice that your breathing is perfectly regular. How do you manage thus to control your emotions?"

"I am no better than other people," replied Sun Shu Ao. "I regard office when it comes as something which may not be declined; when it goes, as something which cannot be kept. To me both the getting and losing are outside my own self; and therefore I feel no chagrin. How am I better than other people?

"Besides, I am not conscious of office being either in the hands of others or in my own. If it is in the hands of others, my own personality disappears; if in mine, theirs. And amidst the cares of deliberation and investigation, what leisure has one for troubling about rank?"

When Confucius heard this, he said, "The perfect Sages of old!—cunning men could not defeat them; beautiful women could not seduce them; robbers could not steal from them;

They were unmoved in the face of danger.

Fu Hsi and the Yellow Emperor could not make friends of them. Life and death are great; yet these gave them no pang.

That would cause them to sacrifice truth.

How much less then rank and power!

"The souls of such men pierced through huge mountains as though they had been nothing; descended into the abyss without getting wet; occupied lowly stations without chagrin. They filled the whole universe; and the more they gave to others, the more they had themselves."

These last words occur in chapter lxxxi. of the Tao-Tê-Ching. It is, to say the least, strange to find them here in the mouth of Confucius without a hint as to their alleged Taoistic source.

The explanation is that when this episode was penned, that patchwork treatise which passes under the name of the Tao-Tê-Ching had not been pieced together.

The Prince of Ch'u was sitting with the Prince of Fan. By and by, one of the officials of Ch'u said, "There were three indications of the destruction of the Fan State."

"The destruction of the Fan State," cried the Prince of Fan, "did not suffice to injure my existence.

Which was already, by virtue of Tao, beyond the reach of mundane influences.

And while the destruction of the Fan State did not suffice to injure my existence, the preservation of the Ch'u State will not be enough to preserve yours.

You being without Tao.

From this point of view it will be seen that while we Fans have not begun to be destroyed, you Ch'us have not begun to exist."

A good specimen of the Fallacia Amphiboliæ.

CHAPTER XXII

Knowledge Travels North

Argument:—Inaction and Tao—The universe our model—Spontaneity our watchword—Omnipresence and indivisibility of Tao—External activity, internal passivity—Man's knowledge finite—Illustrations.

[This chapter is supplementary to chapter vi.]

When Knowledge travelled north, across the Black Water, and over the Dark-Steep Mountain, he met Do-nothing Say-nothing and asked of him as follows:—

"Kindly tell me by what thoughts, by what cogitations, may Tao be known? By resting in what, by according in what, may Tao be approached? By following what, by pursuing what, may Tao be attained?"

To these three questions, Do-nothing Say-nothing returned no answer. Not that he would not answer, but that he could not. So when Knowledge got no reply, he turned round and went off to the south of the White Water and up the Ku-chüeh Mountain, where he saw All-in-extremes, and to him he put the same questions.

"Ha!" cried All-in-extremes, "I know. I will tell you...."

But just as he was about to speak he forgot what he wanted to say. So when Knowledge got no reply, he went back to the palace and asked the Yellow Emperor. The latter said, "By no thoughts, by no cogitations, Tao may be known. By resting in nothing, by according in nothing, Tao may be approached. By following nothing, by pursuing nothing, Tao may be attained."

Then Knowledge said to the Yellow Emperor, "Now you and I know this, but those two know it not. Who is right?"

"Of those two," replied the Yellow Emperor, "Do-nothing Say-nothing is genuinely right, and All-in-extremes is near. You and I are wholly wrong. Those who understand it do not speak about it, those who speak about it do not understand it.

These words occur in the Tao-Tê-Ching, ch. vi. See also ante, p.78.

Therefore the Sage teaches a doctrine which does not find expression in words.

See ante, ch. v. Also The Remains of Lao Tzŭ, p. 7.

Tao cannot be made to come. Virtue cannot be reached.

Virtue (Tê), here the exemplification of Tao.

Charity can be evoked. Duty to one's neighbour can be wrongly directed. Ceremonies are mere shams.

"Therefore it has been said, 'If Tao perishes, then Tê will perish. If Tê perishes, then charity will perish. If charity perishes, then duty to one's neighbour will perish. If duty to one's neighbour perishes, then ceremonies will perish. Ceremonies are but a showy ornament of Tao, while oft-times the source of trouble.'

The above is from the Tao-Tê-Ching, ch. xxxviii. It is interesting to note how the Yellow Emperor annihilates time by quoting a work not written until many centuries after his date.

"Therefore it has been said, 'Those who practise Tao suffer daily loss. If that loss proceeds until inaction ensues, then by that very inaction there is nothing which cannot be done.'

Also in the Tao-Tê-Ching, ch. xlviii.

"Now, we are already beings. And if we desire to revert to our original condition, how difficult that is! 'Tis a change to which only the greatest among us are equal.

"Life follows upon death. Death is the beginning of life. Who knows when the end is reached? The life of man results from convergence of the vital fluid. Its convergence is life; its dispersion, death. If then life and death are but consecutive states, what need have I to complain?

"Therefore all things are One. What we love is animation. What we hate is corruption. But corruption in its turn becomes animation, and animation once more becomes corruption.

"Therefore it has been said, The world is permeated by a single vital fluid, and Sages accordingly venerate One."

"Tota formatio procedens ex nomine uno." Liber Jezirah, p. Bi. (Parisiis: G. Postello, 1552.)

Then Knowledge said to the Yellow Emperor, "I asked Do-nothing Say-nothing, but he did not answer me. Not that he, would not; he could not. So I asked All-in-extremes. He was just going to tell me, but he did not tell me. Not that he would not; but just as he was going to do so, he forgot what he wanted to say. Now I ask you, and you tell me. How then are you wholly wrong?"

"Of those two," replied the Yellow Emperor, "the former was genuinely right, inasmuch as he did not know. The latter was near, inasmuch as he forgot. You and I are wholly wrong, inasmuch as we know."

Tao is attained, not by knowledge, but by absence of knowledge.

When All-in-extremes heard of this, he considered that the Yellow Emperor had spoken well.

"Spoken knowingly" gives the only chance of bringing out what is here a forced play upon words.

The universe is very beautiful, yet it says nothing. The four seasons abide by a fixed law, yet they are not heard. All creation is based upon absolute principles, yet nothing speaks.

And the true Sage, taking his stand upon the beauty of the universe, pierces the principles of created things. Hence the saying that the perfect man does nothing, the true Sage performs nothing, beyond gazing at the universe.

In the hope of attaining, by contemplation, a like spontaneity.

For man's intellect, however keen, face to face with the countless evolutions of things, their death and birth, their squareness and roundness,—can never reach the root. There creation is, and there it has ever been.

But the secret of life is withheld.

The six cardinal points, reaching into infinity, are ever included in Tao. An autumn spikelet, in all its minuteness, must carry Tao within itself. There is nothing on earth which does not rise and fall, but it never perishes altogether.

Nihilo nil posse reverti.

The Yin and the Yang, and the four seasons, keep to their proper order. Apparently destroyed, yet really existing; the material gone, the immaterial left;—such is the law of creation, which passeth all understanding. This is called the root, whence a glimpse may be obtained of God.

From this point, upon which the finger of man can never be laid, his mind may perhaps faintly discern the transcendent workings of that Power by which all creation is swayed;—"uncover those secret recesses where Nature is sitting at the fires in the depths of her laboratory." Swedenborg.

Yeh Ch'üeh enquired of P'i I about Tao.

For the former see ch. ii. Of the latter there is no record.

The latter said, "Keep your body under proper control, your gaze concentrated upon One,—and the peace of God will descend upon you. Keep back your knowledge, and concentrate your thoughts upon One,—and the holy spirit shall abide within you. Virtue shall beautify you, Tao shall establish you, aimless as a new-born calf which recks not how it came into the world."

While P'i I was still speaking, Yeh Ch'üeh had gone off to sleep; at which the former rejoiced greatly, and departed singing,

> *"Body like dry bone,*
> *Mind like dead ashes;*
> *This is true knowledge,*
> *Not to strive after knowing the whence.*
> *In darkness, in obscurity,*
> *The mindless cannot plan;—*
> *What manner of man is that?"*

His mortal trammels had fallen off by his absorption into Tao.

Shun asked Ch'êng,

His tutor.

saying, "Can one get Tao so as to have it for one's own?"

"Your very body," replied Ch'êng, "is not your own. How should Tao be?"

"If my body," said Shun, "is not my own, pray whose is it?"

"It is the delegated image of God," replied Ch'êng. "Your life is not your own. It is the delegated harmony of God.

The affinity of the Yin and Yang causes them, when in due proportions, to combine and produce life.

Your individuality is not your own. It is the delegated adaptability of God.

Providing the endless variety of shapes with an endless variety of complexion.

Your posterity is not your own. It is the delegated exuviæ of God.

As God sends us into the world, so He wishes us to "increase and multiply."

You move, but know not how. You are at rest, but know not why. You taste, but know not the cause. These are the operation of God's laws. How then should you get Tao so as to have it for your own?"

Cf. "Know ye not that your body is the temple of the Holy Ghost," etc. I. Corinthians vi. 19.

Confucius said to Lao Tzŭ, "To-day you are at leisure. Pray tell me about perfect Tao."

"Purge your heart by fasting and discipline," answered Lao Tzŭ. "Wash your soul as white as snow. Discard your knowledge. Tao is abstruse and difficult of discussion. I will try, however, to speak to you of its outline.

"Light is born of darkness. Classification is born of formlessness. The soul is born of Tao. The body is born of the vital essence.

Existence springs from non-existence.

"Thus all things produce after their kind. Creatures with nine channels of communication are born from the womb. Creatures with eight are born from the egg.

Nature is always self-similar.

Of their coming there is no trace. In their departure there is no goal. No entrance gate, no dwelling house, they pass this way and that, as though at the meeting of cross-roads.

"Those who enter herein become strong of limb, subtle of thought, and clear of sight and hearing. They suffer no mental fatigue, nor meet with physical resistance.

"Heaven cannot but be high. Earth cannot but be broad. The sun and moon cannot but revolve. All creation cannot but flourish. To do so is their Tao.

"But it is not from extensive study that this may be known, nor by dialectic skill that this may be made clear. The true Sage will have none of these. It is in addition without gain, in diminution without loss, that the true Sage finds salvation.

"Unfathomable as the sea, wondrously ending only to begin again, informing all creation without being exhausted, the Tao of the perfect man is spontaneous in its operation. That all creation can be informed by it without exhaustion, is its Tao.

The Tao of Tao.

"In the Middle Kingdom there are men who recognise neither positive nor negative. They abide between heaven and earth. They act their part as mortals, and then return to the Cause.

"From that standpoint,

Of the Cause, sc. God, which is commensurate with infinity.

life is but a concentration of the vital fluid, whose longest and shortest terms of existence vary by an inappreciable space,—hardly enough for the classification of Yao and Chieh.

As good and bad. See ch. iv.

"Tree-fruits and plant-fruits exhibit order in their varieties; and the relationships of man, though more difficult to be dealt with, may still be reduced to order.

These have been classified as follows:—
1. Sovereign and Subject.
2. Husband " Wife.
3. Father " Son.
4. Elder Brother " Younger Brother.
5. Friend " Friend.

The true Sage who meets with these, does not violate them. Neither does he continue to hold fast by them.

He adapts himself to the exigencies of his environment.

Adaptation by arrangement is Tê. Spontaneous adaptation is Tao, by which sovereigns flourish and princes succeed.

"Man passes through this sublunary life as a white horse passes a crack. Here one moment, gone the next. Neither are there any not equally subject to the ingress and egress of mortality. One modification brings life; then another, and it is death. Living creatures cry out; human beings sorrow. The bow-sheath is slipped off; the clothes-bag is dropped; and in the confusion the soul wings its flight, and the body follows, on the great journey home!

"The reality of the formless, the unreality of that which has form,—this is known to all. Those who are on the road to attainment care not for these things, but the people at large discuss them. Attainment implies non-discussion: discussion implies non-attainment. Manifested, Tao has no objective value; hence silence is better than argument. It cannot be translated into speech; better then say nothing at all. This is called the great attainment."

Tung Kuo Tzŭ asked Chuang Tzŭ, saying, "What you call Tao,—where is it?"

"There is nowhere," replied Chuang Tzŭ, "where it is not."

"Tell me one place at any rate where it is," said Tung Kuo Tzŭ.

"It is in the ant," replied Chuang Tzŭ.

"Why go so low down?" asked Tung Kuo Tzŭ.

"It is in a tare," said Chuang Tzŭ.

"Still lower," objected Tung Kuo Tzŭ.

"It is in a potsherd," said Chuang Tzŭ.

"Worse still!" cried Tung Kuo Tzŭ.

"It is in ordure," said Chuang Tzŭ. And Tung Kuo Tzŭ made no reply.

"Sir," continued Chuang Tzŭ, "your question does not touch the essential. When Huo, inspector of markets, asked the managing director about the fatness of pigs, the test was always made in parts least likely to be fat. Do not therefore insist in any particular direction; for there is nothing which escapes. Such is perfect Tao; and such also is ideal speech. Whole, entire, all, are three words which sound differently but mean the same. Their purport is One.

"Try to reach with me the palace of Nowhere, and there, amidst the identity of all things, carry your discussions into the infinite. Try to practise with me inaction, wherein you may rest motionless, without care, and be happy. For thus my mind becomes an abstraction. It wanders not, and yet is not conscious of being at rest. It goes and comes and is not conscious of stoppages. Backwards and forwards without being conscious of any goal. Up and down the realms of Infinity, wherein even the greatest intellect would fail to find an end.

"That which makes things the things they are, is not limited to such things. The limits of things are their own limits in so far as they are things. The limits of the limitless, the limitlessness of the limited,—these are called fulness and emptiness, renovation and decay. Tao causes fulness and emptiness, but it is not either. It causes renovation and decay, but it is not either. It causes beginning and end, but it is not either. It causes accumulation and dispersion, but it is not either."

O Ho Kan was studying with Shên Nung under Lao Lung Chi.

No record of the first and last. Shên Nung was a legendary emperor who invented agriculture. See p. 89.

Shên Nung used to remain shut up, with his head on the table, absorbed in day-dreams. On one occasion, O Ho Kan knocked at the door, and entering said, "Lao Lung is dead!"

Thereupon Shên Nung, leaning on his staff, arose; and flinging down his staff with a bang, smiled and said, "O my Master, thou knewest me to be worthless and self-sufficient, and thou didst leave me and die. Now I, having no scope for my vain talk, I too will die."

When Yen Kang Tiao
"A man of Tao." Comm.
heard this, he said, "Those who exemplify Tao are sought after by all the best men in the empire. Now if one who has not attained to more Tao than the ten-thousandth part of the tip of an autumn spikelet, is still wise enough to withhold vain talk and die,—how much more those who exemplify Tao? To the eye it is formless, and to the ear it is noiseless. Those who discuss it, speak of it as 'the obscure.' But the mere fact of discussing Tao makes it not Tao."

At this the Empyrean asked Without-end, saying, "Do you know Tao?"

"I do not," replied Without-end; whereupon the Empyrean proceeded to ask Inaction.

"I do know Tao," said Inaction.

"Is there any method," asked the Empyrean, "by which you know Tao?"

"There is," replied Inaction.

"What is it?" asked the Empyrean.

"I know," answered Inaction, "that Tao may honour and dishonour, bind and loose. That is the method by which I know Tao."

The Empyrean repeated these words to No-beginning, and asked him which was right, the ignorance of Without-end or the knowledge of Inaction.

"Not to know," replied No-beginning, "is profound. To know is shallow. Not to know is internal. To know is external."

Here the Empyrean broke in with a sigh, "Then ignorance is knowledge, and knowledge ignorance! But pray whose knowledge is the knowledge of not knowing?"

"Tao," said No-beginning, "cannot be heard. Heard, it is not Tao. It cannot be seen. Seen, it is not Tao. It cannot be spoken. Spoken, it is not Tao. That which imparts form to forms is itself formless; therefore Tao cannot have a name."

Form precedes name.

No-beginning continued, "He who replies to one asking about Tao, does not know Tao. Although one may hear about Tao, he does not really hear about Tao. There is no such thing as asking about Tao. There is no such thing as answering such questions. To ask a question which cannot be asked is vain. To answer a question which cannot be answered is unreal. And one who thus meets the vain with the unreal is one who has no physical perception of the universe, and no mental perception of the origin of existence,—unfit alike to roam over the K'un-lun peak or to soar into the Supreme Void."

Light asked Nothing, saying, "Do you, Sir, exist, or do you not exist?"

But getting no answer to his question, Light set to work to watch for the appearance of Nothing.

Hidden, vacuous,—all day long he looked but could not see it, listened but could not hear it, grasped at but could not seize it.

See The Remains of Lao Tzŭ, p. 31.

"Bravo!" cried Light. "Who can equal this? I can get to be nothing,

Darkness.

but I cannot get as far as the absence of nothing. Assuming that Nothing has an objective existence, how can it reach this next stage?"

The man who forged swords for the Minister of War was eighty years of age. Yet he never made the slightest slip in his work.

The Minister of War said to him, "Is it your skill, Sir, or have you any method?"

Any Tao?—in its earlier sense of way of doing things.

"It is concentration," replied the man. "When twenty years old, I took to forging swords. I cared for nothing else. If a thing was not a sword, I did not notice it. I availed myself of whatever energy I did not use in other directions in order to secure greater efficiency in the direction required. Still more of that which is never without use;—

Tao.

So that there was nothing which did not lend its aid.

Jen Ch'iu asked Confucius, saying, "Can we know about the time before the universe existed?"

"We can," replied Confucius. "Time was of old precisely what it is now."

At this rebuff, Jen Ch'iu withdrew. Next day he again visited Confucius and said, "Yesterday when I asked you that question and you answered me, I was quite clear about it. To-day I am confused. How is this?"

"Your clearness of yesterday," answered Confucius, "was because my answer appealed direct to your natural intelligence. Your confusion of to-day results from the intrusion of something other than the natural intelligence.
You have passed from "simple apprehension" to "judgment."
There is no past, no present, no beginning, no end.
To-day will be the yesterday of to-morrow.
To have posterity before one has posterity,—is that possible?"

Jen Ch'iu made no answer, and Confucius continued, "That will do. Do not reply. If life did not give birth to death, and if death did not put an end to life, surely life and death would be no longer correlates, but would each exist independently. What there was before the universe, was Tao. Tao makes things what they are, but is not itself a thing. Nothing can produce Tao; yet everything has Tao within it, and continues to produce it without end.
In its offspring.
And the endless love of the Sage for his fellow-man is based upon the same principle."

Yen Yüan asked Confucius, saying, "Master, I have heard you declare that there may be no eagerness to conform, no effort to adapt. If so, pray how are we to get along?"
Reach that condition which is only attained by adaptation to environment.
"The men of old," replied Confucius, "practised physical, but not moral, modification.
They adapted themselves to the requirements of matter, while their hearts remained the same.
The men of to-day practise moral, not physical modification.
They allow their hearts to be influenced while resisting the exigencies of the external.
Let your modification extend to the external only. Internally, be constant without modification.
"How shall you modify, and how shall you not modify? How reconcile the divergence?—By not admitting division.
I.e. "by being constant without modification," says Lin Hsi Chung.
"There was the garden of Hsi Wei, the park of the Yellow Emperor, the palace of Shun, the halls of T'ang and Wu.
The allusion appears to be to schools of learning, like the Grove of Academus. See chs. vi, xii.
These were perfect men; but had they been taught by Confucianists and Mihists, they would have hammered one another to pieces over scholastic quibbles. How much more then the men of to-day?
"The perfect Sage, in his relations with the external world, injures nothing. Neither does anything injure him. And only he who is thus exempt can be trusted to conform and to adapt.
"Mountain forests and loamy fields swell my heart with joy. But ere the joy be passed, sorrow is upon me again.

133

Familiarity destroys the charm.

Joy and sorrow come and go, and over them I have no control.

"Alas! the life of man is but as a stoppage at an inn. He knows that which comes within the range of his experience. Otherwise, he knows not. He knows that he can do what he can do, and that he cannot do what he cannot do. But there is always that which he does not know and that which he cannot do; and to struggle that it shall not be so,—is not this a cause for grief?

"The best language is that which is not spoken, the best form of action is that which is without deeds.

Then conformity and adaptation are not required.

Spread out your knowledge and it will be found to be shallow."

It will by no means cover the area of the knowable. "Read this chapter," says one critic, "and the Tripitaka and the Mahâyâna will open out before you as beneath a sharp-edged blade."

CHAPTER XXIII

Kêng Sang Ch'u

Argument:—The operation of Tao is not seen—Spheres of action vary—Tao remains the same—Spontaneity essential—Tao can be divided but remains entire—It is infinite as Time and Space—It is unconditioned—The external and the internal—Illustrations.

Among the disciples of Lao Tzŭ was one named Kêng Sang Ch'u. He alone had attained to the Tao of his Master. He lived up north, on the Wei-lei Mountains. Of his attendants, he dismissed those who were systematically clever or conventionally charitable. The useless remained with him; the incompetent served him. And in three years the district of Wei-lei was greatly benefited.

One of the inhabitants said in conversation, "When Mr. Kêng Sang first came among us, we did not know what to make of him. Now, we could not say enough about him in a day, and even a year would leave something unsaid. Surely he must be a true Sage. Why not pray to him as to the spirits, and honour him as a tutelary god of the land?"

On hearing of this, Kêng Sang Ch'u turned his face to the south

Towards the abode of Lao Tzŭ.

in shame, at which his disciples were astonished. But Kêng Sang said, "What cause have you for astonishment? The influence of spring quickens the life of plants, and autumn brings them to maturity. In the absence of any agent, how is this so? It is the operation of Tao.

"I have heard that the perfect man may be pent up like a corpse in a tomb, yet the people will become unartificial and without care.
So powerful will be his influence.
But now these poor people of Wei-lei wish to exalt me among their wise and good. Surely then I am but a shallow vessel; and therefore I was shamed for the doctrine of Lao Tzǔ."

The disciples said, "Not so. In a sixteen-foot ditch a big fish has not room to turn round; but 'tis the very place for an eel. On a six or seven-foot hillock a large beast finds no shelter, while the uncanny fox gladly makes its lair therein. Besides, ever since the days of Yao and Shun it has always been customary to honour the virtuous, advance the able, give precedence to the good and useful. Why not then among the people of Wei-lei? Let them do it, Sir."

"Come here, my children," said Kêng Sang Ch'u. "A beast big enough to swallow a cart, if it wanders alone from the hills, will not escape the sorrow of the snare. A fish big enough to gulp down a boat, if stranded on the dry shore will become a prey to ants. Therefore it is that birds and beasts love height, and fishes and turtles love depth. And the man who cares for himself hides his body. He loves the occult.
There is a play here upon words.
"As to Yao and Shun, what claim have they to praise? Their fine distinctions simply amounted to knocking a hole in a wall in order to stop it up with brambles;
They had better have left the wall alone.
to combing each individual hair; to counting the grains for a rice pudding! How in the name of goodness did they profit their generation?

"If the virtuous are honoured, emulation will ensue. If knowledge be fostered, the result will be theft.
People will employ their knowledge against each other.
These things are of no use to make people good. The struggle for wealth is so severe. Sons murder their fathers; ministers their princes; men rob in broad daylight, and bore through walls at high noon. I tell you that the root of this great evil is from Yao and Shun, and that its branches will extend into a thousand ages to come. A thousand ages hence, man will be feeding upon man!"

Nan Yung Ch'u
A disciple.
sadly straightened his seat and said, "But what is one of my age to do that he may attain to this?"

"Preserve your form complete," said Kêng Sang, "your vitality secure. Let no anxious thoughts intrude. And then in three years' space you may attain to this."

"I do not know," said Nan Yung, "that there is any difference in the form of eyes; yet blind men cannot see. I do not know that there is any difference in the form of ears; yet deaf men cannot hear. I do not know that there is any difference in the form of hearts;
The seat of the intellect.
yet fools cannot use theirs to any purpose. The forms are alike; yet there is

something which differentiates them. One will succeed, and another will not. Yet you tell me to preserve my form complete, my vitality secure, and let no anxious thoughts intrude. But so far I only hear Tao with my ears."

"Well said!" cried Kêng Sang; and then he added, "Small wasps cannot transform huge caterpillars.

According to Chinese notions, the wasp has no young. It transforms a small caterpillar into the required offspring.

Bantams cannot hatch the eggs of geese. The fowls of Lu can. Not that there is any difference in the hatching power of chickens. One can and another cannot, because one is naturally fitted for working on a large, the other on a small scale. My talents are of the latter order. I cannot transform you. Why not go south and see Lao Tzŭ?"

So Nan Yung took some provisions, and after a seven days' journey arrived at the abode of Lao Tzŭ.

"Have you come from Kêng Sang Ch'u?" said the latter.

"I have," replied Nan Yung.

"But why," said Lao Tzŭ, "bring all these people with you?"

Meaning the questions he was going to ask.

Nan Yung looked back in alarm, and Lao Tzŭ continued, "Do you not understand what I say?"

Nan Yung bent his head abashed, and then looking up, said with a sigh, "I have now forgotten how to answer, in consequence of missing what I came to ask."

He was so confused by Lao Tzŭ's question coming before he had had time to state his mission.

"What do you mean?" said Lao Tzŭ.

"If I do not know," replied Nan Yung, "men call me a fool. If I do know, I injure myself. If I am not charitable, I injure others. If I am, I injure myself. If I do not do my duty to my neighbour, I injure others. If I do it, I injure myself. My trouble lies in not seeing how to escape from these three dilemmas. On the strength of my connection with Kêng Sang, I would venture to ask advice."

"When I saw you," said Lao Tzŭ, "I knew in the twinkling of an eye what was the matter with you. And now what you say confirms my view. You are confused, as a child that has lost its parents. You would fathom the sea with a pole. You are astray. You are struggling to get back to your natural self, but cannot find the way. Alas! alas!"

Nan Yung begged to be allowed to remain, and set to work to cultivate the good and eliminate the evil within him. At the expiration of ten days, with sorrow in his heart, he again sought Lao Tzŭ.

"Have you thoroughly cleansed yourself?" said Lao Tzŭ. "But this grieved look.... There is some evil obstruction yet.

"If the disturbances are external,

Sc. sensual.

do not be always combating them, but close the channels to the mind. If the disturbances are internal, do not strive to oppose them, but close all entrance from without.

And the mind will recover itself.

If the disturbances are both internal and external, then you will not even be able to hold fast to Tao, still less practise it."

"If a rustic is sick," said Nan Yung, "and another rustic goes to see him; and if the sick man can say what is the matter with him,—then he is not seriously ill. Yet my search after Tao is like swallowing drugs which only increase the malady.

Although really not so very far from Tao (sc. health) as evidenced by my being able to describe my complaint, which a man sick of some serious disease is scarcely able to do.

I beg therefore merely to ask the art of preserving life."

"The art of preserving life," replied Lao Tzŭ, "consists in being able to keep all in One,

Sc. Body and soul. See the Tao-Tê-Ching, ch. x, where this idea has been reproduced.

to lose nothing, to estimate good and evil without divination,

To know that each is bound up in the other.

to know when to stop, and how much is enough, to leave others alone and attend to oneself, to be without cares and without knowledge,—to be in fact as a child. A child will cry all day and not become hoarse, because of the perfection of its constitutional harmony.

Also reproduced in the Tao-Tê-Ching, ch. lv.

It will keep its fist tightly closed all day and not open it, because of the concentration of its virtue. It will gaze all day without taking off its eyes, because its sight is not attracted by externals. In motion, it knows not whither it is bound; at rest, it is not conscious of doing anything; but unconsciously adapts itself to the exigencies of its environment. This is the art of preserving life."

"Is this then the virtue of the perfect man?" cried Nan Yung.

"Not so," said Lao Tzŭ. "I am, as it were, but breaking the ice.

"The perfect man shares the food of this earth, but the happiness of God. He does not incur trouble either from men or things. He does not join in censuring, in plotting, in toadying. Free from care he comes, and unconscious he goes;—this is the art of preserving life."

"This then is perfection?" inquired Nan Yung.

"Not yet," said Lao Tzŭ. "I specially asked if you could be as a child. A child acts without knowing what it does; moves without knowing whither. Its body is like a dry branch; its heart like dead ashes. Thus, good and evil fortune find no lodgment therein; and there where good and evil fortune are not, how can the troubles of mortality be?

"Those whose hearts are in a state of repose give forth a divine radiance, by the light of which they see themselves as they are. And only by cultivating such repose can man attain to the constant.

"Those who are constant are sought after by men and assisted by God. Those who are sought after by men are the people of God; those who are assisted by God are his chosen children.

The stuff of which rulers are made.

"To study this is to study what cannot be learnt. To practise this is to practise what cannot be accomplished. To discuss this is to discuss what can never be proved. Let knowledge stop at the unknowable. That is perfection. And for those who do not follow this, God will destroy them!

"Knowledge," says Emerson in his Montaigne, or the Sceptic, "is the knowing that we cannot know."

"With such defences for the body, ever prepared for the unexpected, deferential to the rights of others,—if then calamities overtake you, these are from God, not from man. Let them not disturb what you have already achieved. Let them not penetrate into the soul's abode. For there resides the Will. And if the will knows not what to will, it will not be able to will.

Inability to exercise the functions of will is Tao.

"Whatsoever is not said in all sincerity, is wrongly said. And not to be able to rid oneself of this vice is only to sink deeper towards perdition.

"Those who do evil in the open light of day,—men will punish them. Those who do evil in secret,—God will punish them. Who fears both man and God, he is fit to walk alone.

The term here used for "God" means strictly those "spirits" which are the avenging emissaries of the Deity.

Those who are devoted to the internal,

To self-culture.

in practice acquire no reputation. Those who are devoted to the external, strive for pre-eminence among their fellows. Practice without reputation throws a halo around the meanest. But he who strives for pre-eminence among his fellows, he is as a huckster whose weariness all perceive though he himself puts on an air of gaiety.

"He who is naturally in sympathy with man, to him all men come. But he who forcedly adapts, has no room even for himself, still less for others. And he who has no room for others, has no ties. It is all over with him.

"There is no weapon so deadly as man's will. Excalibur is second to it. There is no bandit so powerful as Nature.

The interaction of the Positive and Negative principles, which produces the visible universe.

In the whole universe there is no escape from it. Yet it is not Nature which does the injury. It is man's own heart.

"Tao informs its own subdivisions, their successes and their failures. What is feared in subdivision is separation.

From the parent stock of Tao.

What is feared in separation, is further separation.

So that all connection is severed.

Thus, to issue forth without return, this is development of the supernatural. To issue forth and attain the goal, this is called death. To be annihilated and yet to exist, this is convergence of the supernatural into One. To make things which have form appear to all intents and purposes formless,—this is the sum of all things.

Man's final triumph over matter.

"Birth is not a beginning; death is not an end. There is existence without limitation; there is continuity without a starting-point. Existence without limitation is Space. Continuity without a starting-point is Time.

There is birth, there is death, there is issuing forth, there is entering in. That through which one passes in and out without seeing its form, that is the Portal of God.

"The Portal of God is Non-Existence. All things sprang from Non-Existence. Existence could not make existence existence. It must have proceeded from Non-Existence,

The idea of existence, independent of its correlate, cannot be apprehended by the human intellect.

And Non-Existence and Nothing are One.

If all things sprang from non-existence, it might be urged that non-existence had an objective existence. But non-existence is nothing, and nothing excludes the idea of something, making subjective and objective nothings One.

Herein is the abiding-place of the Sage.

There where the matter of mortality shares the tenuity of the formless.

"The knowledge of the ancients reached the highest point,—the time before anything existed. This is the highest point. It is exhaustive. There is no adding to it.

"The second best was that of those who started from existence. Life was to them a misfortune. Death was a return home. There was already separation.

"The next in the scale said that at the beginning there was nothing. Then life came, to be quickly followed by death. They made Nothing the head, Life the trunk, and Death the tail of existence, claiming as friends whoever knew that existence and non-existence, and life and death were all One.

"These three classes, though different, were of the same clan; as were Chao Ching who inherited fame, and Chia who inherited territory.

The fact of inheritance was the same, but not the thing inherited,—by these men of Ch'u.

There are various interpretations of this passage. No two commentators agree.

"Man's life is as the soot on a kettle.

Meaning, concentrated smoke.

Yet men speak of the subjective point of view. But this subjective point of view will not bear the test. It is a point of knowledge we cannot reach.

Individual standards are fallacious. What is subjective from one point of view is objective from another.

"At the winter sacrifice, the tripe may be separated from the great toe; yet these cannot be separated.

Each carries away the characteristics of the whole.

He who looks at a house, visits the ancestral hall, and even the latrines. Thus every point is the subjective point of view.

Or else he has not seen the house but only a part. Where then is the subjective point of view of the house, and by analogy, of the man?

"Let us try to formulate this subjective point of view. It originates with life, and, with knowledge as its tutor, drifts into the admission of right and wrong.

In the abstract.

But one's own standard of right is the standard, and others have to adapt themselves to it. Men will die for this. Such people look upon the useful as appertaining to wisdom, the useless as appertaining to folly; upon success in life as honourable, upon failure as dishonourable.

Not knowing the value of the useless, or perceiving that what is so at one time is not so at another.

The subjective point of view is that of the present generation, who like the cicada and the young dove see things only from their own standpoint.

See ch. i.

"If a man treads upon a stranger's toe in the market-place, he apologises on the score of hurry. If an elder brother does this, he is quit with an exclamation of sympathy. And if a parent does so, nothing whatever is done.

The child being part of himself.

"Therefore it has been said, 'Perfect politeness is not artificial;

Kuo Hsiang says this means treating others as oneself. Lin Hsi Chung takes the "natural" or "spontaneous" view which is here adopted.

perfect duty to one's neighbour is not a matter of calculation; perfect wisdom takes no thought; perfect charity recognises no ties; perfect trust requires no pledges.'

"Discard the stimuli of purpose. Free the mind from disturbances. Get rid of entanglements to virtue. Pierce the obstructions to Tao.

"Honours, wealth, distinction, power, fame, gain,—these six stimulate purpose.

"Mien, carriage, beauty, arguments, influence, opinions,—these six disturb the mind.

Referring, of course, to the mien, carriage, etc. of others.

"Hate, ambition, joy, anger, sorrow, pleasure,—these six are entanglements to virtue.

"Rejecting, adopting, receiving, giving, knowledge, ability,—these six are obstructions to Tao.

The key to which is inaction.

"If these twenty-four be not allowed to run riot, then the mind will be duly ordered. And being duly ordered, it will be in repose. And being in repose, it will be clear of perception. And being clear of perception, it will be unconditioned. And being unconditioned, it will be in that state of inaction by which there is nothing which cannot be accomplished.

"Tao is the sovereign lord of Tê.

Tê is the "virtue" of spontaneity.

Life is the glorifier of Tê.

By means of which it can be manifested.

Nature is the substance of life.

The code of which life is the embodiment.

The operation of that nature is action. The perversion of that action is error.

"People who know put forth physical power. People who know employ mental effort. But what people who know do not know is to be as the eye.

Which sees without looking.

"Emotion which is spontaneous is called virtue passive. Emotion which is not evoked by the external is called virtue active. The names of these are antagonistic; but essentially they are in accord.

All "virtue" should proceed from the real self, sc. from God.

"Yi was skilled in hitting the bull's-eye; but stupid at preventing people from praising him for so doing.

See ch. v.

The Sage devotes himself to the natural and neglects the artificial. For only the Perfect Man can devote himself profitably to the natural and artificial alike. Insects influence insects;

So as to make others like themselves

because insects are natural. When the Perfect Man hates the natural, it is the artificially natural which he hates. How much more man's alternate naturalness and artificiality?

"If a bird falls in with Yi, Yi will get it. Such is his skill. And if the world were made into a cage, birds would have no place of escape. So it was that by cookery T'ang got hold of I Yin, and by five rams' skins Duke Mu of Ch'in got Po Li Ch'i. But had these princes not been themselves successful at getting, they never would have got these men.

Apocryphal stories both. I Yin was the successful and famous minister of the founder of the Shang dynasty. For Poh Li Ch'i, see pp. 122-123.

"A one-legged man discards ornament, his exterior not being open to commendation. Condemned criminals will go up to great heights without fear, for they no longer regard life and death from their former point of view. And those who pay no attention to their moral clothing

Artificial virtues.

and condition become oblivious of their own personality; and by thus becoming oblivious of their personality, they proceed to be the people of God.

"Wherefore, if men revere them, they rejoice not. If men insult them, they are not angered. But only those who have passed into the eternal harmony of God are capable of this.

"If your anger is external, not internal, it will be anger proceeding from not-anger. If your actions are external, not internal, they will be actions proceeding from inaction.

"If you would attain peace, level down your emotional nature. If you desire spirituality, cultivate adaptation of the intelligence. If you would have your actions in accordance with what is right, allow yourself to fall in with the dictates of necessity. For necessity is the Tao of the Sage."

Do nothing save what you cannot help doing.

The authorship of this chapter has been disputed. Lin Hsi Chung regards the question as by no means settled.

CHAPTER XXIV

Hsü Wu Kuei

Argument:—Tao is passionless—Immorality of the moral—Obstructions to natural virtue—The evils of action—Too much zeal—The outward and visible—The inward and spiritual—Illustrations.

Hsü Wu Kuei, introduced by Nü Shang, went to see Wu Hou of Wei.
A hermit, a minister, and a prince, respectively.
The Prince greeted him sympathisingly, and said, "You are suffering, Sir. You must have endured great hardships in your mountain life that you should be willing to leave it and visit me."

"It is I who should sympathise with your Highness, not your Highness with me," answered Hsü Wu Kuei. "If your Highness gives free play to passion and yields to loves and hates, then the natural conditions of your existence will suffer.
Internally.
And if your Highness puts aside passion and abjures loves and hates, then your senses of sight and hearing will suffer.
Externally.
It is I who should sympathise with your Highness, not your Highness with me."

The Prince was too astonished to reply; and after a while Hsü Wu Kuei continued, "I will try to explain to your Highness how I judge of dogs. The lowest in the scale will eat their fill and then stop, like a cat. Those of the middle class are as though staring at the sun. The highest class are as though they had parted with their own individuality.

"But I do not judge of dogs as well as I judge of horses. I judge of horses as follows. Their straightness
In running.
must be that of a line. Their curve must be that of an arc. Their squareness, that of the square. Their roundness, that of the compasses.
One commentator applies all this to the shape of the animals.
These are the horses of the State. They are not equal to the horses of the Empire. The horses of the Empire are splendid. They move as though anxious to get along, as though they had lost the way, as though they had parted with their own individuality. Thus, they outstrip all competitors, over the unstirred dust, out of sight!"

The Prince was greatly pleased and smiled. But when Hsü Wu Kuei went out, Nü Shang asked him, saying, "What can you have been saying to his Highness? Whenever I address him, it is either in a pacific sense, based upon the Canons of Poetry, History, Rites, and Music; or in a belligerent sense, based upon the Golden Roster or the Six Plans of Battle.
Ancient military treatises.
I have transacted with great success innumerable matters entrusted

to me, yet his Highness has never vouchsafed a smile. What can you have been saying to make him so pleased as all this?"

"I merely told him," replied Hsü Wu Kuei, "how I judged of dogs and horses."

"Was that all?" enquired Nü Shang, incredulously.

"Have you not heard," said Hsü Wu Kuei, "of the outlaw of Yüeh? After several days' absence from his State, he was glad to meet any one he had known there. After a month, he was glad to meet any one he had even seen there. And after a year, he was glad to meet any one who was in any way like to his fellow-countrymen. Is not this a case of absence from one's kind increasing the desire to be with them?

"Thus a man who had fled into the wilderness, where bishop-wort chokes the path of the weasel and stoat, now advancing, now stopping,—how he would rejoice if the footfall of a fellow-creature broke upon his ear. And how much more were he to hear the sound of a brother's, of a relative's voice at his side. Long it is, I ween, since his Highness has heard the voice of a pure man at his side!"

Hsü Wu Kuei went to visit the Prince. The latter said, "Living, Sir, up in the hills, and feeding upon berries or satisfying yourself with leeks, you have long neglected me. Are you now growing old? Or do you hanker after flesh-pots and wine? Or is it that mine is such a well-governed State?"

"I am of lowly birth," replied Hsü Wu Kuei. "I could not venture to eat and drink your Highness' meat and wine. I came to sympathise with your Highness."

"What do you mean?" cried the Prince? "What is there to sympathise about?"

"About your Highness' soul and body," replied Hsü Wu Kuei.

"Pray explain," said the Prince.

"Nourishment is nourishment," said Hsü Wu Kuei.

To a peasant as to a prince.

"Being high up does not make one high, nor does being low make one low. Your Highness is the ruler of a large State, and you oppress the whole population thereof in order to satisfy your sensualities. But your soul is not a party to this. The soul loves harmony and hates disorder. For disorder is a disease. Therefore I came to sympathise. How is it that your Highness alone is suffering?"

"I have long desired to see you," answered the Prince. "I wish to love my people, and by cultivation of duty towards one's neighbour to put an end to war. Can this be done?"

"It cannot," replied Hsü Wu Kuei. "Love for the people is the root of all evil to the people. Cultivation of duty towards one's neighbour in order to put an end to war is the origin of all fighting. If your Highness starts from this basis, the result can only be disastrous.

Why try to "do" anything?

"Everything that is made good, turns out bad.

The artificial is impermanent.

And although your Highness should make charity and duty to one's neighbour, I fear they would be spurious articles. For the inward intention would appear in the outward manifestation. The adoption of a fixed standard

I.e. of the personal standard of individuals. See p. 139.

would lead to complications. And revolutions within lead to fighting without. Surely your Highness would not make a bower into a battlefield, nor a shrine of prayer into a scene of warfare!

This, of course, refers to the mind.

"Have nothing within which is obstructive of virtue. Seek not to vanquish others in cunning, in plotting, in war. If I slay a whole nation and annex the territory in order to find nourishment for my passions and for my soul,—irrespective of military skill, wherein does the victory lie?

"What shall it profit a man, if he shall gain the whole world, and lose his own soul?"

"If your Highness will only abstain, that will be enough. Cultivate the sincerity that is within your breast, so as to be responsive to the conditions of your environment, and be not aggressive. The people will thus escape death;

From oppression.

and what need then to put an end to war?"

When the Yellow Emperor went to see Tao upon the Chü-tz'ŭ Mountain, Fang Ming was his charioteer, Ch'ang Yü sat on his right, Chang Jo and Hsi P'êng were his outriders, and K'un Hun and Hua Chi brought up the rear.

Commentators tear this passage to tatters.

On reaching the wilds of Hsiang-ch'êng,

The limit of the known.

these seven Sages lost their way and there was no one of whom to ask the road. By and by, they fell in with a boy who was grazing horses, and asked him, saying, "Do you know the Chü-tz'ŭ Mountain?"

"I do," replied the boy.

"And can you tell us," continued the Sages, "where Tao abides?"

"I can," replied the boy.

"This is a strange lad," cried the Yellow Emperor. "Not only does he know where the Chü-tz'ŭ Mountain is, but also where Tao abides! Come tell me, pray, how would you govern the empire?"

"I should govern the empire," said the boy, "just the same as I look after my horses. What else should I do?

"When I was a little boy and used to live within the points of the compass,

In Vanity Fair.

my eyes got dim of sight. An old man advised me to mount the chariot of the sun

I.e. of Intelligence.

and visit the wilds of Hsiang-ch'êng. My sight is now much better, and I continue to dwell without the points of the compass. I should govern the empire in just the same way. What else should I do?"

"Of course," said the Yellow Emperor, "government is not your trade. Still I should be glad to hear what you would do."

The boy declined to answer, but on being again urged, cried out, "What difference is there between governing the empire and looking after horses? See that no harm comes to the horses, that is all!"

Thereupon the Emperor prostrated himself before the boy; and addressing him as Divine Teacher, took his leave.

Divine Teacher means "inspired by God." The term used is that employed in modern times for the head or Pope of debased Taoism, often wrongly rendered as the "Master of Heaven."

If schemers have nothing to give them anxiety, they are not happy. If dialecticians have not their premises and conclusion, they are not happy. If critics have none on whom to vent their spleen, they are not happy. Such men are the slaves of objective existences.

Those who attract the sympathies of the world, start new dynasties. Those who win the people's hearts, take high official rank. Those who are strong undertake difficulties. Those who are brave encounter dangers. Men of arms delight in war. Men of peace think of nothing but reputation. Men of law strive to improve the administration. Professors of ceremony and music cultivate deportment. Moralists devote themselves to the obligations between man and man.

Take away agriculture from the husbandman, and his classification is gone. Take away trade from the merchant, and his classification is gone. Daily work is the stimulus of the labourer. The skill of the artisan is his pride. If money cannot be made, the avaricious man is sad. If his power meets with a check, the boaster will repine. Ambitious men love change.

Thus, men are always doing something; inaction is to them impossible. They observe in this the same regularity as the seasons, ever without change. They hurry to destruction, dissipating in all directions their vital forces, alas! never to return.

Chuang Tzŭ said, "If archers who aimed at nothing and hit something were accounted good shots, everybody in the world would be another Yi.

See p.140.

Could this be so?"

"It could," replied Hui Tzŭ.

"If there was no general standard of right in the world," continued Chuang Tzŭ, "but each man had his own, then everybody would be a Yao. Could this be so?"

"It could," replied Hui Tzŭ.

"Very well," said Chuang Tzŭ. "Now there are the Confucianists, the Mihists, the schools of Yang

Yang Chu. See ch. viii.

and Ping,

Kung Sun Lung. See ch. xvii.

making with your own five in all. Pray which of these is right?

"Possibly it is a similar case to that of Lu Chü?

Of whom there is no record.

—A disciple said to him, 'Master, I have attained to your Tao. I can do without fire in winter: I can make ice in summer.'

"'You merely avail yourself of latent heat and latent cold,' replied Lu Chü. 'That is not what I call Tao. I will demonstrate to you what my Tao is.'

"Thereupon he tuned two lutes, and placed one in the hall and the other in the adjoining room. And when he struck the Kung note on one, the Kung note on the other sounded; when he struck the chio note on one, the chio note on the other sounded. This because they were both tuned to the same pitch.

"But if he changed the interval of one string, so that it no longer kept its place in the octave, and then struck it, the result was that all the twenty-five strings jangled together. There was sound as before, but the influence of the key-note was gone. Is this your case?"

"The Confucianists, the Mihists, and the followers of Yang and Ping," replied Hui Tzŭ, "are just now engaged in discussing this matter with me. They try to overwhelm me with argument or howl me down with noise. Yet they have not proved me wrong. Why then should you?"

"A man of the Ch'i State," replied Chuang Tzŭ, "sent away his son into the Sung State, to be a door-keeper, with maimed body.

Doorkeepers in ancient times were, for obvious reasons, deprived of their feet.

But a vase, which he valued highly, he kept carefully wrapped up.

Thus Hui Tzŭ sacrifices the greater to the less.

"He who would seek for a stray child, but will not leave his home, is like to lose him.

Thus restricted to his four antagonistic schools is Hui Tzŭ's search for Tao.

"If a man of Ch'u, who was sent away to be a door-keeper, began, in the middle of the night, when no one was about, to fight with the boatman, I should say that before his boat left the shore he would already have got himself into considerable trouble."

A maimed man (Hui Tzŭ) should avoid quarrels. His own share of Tao is insufficient even for himself.

Chuang Tzŭ was once attending a funeral, when he passed by the grave of Hui Tzŭ. Turning to his attendants, he said, "A man of Ying

Capital of the Ch'u state.

who had his nose covered with a hard scab, no thicker than a fly's wing, sent for a stone-mason to chip it off. The stone-mason plied his adze with great dexterity while the patient sat still and let him chip. When the scab was all off, the nose was found to be uninjured, the man of Ying never having moved a muscle.

"When Yüan, prince of Sung, heard of this, he summoned the stone-mason and said, 'Try to do the same for me.'

"'I used to be able to do it Sire,' replied the stone-mason, 'but my material has long since perished.'

"And I too, ever since he perished, have been without my material, having no one with whom I can speak."

A generous compliment to an old adversary.

"There was no one," says Lin Hsi Chung, "in all Chuang Tzŭ's generation who could understand him; neither is there any one now, at this late date, any more than there was then."

Kuan Chung being at the point of death, Duke Huan went to see him.

See p.103.

"You are ill, venerable Sir," said the Duke, "really ill. You had better say to whom, in the event of your getting worse, I am to entrust the administration of the State."

"Whom does your Highness wish to choose?" enquired Kuan Chung.

"Will Pao Yü do?" asked the Duke.

Kuan Chung and Pao Yü are the "Damon and Pythias" of China.

"He will not," said Kuan Chung. "He is pure, incorruptible, and good. With those who are not like himself, he will not associate. And if he has once heard of a man's wrong-doing, he never forgets it. If you employ him in the administration of the empire, he will get to loggerheads with his prince and to sixes and sevens with the people. It would not be long before he and your Highness fell out."

"Whom then can we have?" asked the Duke.

"There is no alternative," replied Kuan Chung; "it must be Hsi P'êng. He is a man who forgets the authority of those above him, and makes those below him forget his. Ashamed that he is not the peer of the Yellow Emperor,

In virtue.

he grieves over those who are not the peers of himself.

"To share one's virtue with others is called true wisdom. To share one's wealth with others is reckoned meritorious. To exhibit superior merit is not the way to win men's hearts. To exhibit inferior merit is the way. There are things in the State he does not hear; there are things in the family he does not see.

Purposely ignoring petty faults.

There is no alternative; it must be Hsi P'êng."

Of whom commentators give no further notice.

The prince of Wu took a boat and went to the Monkey Mountain, which he ascended. When the monkeys saw him, they fled in terror and hid themselves in the thicket. One of them, however, disported himself carelessly, as though showing off its skill before the prince. The prince took a shot at it; but the monkey, with great rapidity, seized the flying arrow with its hand. Then the prince bade his guards try, the result being that the monkey was killed.

The skill of the poor monkey availed nothing against the cloud of arrows discharged by the guards. On peut être plus fin qu'un autre, mais on ne peut pas être plus fin que tous les autres.

Thereupon the prince turned to his friend Yen Pu I, and said, "That monkey flaunted its skill and its dexterity in my face. Therefore it has come to this pass. Beware! Do not flaunt your superiority in the faces of others."

Yen Pu I went home, and put himself under the tuition of Tung Wu,

A professor of Tao.

with a view to get rid of such superiority. He put aside all that gave him pleasure and avoided gaining reputation. And in three years his praise was in everybody's mouth.

Tzŭ Chi of Nan-poh

See ch. iv.
was sitting leaning on a table. He looked up to heaven and sighed, at which juncture Yen Ch'êng Tzŭ entered and said, "How, Sir, can such an important person as yourself be in body like dry wood, in mind like dead ashes?"
Instead of exerting yourself for the benefit of mankind. The speaker, says one commentator, was "a disciple."
"I used to live in a cave on the hills," replied Tzŭ Chi. "At that time, T'ien Ho,
The famous founder of the later House of Ch'i.
because he once saw me, was thrice congratulated by the people of Ch'i. Now I must have given some indication by which he recognised me.
As a Sage.
I must have sold for him to buy. For had I not manifested myself, how would he have recognised me? Had I not sold, how could he have bought?
"Alas! I grieve over man's self-destruction.
As reputation comes, reality goes.
And then I grieve over one who grieves for another. And then I grieve over him who grieves over one who grieves for another! And so I get daily farther and farther away."
And become like dry wood, my soul absorbed into Tao.
When Confucius went to Ch'u, the prince entertained him at a banquet. Sun Shu Ao stood up with a goblet of wine in his hand, and I Liao of Shih-nan poured a libation, saying, "On such occasions as this, the men of old were wont to make some utterance."
"Mine," replied Confucius, "is the doctrine of wordless utterances. Shall I who make no utterances, make utterance now?
"I Liao of Shih-nan played with his ball, and the trouble of two houses was arranged.
A man of great strength who refused to aid in settling a State quarrel. He was a great ball player,—whatever that may have been.
Sun Shu Ao remained quietly in repose, and the men of Ying threw down their arms.
No one dared attack them, so powerful was the prestige of their minister.
I should want a three-foot tongue indeed!
To achieve more by talk than these two achieved by inaction.
"Theirs was the Tao of inaction. His was the argument of silence. Wherefore, for Tê
The manifestation of Tao.
to rest in undivided Tao,
By which all things are One.
and for speech to stop at the unknowable,—this is perfection.
"With undivided Tao, Tê cannot be coincident.
The latter is multiform.
No argument can demonstrate the unknowable. Subdivision into Confucianists and Mihists only makes confusion worse confounded.
"The sea does not reject the streams which flow eastward into it.

Therefore it is immeasurably great. The true Sage folds the universe in his bosom. His good influence benefits all throughout the empire, without respect to persons. Born without rank, he dies without titles. He does not take credit for realities.

But attributes it all to circumstances.

He does not establish a name.

For what he has done.

This is to be a great man.

"A dog is not considered a good dog because he is a good barker.

He must also bite.

A man is not considered a good man because he is a good talker. How much less in the case of greatness? And if doing great things is not enough to secure greatness, how much less shall it secure virtue?

"In point of greatness, there is nothing to be compared with the universe. Yet what does the universe seek in order to be great?

"He who understands greatness in this sense, seeks nothing, loses nothing, rejects nothing, never suffers injury from without. He takes refuge in his own inexhaustibility. He finds safety in according with his nature. This is the essence of true greatness."

Tzǔ Chi had eight sons. He ranged them before him, and summoning Chiu Fang Yin, said to him, "Examine my sons physiognomically, and tell me which will be the fortunate one."

"K'un," replied Chiu Fang Yin, "will be the fortunate one."

"In what sense?" asked the father, beaming with delight.

"K'un," said Chiu Fang Yin, "will eat at the table of a prince, and so end his days."

Thereupon Tzǔ Chi burst into tears and said, "What has my son done that this should be his fate?"

"Eating at the table of a prince," replied Chiu Fang Yin, "will benefit the family for three generations. How much more his father and mother! But for you, Sir, to go and weep is enough to turn back the luck from you. The son's fortune is good, but the father's bad."

"Yin," said Tzǔ Chi, "I should like to know what you mean by calling K'un fortunate. Wine and meat gratify the palate, but you do not say how these are to come.

"Supposing that to me, not being a shepherd, a lamb were born in the south-west corner of my hall; or that to me, not being a sportsman, quails were hatched in the north-east corner. If you did not call that uncanny, what would you call it?

"My sons and I do but roam through the universe. With them I seek the joys of heaven; with them I seek the fruits of earth. With them I engage in no business; with them I concoct no plots; with them I attempt nothing out-of-the-way. With them I mount upon the truth of the universe, and do not offer opposition to the exigencies of our environment. With them I accommodate myself naturally; but with them I do not become a slave to circumstances. Yet now the world is rewarding me!

"Every uncanny effect must be preceded by some uncanny cause. Alas! my sons and I have done nothing. It must be the will of God. Therefore I weep."

Shortly afterwards, when K'un was on his way to the Yen State, he was captured by brigands. To sell him as he was, would be no easy matter. To sell him without his feet would be easy enough. So they cut off his feet and sold him into the Ch'i State, where he became door-keeper to Duke Chü and had meat to his dinner for the rest of his life.

Commentators make terrible havoc here.

Yeh Ch'üeh meeting Hsü Yu, said to him, "Where are you going?"

"Away from Yao!" replied the latter.

"What do you mean?" asked Yeh Ch'üeh.

"Yao," said Hsü Yu, "thinks of nothing but charity. I fear he will become a laughing-stock to the world, and that in future ages men will eat one another.

See p.135.

"There is no difficulty in winning the people. Love them and they will draw near. Profit them and they will come up. Praise them and they will vie with one another. But introduce something they dislike, and they will be gone.

"Love and profit are born of charity and duty to one's neighbour. Those who ignore charity and duty to one's neighbour are few; those who make capital out of them are many.

"For the operation of these virtues is not disinterested. It is like lending gear to a sportsman.

With a view to share the game.

Wherefore, for one man to dogmatise for the good of the whole empire, is like splitting a thing at a single blow.

Without reference to method or the requirements of the case in point.

"Yao knows that good men benefit the empire. But he does not know that they injure it. Only those on a higher level than good men know this.

"There are nincompoops; there are parasites; there are enthusiasts.

"A man who learns from a single teacher, and then goes off exultant, satisfied with his acquirements though ignorant that there was a time when nothing existed,—such a one is a nincompoop.

"Parasites are like the lice on a pig's back. They choose bald patches, which are to them palaces and parks. The parts between the toes, the joints, the dugs, and the buttocks, are to them so many comfortable and convenient resting-places. They know not that one day the butcher will tuck up his sleeves and spread straw and apply fire, and that they will perish in the singeing of the pig. As they sow, so do they reap. This is to be a parasite.

"Of enthusiasts, Shun is an example. Mutton does not care for ants; it is the ants which care for the mutton. Mutton has a frowsy smell; and there is a frowsiness about Shun which attracts the people. Therefore it was that after three changes of residence, when he came to the Têng district, he had some hundred thousand families with him.

"Then Yao, hearing of his goodness, appointed him to a barren region, trusting, as he said, that Shun's arrival would enrich it. When Shun took up this appointment, he was already old, and his intellect was failing;

yet he would not cease work and retire from office. He was, in fact, an enthusiast.

"So it is that the spiritual man dislikes a crowd. For where there is a crowd there is diversity, and where there is diversity advantage does not accrue. He is therefore neither very intimate, nor very distant. He clings to virtue and nourishes a spirit of harmony, in order to be in accord with his fellow-men. This is to be a divine man.

"Leave wisdom to ants. Strive for what fishes desire.

To be left alone in the water.

"Leave attractiveness to mutton. Use your eyes to contemplate, your ears to listen to, your mind to consider, their own internal workings. For him who can do these things, his level will be that of a line, his modifications in due and proper season.

"Therefore, the divine man trusts to the natural development of events. He does not strive to introduce the artificial into the domain of the natural. Accordingly, life is a gain and death a loss, or death is a gain and life a loss.

According to circumstances.

"For instance, drugs. They are characteristically poisonous. Such are Chieh-Kêng, Chi-Yung, and Shih-Ling. Circumstances, however, make of each a sovereign remedy. The list is inexhaustible.

Chieh-Kêng is the Platycodon grandiflorum. It is used by Chinese doctors as a tonic, astringent, and vermifuge.

"When Kou Chien encamped with three thousand armed warriors at Kuei-ch'i,

Leading the men of Wu to attack the Yüeh State.

only Chung

Wên Chung, minister of Yüeh.

saw that defeat would be followed by a rally. Yet he could not foresee the evil that was to come upon himself. Wherefore it has been said, 'An owl's eyes are adapted to their use. A crane's leg is of the length required. 'Twould be disastrous to shorten it.'

This illustration has been used in ch. viii, p.47.

"Thus it has been said, 'The wind blows and the river suffers. The sun shines and the river suffers.' But though wind and sun be both brought into relation with the river, it does not really suffer therefrom. Fed from its source, it still continues to flow on.

The Sage too has a source from which the nourishment of his soul is supplied.

"The relation between water and earth is determinate. The relation between a man and his shadow is determinate. The relation between thing and thing is determinate.

"The relation between eye and vision is baneful.

Because indeterminate.

The relation between ear and hearing is baneful. The relation between mind and object is baneful. The relation between all kinds of capacity and man's inner self is baneful. If such banefulness be not corrected, disasters will spring up on all sides. Retrogression is hard to achieve, and success long in coming. Yet alas! men regard such capacities as valuable possessions.

"The destruction of States and the ceaseless slaughter of human beings result from an inability to examine into this.

"The foot treads the ground in walking; nevertheless it is the ground not trodden on which makes up the good walk. A man's knowledge is limited; but it is upon what he does not know that he depends to extend his knowledge to the apprehension of God.

"Knowledge of the great One, of the great Negative, of the great Nomenclature, of the great Uniformity, of the great Space, of the great Truth, of the great Law,—this is perfection.

"The great One is omnipresent. The great Negative is omnipotent. The great Nomenclature is all-inclusive. The great Uniformity is all-assimilative. The great Space is all-receptive. The great Truth is all-exacting. The great Law is all-binding.

"The ultimate end is God. He is manifested in the laws of nature. He is the hidden spring. At the beginning, he was.

Had an objective existence.

This, however, is inexplicable. It is unknowable. But from the unknowable we reach the known.

"Investigation must not be limited, nor must it be unlimited.

It must be undertaken from the standpoint of the unconditioned.

In this vague undefinedness there is an actuality. Time does not change it. It cannot suffer diminution. May we not then call it our great Guide?

"Why not bring our doubting hearts to investigation thereof? And then, using certainty to dispel doubt, revert to a state without doubt, in which doubt is doubly dead?"

Doubt dispelled leaves conviction firmer still.

Lin Hsi Chung says that this essay begins with the subtle to end in the abstruse. "The force of language," adds he, "can no farther go!"

CHAPTER XXV

Tsê Yang

Argument:—Influence of virtue concealed—The true Sage a negative quantity—The great, the small, the infinite—Crime and Capital—Rulers and their vices—What is Society? Predestination or Chance? Illustrations.

When Tsê Yang visited the Ch'u State, I Chieh

An official of Ch'u.

spoke of him to the prince; but the latter refused an audience.

Upon I Chieh's return, Tsê Yang went to see Wang Kuo,

A local Sage.

and asked him to obtain an interview with the prince.

"I am not so fitted for that," replied Wang Kuo, "as Kung Yüeh Hsiu."

A hermit.

"What sort of a man is he?" enquired Tsê Yang.

"In winter," said Wang Kuo, "he catches turtles on the river. In summer, he reposes in some mountain copse. If any passers-by ask of him, he tells them, "This is my home." Where I Chieh could not succeed, still less should I. I am not equal even to him.

"He is a man without virtue, but possessed of knowledge. Were it not for an air of arrogance, he would be very popular with his superiors. But help without virtue is a hindrance. Shivering people borrowing clothes in the coming spring! Hot people thinking of last winter's icy blast!

"The prince of Ch'u is dignified and severe. In punishing, he is merciless as a tiger. Only a very practised or a very perfect man could influence him.

"The true Sage, when in obscurity, causes those around him to forget their poverty. When in power, he causes princes to forget ranks and emoluments, and to become as though of low estate. He rejoices exceedingly in all creation. He exults to see Tao diffused among his fellow-men, while suffering no loss himself.

Tao is a constant quantity. It can be shared, but cannot be divided.

"Thus, although silent, he can instil peace; and by his mere presence cause men to be to each other as father and son. From his very return to passivity comes this active influence for good. So widely does he differ in heart from ordinary men. Wherefore I said, 'Wait for Kung Yüeh Hsiu.'

"The true Sage is free from all embarrassments. All things are to him as One. Yet he knows not that this is so. It is simply nature. In the midst of action he remains the same. He makes God his guide, and men make him theirs. He grieves that wisdom carries one but a short distance, and at times comes altogether to a deadlock.

"To a beauty, mankind is the mirror in which she sees herself. If no one tells her she is beautiful, she does not know that she is so. But whether she knows it or whether she does not know it, whether she hears it or whether she does not hear it, her joy will never cease, neither will mankind ever cease to take pleasure therein. It is nature.

"The love of a Sage for his fellows likewise finds expression among mankind. Were he not told so, he would not know that he loved his fellows. But whether he knows it or whether he does not know it, whether he hears it or whether he does not hear it, his love for his fellows is without end, and mankind cease not to repose therein.

"The old country, the old home, gladden a wanderer's eyes. Nay, though nine-tenths of it be a howling wilderness, still his eye will be glad.

How much more to see sight and hear hearing, from a lofty dais suspended in their very midst!"

The joy of the wanderer is as that of the mind returning to a consciousness only of itself.

Jen Hsiang Shih reached the centre and attained.

The centre at which all Infinities converge. See p.8. This individual was a legendary ruler of old.

He recognised no beginning, no end, no quantity, no time. Daily modified together with his environment, as part of One he knew no modification. Why not rest in this?

To strive to follow God and not to succeed is to display an activity fatal to itself. How can success ever be thus achieved?

The true Sage ignores God. He ignores man. He ignores a beginning. He ignores matter. He moves in harmony with his generation and suffers not. He takes things as they come and is not overwhelmed. How are we to become like him?

T'ang appointed his Equerry, Mên Yin Têng Hêng, to be his tutor, listening to his counsels but not being restricted by them. He got Tao for himself and a reputation for his tutor. But the reputation was a violation of principle, and landed him in the domain of alternatives.

Instead of One. No ingenuity of commentator has here succeeded in making sense.

As a tutor, Confucius pushed care and anxiety to an extreme limit.

Yung Ch'êng Shih

Lao Tzŭ's tutor.

said, "Take away days, and there would be no years. No inside, no outside."

Prince Hui of Wei had made a treaty with prince Wei of Ch'i, which the latter broke.

Thereupon prince Hui was wroth, and was about to send a man to assassinate him. But the Captain-General heard of this, and cried out in shame, "Sire, you are ruler over a mighty State, yet you would seek the vengeance of a common man. Give me two hundred thousand warriors, and I will do the work for you. I will take his people prisoners, and carry off their oxen and horses. I will make the heat of the prince's mind break out on his back. Then I will seize his country, and he will flee. Then you can wring his neck as you please."

When Chi Tzŭ heard this, he cried out in shame and said, "If you are building a ten-perch wall, and when the wall is near completion, destroy it, you inflict great hardship on the workmen.

Alluding to the corvée system of public works. The speaker was an official of Wei.

Now for seven years the troops have not been called out. That is, as it were, your Highness' foundation work. Listen not to the Captain-General. He is a mischievous fellow."

When Hua Tzŭ

Also an official of Wei.

heard this, he was very indignant and said, "He who argued in favour of punishing the Ch'i State was a mischievous fellow. And he who argued against punishing the Ch'i State was a mischievous fellow. And he who says that either of the above is a mischievous fellow, is a mischievous fellow himself."

"Where then shall I find what to do?" enquired the prince.

"In Tao alone," said Hua Tzŭ.

When Hui Tzŭ heard this, he introduced Tai Chin Jen to the prince.

A Sage of the Liang State. For Hui Tzŭ, see p. 8.

"There is a creature called a snail," said Tai Chin Jen. "Does your Highness know what I mean?"

"I do," replied the prince.

"There is a kingdom on its left horn," continued Tai Chin Jen, "ruled over by Aggression, and another on its right horn, ruled over by Violence. These two rulers are constantly fighting for territory. In such cases, corpses lie about by thousands, and one party will pursue the other for fifteen days before returning."

"Whew!" cried the prince. "Surely you are joking."

"Sire," replied Tai Chin Jen, "I beg you to regard it as fact. Does your Highness recognise any limit to space?"

"None," said the prince, "It is boundless."

"When, therefore," continued Tai Chin Jen, "the mind descends from the contemplation of boundless space to the contemplation of a kingdom with fixed boundaries, that kingdom must seem to be of dimensions infinitesimally small?"

"Of course," replied the prince.

"Well then," said Tai Chin Jen, "in a kingdom with fixed boundaries
Meaning the then empire of the Chous.
there is the Wei State. In the Wei State there is the city of Liang. In the city of Liang there is a prince. In what does that prince differ from Violence?"

In his pettiness.

"There is no difference," said the prince.

Thereupon Tai Chin Jen took his leave, and the prince remained in a state of mental perturbation, as though he had lost something.

When Tai Chin Jen had gone, Hui Tzŭ presented himself, and the prince said, "Our friend is truly a great man. Sages are not his equal."

"If you blow through a tube," replied Hui Tzŭ, "the result will be a note. If you blow through the hole in a sword-hilt, the result will be simply whssh. Yao and Shun have been belauded by mankind; yet compared with Tai Chin Jen they are but whssh."

When Confucius went to Ch'u, he stopped at a restaurant on Mount I. The servant to a man and his wife who lived next door, got up on top of the house.

"Whatever is he doing up there?" asked Tzŭ Lu.

"He is a Sage," replied Confucius, "under the garb of a menial. He buries himself among the people.

So as to get into closer relation with them.

He effaces himself at the wayside. Fame, he has none; but his perseverance is inexhaustible. Though his mouth speaks, his heart speaks not. He has turned his back upon mankind, not caring to abide amongst them. He has drowned himself on dry land. I think 'tis I Liao of Shih-nan."

See p.148.

Tzŭ Lu asked to be allowed to go and call him; but Confucius stopped him, saying, "No. He knows that I know what he is. He knows that I have come to Ch'u to recommend him to the prince. And he looks on me as a toady. Under the circumstances, as he would scorn to hear the words of a toady, how much more would he scorn to see him in the flesh! How could you keep him?"

Tzŭ Lu went to see, but the house was empty.

The border-warden of Ch'ang-wu said to Tzŭ Lao,

Ch'in Lao, or Ch'in Chang, a disciple of Confucius.

"A prince in his administrative details must not lack thoroughness; in his executive details he must not be inefficient. Formerly, in my ploughing I lacked thoroughness, and the results also lacked thoroughness. In my weeding I was inefficient, and the results were also inefficient. By and by, I changed my system. I ploughed deep, and weeded carefully, the result being an excellent harvest, more than I could get through in a year."

Chuang Tzŭ, upon hearing this, observed, "The men of to-day in their self-regulation and their self-organisation are mostly as the Border-warden has described. They put their Godhead out of sight. They abandon their natural dispositions. They get rid of all feeling. They part with their souls, carried away by the fashion of the hour.

"Those who lack thoroughness in regard to their natural dispositions suffer an evil tribe to take the place thereof.

The physical senses.

These grow up rank as reeds and rushes, at first of apparent value to the body, but afterwards to destroy the natural disposition. Then they break out, at random, like sores and ulcers carrying off pent-up humours."

Poh Chü was studying under Lao Tzŭ. "Let us go," said he, "and wander over the world."

One commentator says Poh Chü was a "criminal," probably from his sympathetic remarks in the context.

"No," replied Lao Tzŭ, "the world is just as you see it here."

But as he again urged it, Lao Tzŭ said, "Where would you go to begin with?"

"I would begin," answered Poh Chü, "by going to the Ch'i State. There I would view the dead bodies of their malefactors. I would push them to make them rise. I would take off my robes and cover them. I would cry to God and bemoan their lot, as follows:—'O sirs, O sirs, there was trouble upon earth, and you were the first to fall into it!'

"I would say, 'Perhaps you were robbers, or perhaps murderers?' ... Honour and disgrace were set up, and evil followed. Wealth was accumulated, and contentions began. Now the evil which has been set up and the contentions which have accumulated, endlessly weary man's body and give him no rest. What escape is there from this?

This might almost have come from The Curse of Capital, (Aveling) or from one of Mr. Hyndman's discourses.

"The rulers of old set off all success to the credit of their people, attributing all failure to themselves. All that was right went to the credit of their people, all that was wrong they attributed to themselves. Therefore, if any matter fell short of achievement, they turned and blamed themselves.

"Not so the rulers of to-day. They conceal a thing and blame those who cannot see it. They impose dangerous tasks and punish those who dare not undertake them. They inflict heavy burdens and chastise those who cannot bear them. They ordain long marches and slay those who cannot make them.

"And the people, feeling that their powers are inadequate, have recourse to fraud. For when there is so much fraud about,

In the rulers.

how can the people be otherwise than fraudulent? If their strength is insufficient, they will have recourse to fraud. If their knowledge is insufficient, they will have recourse to deceit. If their means are insufficient, they will steal. And for such robbery and theft, who is really responsible?"

When Chü Poh Yü

See p. 22.

reached his sixtieth year, he changed his opinions. What he had previously regarded as right, he now came to regard as wrong. But who shall say whether the right of to-day may not be as wrong as the wrong of the previous fifty-nine years?

See p. 166.

Things are produced around us, but no one knows the whence. They issue forth, but no one sees the portal. Men one and all value that part of knowledge which is known. They do not know how to avail themselves of the unknown in order to reach knowledge. Is not this misguided?

Men value the phenomena of which the senses make them conscious, but not the phenomena of the senses themselves.

Alas! alas! the impossibility of escaping from this state results in what is known as elective affinity.

Adaptation to the suitable; being as one is because more adapted to that than to something to which one is not adapted. See ch. ii, where this idea is first broached.

Confucius asked the historiographers Ta T'ao, Poh Ch'ang Ch'ien, and Hsi Wei, saying, "Duke Ling was fond of wine and given up to pleasure, and neglected the administration of his State. He spent his time in hunting, and did not cultivate the goodwill of the other feudal princes. How was it he came to be called Ling?"

The name Ling means "knowing," which may be taken in two senses.

"For those very reasons," replied Ta T'ao.

"The Duke," said Poh Ch'ang Ch'ien, "had three wives. He was having a bath together with them when Shih Ch'in, summoned by his Highness, entered the apartment. Thereupon the Duke covered himself and the ladies. So outrageously did he behave on the one hand, and yet so respectful was he towards a virtuous man. Hence he was called Ling."

"When the Duke died," said Hsi Wei, "divination showed that it would be inauspicious to bury him in the old family burying-ground, but auspicious to bury him at Sha-ch'iu. And upon digging a grave there, several fathoms deep, a stone coffin was found, which, being cleaned, yielded the following inscription:—Posterity cannot be trusted. Duke Ling will seize this for his tomb.

"As a matter of fact, Duke Ling had been named Ling long before. What should these two persons know about it?"

As evidenced by the inscription, the Duke had been so named long before, in the Book of Fate.

Shao Chih asked T'ai Kung Tiao, saying, "What is meant by society?"

The first name signifies Small Knowledge. Of the second personage there is no record.

"Society," replied T'ai Kung Tiao, "is an agreement of a certain number of families and individuals to abide by certain customs. Discordant elements unite to form a harmonious whole. Take away this unity and each has a separate individuality.

"Point at any one of the many parts of a horse, and that is not a horse, although there is the horse before you. It is the combination of all which makes the horse.

"Similarly, a mountain is high because of its individual particles. A river is large because of its individual drops. And he is a just man who regards all parts from the point of view of the whole.

"Thus, in regard to the views of others, he holds his own opinion, but not obstinately. In regard to his own views, while conscious of their truth, he does not despise the opinions of others.

"The four seasons have different characteristics, but God shows no preference for either, and therefore we have the year complete.

With results which could not be otherwise achieved.

The functions of the various classes of officials differ; but the sovereign shows no partiality, and therefore the empire is governed. There are the civil and the military; but the truly great man shows no preference for either, and therefore their efficacy is complete. All things are under the operation of varying laws; but Tao shows no partiality and therefore it cannot be identified.

As the given part of anything.

Not being able to be identified, it consequently does nothing. And by doing nothing all things can be done.

"Seasons have their beginnings and their ends. Generations change and change. Good and evil fortune alternate, bringing sorrow here, happiness there.

Nunc mihi, nunc alio, benigna.

He who obstinately views things from his own standpoint only, may be right in one case and wrong in another. Just as in a great jungle all kinds of shrubs are found together; or as on a mountain you see trees and stones indiscriminately mixed,—so is what we call society."

"Would it not do then," asked Shao Chih, "if we were to call this Tao?"

"It would not," replied T'ai Kung Tiao. "All creation is made up of more than ten thousand things. We speak of creation as the Ten Thousand

Things merely because it is a convenient term by which to express a large number. In point of outward shape the universe is vast. In point of influence the Positive and Negative principles are mighty. Yet Tao folds them all in its embrace. For convenience' sake the bond of society is called great. But how can that which is thus conditioned

By having a name.

be compared with Tao? There is as wide a difference between them as there is between a horse and a dog."

"Whence then," enquired Shao Chih, "comes the vitality of all things between the four points of the compass, between heaven above and earth beneath?"

"The Positive and Negative principles," answered T'ai Kung Tiao, "influence, act upon, and regulate each other. The four seasons alternate with, give birth to, and destroy one another. Hence, loves and hates, and courses rejected and courses adopted. Hence too, the intercourse of the sexes.

"States of peril and safety alternate. Good and evil fortune give birth to one another. Slowness and speed are mutually exclusive. Collection and dispersion are correlates. The actuality of these may be noted.

There is the name and the embodiment.

The essence of each can be verified. There is regular movement forward, modified by deflection into a curve. Exhaustion leads to renewal. The end introduces a new beginning. This is the law of material existences. The force of language, the reach of knowledge, cannot pass beyond the bounds of such material existences. The disciple of Tao refrains from prying into the states after or before. Human speculation stops short of this."

"Chi Chên," said Shao Chih, "taught Chance; Chieh Tzŭ taught Predestination.

"Two Sages." Comm.

In the speculations of these two schools, on which side did right lie?"

"The cock crows," replied T'ai Kung Tiao, "and the dog barks. So much we know. But the wisest of us could not say why one crows and the other barks, nor guess why they crow or bark at all.

"Let me explain. The infinitely small is inappreciable; the infinitely great is immeasurable. Chance and Predestination must refer to the conditioned. Consequently, both are wrong.

"Predestination involves a real existence.

Of a God.

Chance implies an absolute absence of any principle. To have a name and the embodiment thereof,—this is to have a material existence. To have no name and no embodiment,—of this one can speak and think; but the more one speaks the farther off one gets.

"The unborn creature cannot be kept from life.

So powerful is its "will to live."

The dead cannot be tracked. From birth to death is but a span; yet the secret cannot be known. Chance and Predestination are but à priori solutions.

"When I seek for a beginning, I find only time infinite. When I look forward to an end, I see only time infinite. Infinity of time past and to come implies no beginning and is in accordance with the laws of material existences. Predestination and Chance give us a beginning, but one which is compatible only with the existence of matter.

And not with the time before matter was.

"Tao cannot be existent. If it were existent, it could not be non-existent. The very name of Tao is only adopted for convenience' sake. Predestination and Chance are limited to material existences. How can they bear upon the infinite?

"Were language adequate, it would take but a day to fully set forth Tao. Not being adequate, it takes that time to explain material existences. Tao is something beyond material existences. It cannot be conveyed either by words or by silence. In that state which is neither speech nor silence, its transcendental nature may be apprehended."

"With this essay in China," says Lin Hsi Chung, "what need to fetch Buddhist books from the West?"

CHAPTER XXVI

Contingencies

Argument:—The external uncertain—The internal alone without harm—Life and death are external—The soul only is under man's control—Folly of worldliness—Illustrations.

Contingencies are uncertain. Hence the decapitation of Lung Fêng, the disembowelment of Pi Kan, the enthusiasm of Chi Tzŭ, the death of Wu Lai, the flights of Chieh and Chou.

See pp. 18, 33. Wu Lai was an intriguing official who held office under the tyrant Chou Hsin.

No sovereign but would have loyal ministers; yet loyalty does not necessarily inspire confidence. Hence Wu Yüan found a grave in the river;

See p. 101.

and Ch'ang Hung perished in Shu, his blood, after being preserved three years, turning into green jade.

No parent but would have filial sons; yet filial piety does not necessarily inspire love. Hence Hsiao Chi sorrowed, and Tsêng Shên grieved.

The first, prince of the House of Yin, was turned out of doors by his stepmother. The second, one of the disciples of Confucius and a rare pattern of filial piety, grieved because his mother was too old to hit him hard enough. See p.46.

Wood rubbed with wood produces fire. Metal exposed to fire will liquefy. If the Positive and Negative principles operate inharmoniously, heaven and earth are greatly disturbed. Thunder crashes, and with rain comes lightning, scorching up the tall locust-trees. One fears lest sky and land should collapse and leave no escape. Unable to lie perdu, the heart feels as though suspended between heaven and earth.

So in the struggle between peace and unrest, the friction between good and evil, much fire is evolved which consumes the inner harmony of man. But the mind is unable to resist fire. It is destroyed, and with it Tao comes to an end.

Chuang Tzŭ's family being poor, he went to borrow some corn from the prince of Chien-ho.

"Yes," said the prince. "I am just about collecting the revenue of my fief, and will then lend you three hundred ounces of silver. Will that do?"

At this Chuang Tzŭ flushed with anger and said, "Yesterday, as I was coming along, I heard a voice calling me. I looked round, and in the cart-rut I saw a stickleback.

"'And what do you want, stickleback?' said I.

"'I am a denizen of the eastern ocean,' replied the stickleback. 'Pray, Sir, a pint of water to save my life.'

"'Yes,' said I. 'I am just going south to visit the princes of Wu and Yüeh. I will bring you some from the west river. Will that do?'

"At this the stickleback flushed with anger and said, 'I am out of my element. I have nowhere to go. A pint of water would save me. But to talk to me like this,—you might as well put me in a dried-fish shop at once.'"

The above episode is condemned by Lin Hsi Chung on the score of style.

Jên Kung Tzŭ

A young noble of the Jen State. Comm.

got a huge hook on a big line, which he baited with fifty oxen. He squatted down at Kuei-chi, and cast into the eastern ocean. Every day he fished, but for a whole year he caught nothing. Then came a great fish which swallowed the bait, and dragging the huge hook dived down below. This way and that way it plunged about, erecting the dorsal fin. The white waves rolled mountain high. The great deep was shaken up. The noise was like that of so many devils, terrifying people for many miles around.

But when Jên Kung Tzŭ had secured his fish, he cut it up and salted it. And from Chih-ho eastwards, and from Ts'ang-wu northwards, there was none but ate his fill of that fish. Even among succeeding generations, gobemouches of the day recounted the marvellous tale.

To take a rod and line, and go to a pool, and catch small fry is a very different thing from catching big fish. And by means of a little show of ability to secure some small billet is a very different thing from really pushing one's way to the front. So that those who do not imitate the example of Jên Kung Tzŭ will be very far from becoming leaders in their generation.

Also spurious.

When some Confucianists were opening a grave in accordance with their Canons of Poetry and Rites, the master shouted out, "Day is breaking. How are you getting on with the work?"

"Not got off the burial-clothes yet," answered an apprentice. "There is a pearl in the mouth."

Now the Canon of Poetry says—

> *The greenest corn*
> *Grows over graves.*
> *In life, no charity;*
> *In death, no pearl.*

So seizing the corpse's brow with one hand, and forcing down its chin with the other, these Confucianists proceed to tap its cheeks with a metal hammer, in order to make the jaws open gently and not injure the pearl!

The above, pronounced by Lin Hsi Chung to be spurious, is aimed at the Confucianists, who are ready to commit any outrage on natural feeling so long as there is no violation of the details of their own artificial system.

A disciple of Lao Lai Tzŭ

A sage of the Ch'u State.

while out gathering fuel, chanced to meet Confucius. On his return, he said, "There is a man over there with a long body and short legs, round shoulders and drooping ears. He looks as though he were sorrowing over mankind. I know not who he can be."

"It is Confucius!" cried Lao Lai Tzŭ. "Bid him come hither."

When Confucius arrived, Lao Lai Tzŭ addressed him as follows:—

"Ch'iu! Get rid of your dogmatism and your specious knowledge, and you will be really a superior man."

Confucius bowed and was about to retire, when suddenly his countenance changed and he enquired, "Shall I then be able to enter upon Tao?"

"The wounds of one generation being too much," answered Lao Lai Tzŭ, "you would take to yourself the sorrows of all time. Are you not weary? Is your strength equal to the task?

"To employ goodness as a passport to influence through the gratification of others, is an everlasting shame. Yet this is the common way of all, to lure people by fame, to bind them by ties of gratification.

"Better than extolling Yao and cursing Chieh is oblivion of both, keeping one's praises to oneself. These things react injuriously on self; the agitation of movement results in deflection.

"The true Sage is a passive agent. If he succeeds, he simply feels that he was provided by no effort of his own with the energy necessary to success."

Prince Yüan of Sung dreamed one night that a man with dishevelled hair peeped through a side door and said, "I have come from the waters of Tsai-lu. I am a marine messenger attached to the staff of the River God. A fisherman, named Yü Ch'ieh, has caught me."

When the prince awaked, he referred his dream to the soothsayers, who said, "This is a divine tortoise."

"Is there any fisherman," asked the prince, "whose name is Yü Ch'ieh?"

Being told there was, the prince gave orders for his appearance at court; and the next day Yü Ch'ieh had an audience.

"Fisherman," said the prince, "what have you caught?"

"I have netted a white tortoise," replied the fisherman, "five feet in semi-circumference."

"Bring your tortoise," said the prince. But when it came, the prince could not make up his mind whether to kill it or keep it alive. Thus in doubt, he had recourse to divination, and received the following response:—

Slay the tortoise for purposes of divination and good fortune will result.

So the tortoise was despatched. After which, out of seventy-two omens taken, not a single one proved false.

"A divine tortoise," said Confucius, "can appear to prince Yüan in a dream, yet it cannot escape the net of Yü Ch'ieh. Its wisdom can yield seventy-two faultless omens, yet it cannot escape the misery of being cut to pieces. Truly wisdom has its limits; spirituality, that which it cannot reach.

"In spite of the highest wisdom, there are countless snares to be avoided; If a fish has not to fear nets, there are always pelicans. Get rid of small wisdom, and great wisdom will shine upon you. Put away goodness and you will be naturally good. A child does not learn to speak because taught by professors of the art, but because it lives among people who can themselves speak."

Hui Tzŭ said to Chuang Tzŭ, "Your theme, Sir, is the useless."

"You must understand the useless," replied Chuang Tzŭ, "before you can discuss the useful.

"For instance, the earth is of huge proportions, yet man uses of it only as much as is covered by the sole of his foot. By and by, he turns up his toes and goes beneath it to the Yellow Spring. Has he any further use for it?"

"He has none," replied Hui Tzŭ.

"And in like manner," replied Chuang Tzŭ, "may be demonstrated the use of the useless.

"Could a man transcend the limits of the human," said Chuang Tzŭ, "would he not do so? Unable to do so, how should he succeed?

"The determination to retire, to renounce the world,—such alas! is not the fruit of perfect wisdom or immaculate virtue. From cataclysms ahead, these do not turn back; nor do they heed the approach of devouring flame. Although there are class distinctions of high and low, these are but for a time, and under the changed conditions of a new sphere are unknown.

In the transcendental state.

"Wherefore it has been said, 'The perfect man leaves no trace behind.'

"For instance, to glorify the past and to condemn the present has always been the way of the scholar.

Laudator temporis acti.

Yet if Hsi Wei Shih and individuals of that class

Sc. patriarchs.

were caused to re-appear in the present day, which of them but would accommodate himself to the age?

"Only the perfect man can transcend the limits of the human and yet not withdraw from the world, live in accord with mankind and yet suffer no injury himself. Of the world's teachings he learns nothing. He has that within which makes him independent of others.

"If the eye is unobstructed, the result is sight. If the ear is unobstructed the result is hearing. If the nose is unobstructed, the result is sense of smell. If the mouth is unobstructed, the result is sense of taste. If the mind is unobstructed, the result is wisdom. If wisdom is unobstructed, the result is Tê.

"Tao may not be obstructed. To obstruct is to strangle. This affects the base, and all evils spring into life.

"All sentient beings depend upon breath. If this does not reach them in sufficient quantity, it is not the fault of God. God supplies it day and night without cease, but man stops the passage.

"Man has for himself a spacious domain. His mind may roam to heaven. If there is no room in the house, the wife and her mother-in-law run against one another. If the mind cannot roam to heaven, the faculties will be in a state of antagonism. Those who would benefit mankind from deep forests or lofty mountains are simply unequal to the strain upon their higher natures.

It is for that reason they become hermits.

"Ill-regulated virtue ends in reputation. Ill-regulated reputation ends in notoriety. Scheming leads to confusion. Knowledge begets contentions. Obstinacy produces stupidity. Organised government is for the general good of all.

"Spring rains come in due season, and plants and shrubs burst up from the earth. Weeding and tending do not begin until such plants and shrubs have reached more than half their growth, and without being conscious of the fact.

"Repose gives health to the sick. Rubbing the eyelids removes the wrinkles of old age. Quiet will dispel anxieties. These remedies however are the resource only of those who need them. Others who are free from such ills pay no attention thereto.

"That which the true Sage marvels at in the empire, claims not the attention of the Divine man. That which the truly virtuous man marvels at in his own sphere, claims not the attention of the true Sage. That which the superior man marvels at in his State, claims not the attention of the truly virtuous man. How the mean man adapts himself to his age, claims not the attention of the superior man.

"The keeper of the Yen gate,

Of the capital of the Sung State.

having maltreated himself severely in consequence of the death of his parents, received a high official post.

In reward for his filial piety.

His relatives thereupon maltreated themselves, and some half of them died.

In the vain endeavour to secure like rewards.

"Yao offered the empire to Hsü Yu, but Hsü Yu fled. T'ang offered it to Wu Kuang, but Wu Kuang declined with anger.

See pp. 3, 33.

"When Chi T'o heard of Hsü Yu's flight, he took all his disciples with him and jumped into the river K'uan;

As a tribute to his eminent virtue.

upon which the various feudal princes mourned for three years,

They did not resign their fiefs at his example.

and Shên T'u Ti had the river filled up.

Fearing similar ill-advised acts. For names, see pp.3, 33.

"The raison d'être of a fish-trap is the fish. When the fish is caught, the trap may be ignored. The raison d'être of a rabbit-snare is the rabbit. When the rabbit is caught the snare may be ignored. The raison d'être of language is an idea to be expressed. When the idea is expressed, the language may be ignored. But where shall I find a man to ignore language, with whom I may be able to converse?"

CHAPTER XXVII

Language

Argument:—Speech, natural and artificial—Natural speech in harmony with the divine—Destiny—The ultimate cause—Purification of the soul—Illustrations.

Of language put into other people's mouths, nine tenths will succeed. Of language based upon weighty authority, seven tenths. But language which flows constantly over, as from a full goblet, is in accord with God.

The natural overflowings of the heart.

When language is put into other people's mouths, outside support is sought. Just as a father does not negotiate his son's marriage; for any praise he could bestow would not have the same value as praise by an outsider. Thus, the fault is not mine, but that of others.

Who will not believe the original speaker.

To that which agrees with our own opinions we assent; from that which does not we dissent. We regard that which agrees with our own opinion as right. We regard that which differs from our opinion as wrong. Language based on weighty authority is used to bar further argument. The authorities are our superiors, our elders in years. But if they lack the requisite knowledge and experience, being our superiors only in the sense of age, then they are not our superiors. And if men are not the superiors of their fellows, no one troubles about them. And those about whom no one troubles are merely stale.

Language which flows constantly over, as from a full goblet, is in accord with God.

Embracing both positive and negative in One.

Because it spreads out on all sides, it endures for all time. Without language, contraries are identical. The identity is not identical with its expression: the expression is not identical with its identity. Therefore it has been said, Language not expressed in language is not language. Constantly spoken, it is as though not spoken. Constantly unspoken, it is not as though not spoken.

From the subjective point of view, there are possibilities and impossibilities, there are suitabilities and unsuitabilities. This results from the natural affinity of things for what they are and their natural antagonism to what they are not. For all things have their own particular constitutions and potentialities. Nothing can exist without these.

See p.9.

But for language that constantly flows over, as from a full goblet, and is in accord with God, how should the permanent be attained?

All things spring from germs. Under many diverse forms these things are ever being reproduced. Round and round, like a wheel, no part of which is more the starting-point than any other. This is called the equilibrium of God. And he who holds the scales is God.

Alluding to the Identity-philosophy, which means, in the words of Emerson, "that nature iterates her means perpetually on successive planes.... The whole art of the plant is still to repeat leaf on leaf without end."

Chuang Tzŭ said to Hui Tzŭ, "When Confucius reached his sixtieth year he changed his opinions. What he had previously regarded as right, he ultimately came to regard as wrong. But who shall say whether the right of to-day may not be as wrong as the wrong of the previous fifty-nine years?"

See p.157.

"He was a persevering worker," replied Hui Tzŭ, "and his wisdom increased day by day."

His conversion was no spasmodic act.

"Confucius," replied Chuang Tzŭ, "discarded both perseverance and wisdom, but did not attempt to formulate the doctrine in words. He said, 'Man has received his talents from God, together with a soul to give them life. He should speak in accordance with established laws. His words should be in harmony with fixed order. Personal advantage and duty to one's neighbour lie open before us. Likes and dislikes, rights and wrongs, are but as men choose to call them. But to bring submission into men's hearts, so that they shall not be stiff-necked, and thus fix firmly the foundations of the empire,—to that, alas! I have not attained.'"

"From the above," says Lin Hsi Chung, "we may see that Hui Tzǔ, though skilled in winning debates was unskilled in winning hearts."

Tsêng Tzǔ held office twice. His emotions varied in each case.
See pp.46, 169.
"As long as my parents were alive," said he, "I was happy on a small salary. When I had a large salary, but my parents were no more, I was sad."

A disciple said to Confucius, "Can we call Tsêng Tzǔ a man without cares to trouble him?"
Money being no object to him.
"He had cares to trouble him," replied Confucius. "Can a man who has no cares to trouble him feel grief? His small salary and his large salary were to him like a heron or a mosquito flying past."

Yen Ch'êng Tzǔ Yu said to Tung Kuo Tzǔ Chi,
See p. 147.
"One year after receiving your instructions I became naturally simple. After two years, I could adapt myself as required. After three years, I understood. After four years, my intelligence developed. After five years, it was complete. After six years, the spirit entered into me. After seven, I knew God. After eight, life and death existed for me no more. After nine, perfection.

"Life has its distinctions; but in death we are all made equal. That death should have an origin, but that life should have no origin,—can this be so? What determines its presence in one place, its absence in another?

"Heaven has its fixed order.
Visible to all.
Earth has yielded up its secrets to man. But where to seek whence am I?

"Not knowing the hereafter, how can we deny the operation of Destiny? Not knowing what preceded birth, how can we assert the operation of Destiny? When things turn out as they ought, who shall say that the agency is not supernatural? When things turn out otherwise, who shall say that it is?"

The various Penumbræ said to the Umbra, "Before you were looking down, now you are looking up. Before you had your hair tied up, now it is all loosed. Before you were sitting, now you have got up. Before you were moving, now you are stopping still. How is this?"

"Gentlemen," replied the Umbra, "the question is hardly worth asking.
Ultimate causes being unknowable.
I do these things, but I do not know why. I am like the scaly back of the cicada, the shell of the locust,—apparently independent, but not really so. By firelight or in daylight I am seen: in darkness or by night I am gone. And if I am dependent on these, how much more are they dependent on something else? When they come, I come with them. When they go, I go with them. When they live, I live with them. But who it is that gives the life, how shall we seek to know?"

Repeated, with variations, from ch. ii.
Yang Tzŭ Chü
See p. 46.
went southwards to P'ei, and when Lao Tzŭ was travelling westwards to Ch'in, hastened to receive him outside the city. Arriving at the bridge, he met Lao Tzŭ; and the latter standing in the middle of the road, looked up to heaven and said with a sigh, "At first, I thought you could be taught. I think so no more."

Yang Tzŭ Chü made no reply, but when they reached the inn, handed Lao Tzŭ water for washing and rinsing, and a towel and comb. He then removed his own boots outside the door, and crawling on his knees into the Master's presence, said, "I have been wishing to ask for instruction, Sir, but as you were travelling and not at leisure, I did not venture. You are now, Sir, at leisure. May I enquire the reason of what you said?"

"You have an overbearing look," said Lao Tzŭ. "Who would live with such a man? He who is truly pure behaves as though he were sullied. He who has virtue in abundance behaves as though it were not enough."

These last two sentences occur in the Tao-Tê-Ching, ch. xli, and also in the works of Lieh Tzŭ as part of that author's own text. See The Remains of Lao Tzŭ, p. 29.

Yang Tzŭ Chü changed countenance at this, and replied, "I hear and obey."

Now when Yang Tzŭ Chü first went to the inn, the visitors there had come out to receive him. Mine host had arranged his mat, while the landlady held towel and comb. The visitors had given him up the best seats, and those who were cooking had left the stove free for him. But when he went back,
After his interview with Lao Tzŭ.
the other visitors struggled to get the best seats for themselves.
So changed was he in spirit.
Lin Hsi Chung considers that this chapter should immediately precede what is now ch. xxxii, from which it has been separated by the interpolation of the four following chapters, all admittedly spurious.

CHAPTER XXVIII

On Declining Power

[Spurious.]

Yao offered to resign the empire to Hsü Yu, but the latter declined.

He then offered it to Tzŭ Chou Chih Fu, who said, "There is no objection to making me emperor. But just now I am suffering from a troublesome disease, and am engaged in trying to cure it. I have no leisure to look after the empire."

Now the empire is of paramount importance. Yet here was a man who would not allow it to injure his chance of life. How much less then would he let other things do so? Yet it is only he who would do nothing in the way of government who is fit to be trusted with the empire.

Those personages who have not been previously mentioned may be taken to be allegorical.

Shun offered to resign the empire to Tzŭ Chou Chih Poh. The latter said, "Just now I am suffering from a troublesome disease, and am engaged in trying to cure it. I have no leisure to look after the empire."

Now the empire is a great trust; but not to sacrifice one's life for it is precisely where the man of Tao differs from the man of the world.

Shun offered to resign the empire to Shan Chüan. Shan Chüan said, "I am a unit in the sum of the universe. In winter I wear fur clothes. In summer I wear grass-cloth. In spring I plough and sow, toiling with my body. In autumn I gather in the harvest, and devote myself to rest and enjoyment. At dawn I go to work; at sunset I leave off. Contented with my lot I pass through life with a light heart. Why then should I trouble myself with the empire? Ah, Sir, you do not know me."

So he declined, and subsequently hid himself among the mountains, nobody knew where.

Shun offered the empire to a friend, a labourer of Shih Hu.

"Sire," said the latter, "you exert yourself too much. The chief thing is to husband one's strength;"—meaning that in point of real virtue Shun had not attained.

Then, husband and wife, bearing away their household gods and taking their children with them, went off to the sea and never came back.

When T'ai Wang Shan Fu was occupying Pin, he was attacked by savages. He offered them skins and silk, but they declined these. He offered them dogs and horses, but they declined these also. He then offered them pearls and jade, but these too they declined. What they wanted was the territory.

"To live with a man's elder brother," said T'ai Wang Shan Fu,

Addressing his own people.

"and slay his younger brother; to live with a man's father and slay his son,—this I could not bear to do. Make shift to remain here. To be my subjects or the subjects of these savages, where is the difference? Besides I have heard say that we ought not to let that which is intended to nourish life become injurious to life."

Alluding to the "territory."

Thereupon he took his staff and went off. His people all followed him, and they founded a new State at the foot of Mount Ch'i.

Now T'ai Wang Shan Fu undoubtedly had a proper respect for life. And those who have a proper respect for life, if rich and powerful, do not let that which should nourish injure the body. If poor and lowly, they do not allow gain to involve them in physical wear and tear.

But the men of the present generation who occupy positions of power and influence, are all afraid of losing what they have got. Directly they see a chance of gain, away goes all care for their bodies. Is not that a cause for confusion?

In three successive cases the people of Yüeh had put their prince to death. Accordingly, Shou, the son of the last prince, was much alarmed, and fled to Tan Hsüeh, leaving the State of Yüeh without a ruler.

Shou was at first nowhere to be found, but at length he was traced to Tan Hsüeh. He was, however, unwilling to come forth, so they smoked him out with moxa. They had a royal carriage ready for him; and as Shou seized the cord to mount the chariot, he looked up to heaven and cried, "Oh! ruling, ruling, could I not have been spared this?"

It was not that Shou objected to be a prince. He objected to the dangers associated with such positions. Such a one was incapable of sacrificing life to the State, and for that very reason the people of Yüeh wanted to get him.

The States of Han and Wei were struggling to annex each other's territory when Tzŭ Hua Tzŭ went to see prince Chao Hsi. Finding the latter very downcast, Tzŭ Hua Tzŭ said, "Now suppose the representatives of the various States were to sign an agreement before your Highness, to the effect that although cutting off the left hand would involve loss of the right, while cutting off the right would involve loss of the left, nevertheless that whosoever would cut off either should be emperor over all,—would your Highness cut?"

"I would not," replied the prince.

"Very good," said Tzŭ Hua Tzŭ. "It is clear therefore that one's two arms are worth more than the empire. And one's body is worth more than one's arms, while the State of Han is infinitely less important than the empire. Further, what you are struggling over is of infinitely less importance than the State of Han. Yet your Highness is wearing out body and soul alike in fear and anxiety lest you should not get it."

"Good indeed!" cried the prince. "Many have counselled me, but I have never heard the like of this."

From which we may infer that Tzŭ Hua Tzŭ knew the difference between what was of importance and what was not.

The prince of Lu, hearing that Yen Ho had attained to Tao, despatched messengers with presents to open communications.

Yen Ho lived in a hovel. He wore clothes of coarse grass, and occupied himself in tending oxen.

When the messengers arrived, Yen Ho went out to meet them; whereupon they enquired, "Is this where Yen Ho lives?"

"This is Yen Ho's house," replied the latter.

The messengers then produced the presents; but Yen Ho said, "I fear you have made a mistake. And as you might get into trouble, it would be as well to go back and make sure."

This the messengers accordingly did. When however they returned, there was no trace to be found of Yen Ho. Thus it is that men like Yen Ho hate wealth and power.

Wherefore it has been said that the best part of Tao is for self-culture, the surplus for governing a State, and the dregs for governing the empire. From which we may infer that the great deeds of kings and princes are but the leavings of the Sage. For preserving the body and nourishing vitality, they are of no avail. Yet the superior men of to-day endanger their bodies and throw away their lives in their greed for the things of this world. Is not this pitiable?

The true Sage in all his actions considers the why and the wherefore. But there are those now-a-days who use the pearl of the prince of Sui to shoot a bird a thousand yards off.

A wonderfully brilliant gem, of a "ten chariot" illuminating power.

And the world of course laughs at them. Why? Because they sacrifice the greater to get the less. But surely life is of more importance even than the prince's pearl!

Lieh Tzǔ was poor. His face wore a hungry look.

A visitor one day mentioned this to Tzǔ Yang

Prime Minister.

of Chêng, saying, "Lieh Tzǔ is a scholar who has attained to Tao. He lives in your Excellency's State, and yet he is poor. Can it be said that your Excellency does not love scholars?"

Thereupon Tzǔ Yang gave orders that Lieh Tzǔ should be supplied with food. But when Lieh Tzǔ saw the messengers, he bowed twice and declined.

When the messengers had gone, and Lieh Tzǔ went within, his wife gazed at him, and beating her breast said, "I have heard that the wife and children of a man of Tao are happy and joyful. But see how hungry I am. His Excellency sent you food, and you would not take it. Is not this flying in the face of Providence?"

"His Excellency did not know me personally," answered Lieh Tzǔ with a smile. "It was because of what others said about me that he sent me the food. If then men were to speak ill of me, he would also act upon it. For that reason I refused the food."

Subsequently, there was trouble among the people of Chêng, and Tzǔ Yang was slain.

When Prince Chao of the Ch'u State lost his kingdom, he was followed into exile by his butcher, named Yüeh.

On his restoration, as he was distributing rewards to those who had remained faithful to him, he came to the name of Yüeh.

Yüeh, however, said, "When the prince lost his kingdom, I lost my butchery. Now that the prince has got back his kingdom, I have got back my butchery. I have recovered my office and salary. What need for further reward?"

On hearing this, the prince gave orders that he should be made to take his reward.

"It was not through my fault," argued Yüeh, "that the prince lost his kingdom, and I should not have taken the punishment. Neither was it through me that he got it back, and I cannot therefore accept the reward."

When the prince heard this answer, he commanded Yüeh to be brought before him. But Yüeh said, "The laws of the Ch'u State require that a subject shall have deserved exceptionally well of his prince before being admitted to an audience. Now my wisdom was insufficient to preserve this kingdom, and my courage insufficient to destroy the invaders. When the Wu soldiers entered Ying, I feared for my life and fled. That was why I followed the prince. And if now the prince wishes to set law and custom aside and summon me to an audience, this is not my idea of proper behaviour on the part of the prince."

"Yüeh," said the prince to Tzŭ Chi, his master of the horse, "occupies a lowly position; yet his principles are of the most lofty. Go, make him a San Ching."

"I am aware," replied Yüeh to the master of the horse, "that the post of San Ching is more honourable than that of butcher. And I am aware that the emolument is larger than what I now receive. Still, because I want preferment and salary, I cannot let my prince earn the reputation of being injudicious in his patronage. I must beg to decline. Let me go back to my butchery."

And he adhered to his refusal.

Yüan Hsien dwelt in Lu,—in a mud hut, with a grass-grown roof, an apology for a door, and two mulberry-trees for door-posts. The windows which lighted his two rooms were no bigger than the mouth of a jar, and were closed by a wad of old clothes. The hut leaked from above and was damp under foot; yet Yüan Hsien sat gravely there playing on the guitar.

Tzŭ Kung came driving up in a fine chariot, in a white robe lined with purple; but the hood of the chariot was too big for the street.

When he went to see Yüan Hsien, the latter came to the door in a flowery cap, with his shoes down at heel, and leaning on a stalk.

"Good gracious!" cried Tzŭ Kung, "whatever is the matter with you?"

"I have heard," replied Yüan Hsien, "that he who is without wealth is called poor, and that he who learns without being able to practise is said to have something the matter with him. Now I am merely poor; I have nothing the matter with me."

Tzŭ Kung was much abashed at this reply; upon which Yüan Hsien smiling continued, "To try to thrust myself forward among men; to seek friendship in mutual flattery; to learn for the sake of others; to teach for my own sake; to use benevolence and duty to one's neighbour for evil ends; to make a great show with horses and carriages,—these things I cannot do."

Tsêng Tzŭ lived in the Wei State. His wadded coat had no outside cloth. His face was bloated and rough. His hands and feet were horny hard. For three days he had had no fire; no new clothes for ten years. If he set his cap straight the tassel would come off. If he drew up his sleeve his elbow would poke through. If he pulled up his shoe, the heel would come off. Yet slipshod he sang the Sacrificial Odes of Shang, his voice filling the whole sky, as though it had been some instrument of metal or stone.

The Son of Heaven could not secure him as a minister. The feudal princes could not secure him as a friend. For he who nourishes his purpose becomes oblivious of his body. He who nourishes his body becomes oblivious of gain. And he who has attained Tao becomes oblivious of his mind.

"Come hither," said Confucius to Yen Hui. "Your family is poor, and your position lowly. Why not go into official life?"

"I do not wish to," replied Yen Hui. "I have fifty acres of land beyond the city walls, which are enough to supply me with food. Ten more within the walls provide me with clothes. My lute gives me all the amusement I want; and the study of your doctrines keeps me happy enough. I do not desire to go into official life."

"Bravo! well said!" cried Confucius with beaming countenance. "I have heard say that those who are contented do not entangle themselves in the pursuit of gain. That those who have really obtained do not fear the contingency of loss. That those who devote themselves to cultivation of the inner man, though occupying no position, feel no shame. Thus indeed I have long preached. Only now, that I have seen Yen Hui, am I conscious of the realisation of these words."

Prince Mou of Chung-shan said to Chan Tzŭ, "My body is in the country, but my heart is in town. What am I to do?"

"Make life of paramount importance," answered Chan Tzŭ, "and worldly advantage will cease to have weight."

"That I know," replied the Prince; "but I am not equal to the task."

"If you are not equal to this," said Chan Tzŭ, "then it were well for you to pursue your natural bent. Not to be equal to a task, and yet to force oneself to stick to it,—this is called adding one injury to another. And those who suffer such two-fold injury do not belong to the class of the long-lived."

Prince Mou of Wei was heir to the throne of a large State. For him to become a hermit among the hills was more difficult than for an ordinary cotton-clothed scholar. And although he had not attained to Tao, he may be said to have been on the way thither.

When Confucius was caught between the Ch'êns and the Ts'ais, he went seven days without proper food. He ate soup of herbs, having no rice. He looked very much exhausted, yet he sat within playing his guitar and singing to it.

Yen Hui was picking over the herbs, while Tzŭ Lu and Tzŭ Kung were talking together. One of them said, "Our Master has twice been driven out of Lu. They will have none of him in Wei. His tree was cut down in Sung. He got into trouble in Shang and Chou. And now he is surrounded by the Ch'êns and the Ts'ais. Whoever kills him is to be held guiltless. Whoever takes him prisoner is not to be interfered with. Yet all the time he goes on playing and singing without cease. Is this the right thing for a superior man to do?"

Yen Hui said nothing, but went inside and told Confucius, who laid aside his guitar and said with a loud sigh, "Yu and Tzǔ are ignorant fellows.
These were their personal names.
Bid them come, and I will speak to them."

When they entered Tzǔ Lu said, "We seem to have made a thorough failure."

"What do you mean?" cried Confucius. "The superior man who succeeds in Tao, has success. If he fails in Tao, he makes a failure. Now I, holding fast to the Tao of charity and duty towards one's neighbour, have fallen among the troubles of a disordered age. What failure is there in that?

"Therefore it is that by cultivation of the inner man there is no failure in Tao, and when danger comes there is no loss of virtue. It is the chill winter weather, it is frost, it is snow, which bring out the luxuriance of the pine and the fir.
See Lun Yü, ix, 27.
I regard it as a positive blessing to be thus situated as I am."

Thereupon he turned abruptly round and went on playing and singing.

At this Tzǔ Lu hastily seized a shield and began dancing to the music, while Tzǔ Kung said, "I had no idea of the height of heaven and of the depth of earth."

The ancients who attained Tao were equally happy under success and failure. Their happiness had nothing to do with their failure or their success. Tao once attained, failure and success became mere links in a chain, like cold, heat, wind, and rain. Thus Hsü Yu enjoyed himself at Ying-yang, and Kung Poh found happiness on the hill-top.
Whither he retired after a reign of 14 years.
Shun offered to resign the empire to his friend Pei Jen Wu Tsê.

"What a strange manner of man you are!" cried the latter. "Living in the furrowed fields, you exchanged such a life for the throne of Yao. And as if that was not enough, you now try to heap indignity upon me. I am ashamed of you."

Thereupon he drowned himself in the waters of Ch'ing-ling.

"But how about preservation of life?" asks Lin Hsi Chung with a sneer.

When T'ang was about to attack Chieh, he went to consult with Pien Sui.

"It is not a matter in which I can help you," said the latter.

"Who can?" asked T'ang.

"I do not know," replied Pien Sui.

T'ang then went to consult with Wu Kuang.

"It is not a matter in which I can help you," said the latter.

"Who can?" asked T'ang.

"I do not know," replied Wu Kuang.

"What do you think of I Yin?" asked T'ang.

"He forces himself," said Wu Kuang, "to put up with obloquy. Beyond this I know nothing of him."

So T'ang took I Yin into his counsels. They attacked Chieh, and vanquished him.

Then T'ang offered to resign the empire in favour of Pien Sui. But Pien Sui declined, saying, "When your Majesty consulted with me about attacking Chieh, you evidently looked on me as a robber.

Who would steal territory. But men of Tao wage no wars.

Now that you have vanquished him, and you offer to resign in my favour, you evidently regard me as covetous. I was born indeed in a disordered age. But for a man without Tao to thus insult me twice, is more than I can endure."

So he drowned himself in the river Chou.

Then T'ang offered to resign in favour of Wu Kuang, saying, "The wise plan, the brave execute, the good rest therein,—such was the Tao of the ancients. Why, Sir, should not you occupy the throne?"

But Wu Kuang declined, saying, "To depose a ruler is not to do one's duty to one's neighbour. To slay the people is not charity. For others to suffer these wrongs, while I enjoy the profits, is not honest. I have heard say that one should not accept a wage unless earned in accordance with right; and that if the world is without Tao, one should not put foot upon its soil, still less rule over it! I can bear this no longer."

Thereupon he took a stone on his back and jumped into the river Lu.

At the rise of the Chou dynasty there were two scholars, named Po I and Shu Ch'i, who lived in Ku-tu.

One of these said to the other, "I have heard that in the west there are men who are apparently in possession of Tao. Let us go and see them."

Meaning the men of Chou.

When they arrived at Ch'i-yang, Wu Wang

The writer meant Wên Wang, father of Wu Wang.

heard of their arrival and sent Shu Tan

Chou Kung.

to enter into a treaty with them. They were to receive emoluments of the second degree and rank of the first degree. The treaty was to be sealed with blood and buried.

At this the two looked at each other and smiled. "Ah!" said one of them, "this is strange indeed. It is not what we call Tao.

"When Shên Nung ruled the empire, he worshipped God without asking for any reward. Sometimes it was the law he put in force; sometimes it was his personal influence he brought to bear. He was loyal and faithful to his people without seeking any return. He did not build his success upon another's ruin, nor mount high by means of another's fall, nor seize opportunities to secure his own advantage.

"But now that the Chous, beholding the iniquities of the Yins, have taken upon themselves to govern, we have intrigues above and bribes below. Troops are mobilised to protect prestige. Victims are slaughtered to give good faith to a treaty. A show of virtue is made to amuse the masses. Fighting and slaughter are made the means of gain. Confusion has simply been exchanged for disorder.

"I have heard tell that the men of old, living in quiet times, never shirked their duties; but lighting upon troublous times, nothing could make them stay. The empire is now in darkness. The virtue of the Chous has faded. For the empire to be united under the Chous would be a disgrace to us. Better flee away and keep our actions pure."

Accordingly, these two philosophers went north to Mount Shou-yang, where they subsequently starved themselves to death.

Men like Poh I and Shu Ch'i, if wealth and honour came to them so that they could properly accept, would assuredly not have recourse to such heroic measures, nor would they be content to follow their own bent, without giving their services to their generation. Such was the purity of these two scholars.

CHAPTER XXIX

Robber Chê

[Spurious.]

Confucius was on terms of friendship with Liu Hsia Chi, whose younger brother was known as "Robber Chê."
This is an anachronism. Liu Hsia Chi (or Hui) was a virtuous official of the Lu State. He flourished some 80 and more years before the time of Confucius.

Robber Chê had a band of followers nine thousand strong. He ravaged the whole empire, plundering the various nobles and breaking into people's houses. He drove off oxen and horses. He stole men's wives and daughters. Family ties put no limit to his greed. He had no respect for parents nor for brothers. He neglected the worship of his ancestors. Wherever he passed, the greater States flew to arms, the smaller ones to places of safety. All the people were sore distressed.

"A father," said Confucius to Liu Hsia Chi, "should surely be able to admonish his son; an elder brother to teach his younger brother. If this be not so, there is an end of the value attached to these relationships.

"Now you, Sir, are one of the scholars of the age, while your younger brother is the Robber Chê, the scourge of the empire. You are unable to teach him, and I blush for you. Let me go and have a talk with him on your behalf."

"As to what you say, Sir, about fathers and elder brothers," answered Liu Hsia Chi, "if the son will not listen to his father, nor the younger brother to his elder brother, what becomes of your arguments then?

"Besides, Chê's passions are like a bubbling spring. His thoughts are like a whirlwind. He is strong enough to defy all foes. He can argue until wrong becomes right. If you follow his inclinations, he is pleased. If you oppose them he is angry. He is free with the language of abuse. Do not go near him."

Confucius paid no attention to this advice; but with Yen Hui as charioteer and Tzŭ Kung on his right, went off to see Robber Chê.

The latter had just encamped to the south of T'ai-shan, and was engaged in devouring a dish of minced human liver. Confucius alighted from his chariot, and advancing addressed the doorkeeper as follows:—

"I am Confucius of the Lu State. I have heard of the high character of your captain."

He then twice respectfully saluted the doorkeeper, who went in to announce his arrival.

When Robber Chê heard who it was, he was furious. His eyes glared like stars. His hair raised his cap from his head as he cried out, "What! that crafty scoundrel Confucius of Lu? Go, tell him from me that he is a mere word-mongerer. That he talks nonsense about Wên Wang and Wu Wang. That he wears an extravagant cap, with a thong from the side of a dead ox. That what he says is mostly rhodomontade. That he consumes where he does not sow, and wears clothes he does not weave. That his lips patter and his tongue wags. That his rights and wrongs are of his own coining, whereby he throws dust in the eyes of rulers and prevents the scholars of the empire from reverting to the original source of all things.

Sc. Tao.

That he makes a great stir about filial piety and brotherly love, glad enough himself to secure some fat fief or post of power. Tell him that he deserves the worst, and that if he does not take himself off his liver shall be in my morning stew."

But Confucius sent in again, saying, "I am a friend of Liu Hsia Chi. I am anxious to set eyes upon your captain's shoe-strings."

Another interpretation is "upon your captain's feet visible from beneath the screen."

When the doorkeeper gave this second message, Robber Chê said, "Bring him before me!" Thereupon Confucius hurried in, and avoiding the place of honour stepped back and made two obeisances.

Robber Chê, flaming with anger, straddled out his two legs, and laying his hand upon his sword glared at Confucius and roaring like a tigress with young, said, "Ch'iu! come here. If what you say suits my ideas, you will live. Otherwise you will die."

"I have heard," replied Confucius, "that the world contains three classes of virtue. To grow up tall, of a beauty without compare, and thus to be the idol of young and old, of noble and lowly alike,—this is the highest class. To be possessed of wisdom which embraces the universe and can explain all things,—this is the middle class. To be possessed of courage which will stand test and gather followers around,—this is the lowest class.

"Now any man whose virtue belongs to either of these classes is fit to occupy the place and title of ruler. But you, Captain, unite all three in yourself. You are eight feet two in height. Your expression is very bright. Your lips are like vermilion. Your teeth like a row of shells. Your voice is like a beautiful bell;—yet you are known as Robber Chê. Captain, I blush for you.

"Captain, if you will hearken to me I will go south for you to Wu and Yüeh, north to Ch'i and Lu, east to Sung and Wei, and west to Chin and Ch'u. I will have a great wall built for you of many li in extent, enclosing hamlets of many hundreds of thousands of inhabitants, over which State you shall be ruler. Your relations with the empire will enter upon a new phase. You will disband your men. You will gather your brothers around you. You will join in worship of your ancestors. Such is the behaviour of the true Sage and the man of parts, and such is what the world desires."

"Ch'iu! come here," cried Robber Chê in a great rage. "Those who are squared by offers and corrected by words are the stupid vulgar masses. The height and the beauty which you praise in me are legacies from my parents. Even though you did not praise them, do you think I should be ignorant of their existence? Besides, those who flatter to the face speak evil behind the back. Now all you have been saying about the great State and its numerous population simply means squaring me by offers as though one of the common herd. And of course it would not last.

"There is no State bigger than the empire. Yao and Shun both got this, yet their descendants have not territory enough to insert an awl's point. T'ang and Wu Wang both sat upon the Imperial throne, yet their posterity has been obliterated from the face of the earth.

Hardly in Chuang Tzŭ's time.
Was not this because of the very magnitude of the prize?
"I have also heard that in olden times the birds and animals outnumbered man, and that the latter was obliged to seek his safety by building his domicile in trees. By day he picked up acorns and chestnuts. At night he slept upon a branch. Hence the name Nest-builders.

"Of old, the people did not know how to make clothes. In summer they collected quantities of fuel, and in winter warmed themselves by fire. Hence the name Provident.

"In the days of Shên Nung, they lay down without caring where they were and got up without caring whither they might go. A man knew his mother but not his father. He lived among the wild deer. He tilled the ground for food. He wove cloth to cover his body. He harboured no thought of injury to others. These were the glorious results of an age of perfect virtue.

"The Yellow Emperor, however, could not attain to this virtue. He fought with Ch'ih Yu at Chŏ-lu, and blood flowed for a hundred li. Then came Yao and Shun with their crowd of ministers. Then T'ang who deposed his sovereign, and Wu Wang who slew Chou. After which time the strong took to oppressing the weak, the many to coercing the few. In fact, ever since T'ang and Wu Wang we have had none other than disturbers of the peace.

"And now you come forward preaching the old dogmas of Wên Wang and palming off sophistries without end, in order to teach future generations. You wear patched clothes and a narrow girdle, you talk big and act falsely, in order to deceive the rulers of the land, while all the time you yourself are aiming at wealth and power! You are the biggest thief I know of; and if the world calls me Robber Chê, it most certainly ought to call you Robber Ch'iu.

"By fair words you enticed Tzǔ Lu to follow you. You made him doff his martial cap,
Shaped like a cock's comb.
and ungird his long sword, and sit a disciple at your feet. And all the world cried out that Confucius could stop violence and prevent wrong-doing. By and by, when Tzǔ Lu wished to slay the prince of Wei, but failed, and was himself hacked to pieces and exposed over the eastern gate of Wei,—that was because you had not properly instructed him.
See the account in the Tso Chuan.
"You call yourself a man of talent and a Sage forsooth! Twice you have been driven out of Lu. You were tabooed in Wei. You were a failure in Ch'i. You were surrounded by the Ch'êns and the Ts'ais. In fact, the empire won't have you anywhere. It was your teaching which brought Tzǔ Lu to his tragical end. You cannot take care, in the first place, of yourself, nor, in the second place, of others. Of what value can your doctrine be?

"There is none to whom mankind has accorded a higher place than to the Yellow Emperor. Yet his virtue was not complete. He fought at Chŏ-lu, and blood ran for a hundred li. Yao was not paternal.
He killed his eldest son.
Shun was not filial.
He banished his mother's younger brother.
The great Yü was deficient in one respect.
He was wanting in natural feeling. When engaged in his great engineering work of draining the empire, he even passed his own door without going in to see his family.
T'ang deposed his sovereign. Wu Wang vanquished Chou. Wên Wang was imprisoned at Yin Li.

"Now these six worthies enjoy a high reputation among men. Yet a fuller investigation shows that in each case a desire for advantage disturbed their original purity and forced it into a contrary direction. Hence the shamelessness of their deeds.

"Among those whom the world calls virtuous were Poh I and Shu Ch'i. They declined the sovereignty of Ku-chu and died of starvation on Mount Shou-yang, their corpses deprived of burial.

"Pao Chiao made a great show of virtue and abused the world in general. He grasped a tree and died.
Tzǔ Kung, one of Confucius' disciples, is said to have scolded Pao Chiao so vigorously that the latter withered up into dead wood.
"Shên T'u Ti, when no heed was paid to his counsels, jumped into the river with a stone on his back and became food for fishes.
See p. 33.
"Chieh Tzǔ T'ui was truly loyal. He cut a slice from his thigh to feed Wên Wang. Afterwards, when Wên Wang turned his back upon him, he retired in anger, and grasping a tree, was burnt to death.
He took refuge in a forest, from which Wên Wang, anxious to recover his friend, tried to smoke him out!
"Wei Shêng made an assignation with a girl beneath a bridge. The girl did not come, and the water rose. But Wei Shêng would not leave. He grasped a buttress and died.

"These four differed in no way from dogs and pigs going about begging to be slaughtered. They all exaggerated reputation and disregarded death. They did not reflect upon their original nature and seek to preserve life into the old age allotted.

"Among ministers whom the world calls loyal, none can compare with Wang Tzŭ, Pi Kan, and Wu Tzŭ Hsü. The last-mentioned drowned himself. Pi Kan was disembowelled. These two worthies are what men call loyal ministers; yet, as a matter of fact, all the world laughs at them!

"Thus, from the most ancient times down to Tzŭ Hsü and Pi Kan, there have been none deserving of honour. And as to the sermon you, Ch'iu, propose to preach to me,—if it is on ghostly subjects, I shan't understand them, and if it is on human affairs, why there is nothing more to be said. I know it all already.

"I will now tell you a few things. The lust of the eye is for beauty. The lust of the ear is for music. The lust of the palate is for flavour. The lust of ambition is for gratification. Man's greatest age is one hundred years. A medium old age is eighty years. The lowest estimate is sixty years. Take away from this the hours of sickness, disease, death, mourning, sorrow, and trouble, and there will not remain more than four or five days a month upon which a man may open his mouth to laugh. Heaven and Earth are everlasting. Sooner or later every man has to die. That which thus has a limit, as compared with that which is everlasting, is a mere flash, like the passage of some swift steed seen through a crack. And those who cannot gratify their ambition and live through their allotted span, are men who have not attained to Tao.

"Ch'iu! all your teachings are nothing to me. Begone! Go home! Say no more! Your doctrine is a random jargon, full of falsity and deceit. It can never preserve the original purity of man. Why discuss it further?"

Confucius made two obeisances and hurriedly took his leave. On mounting his chariot, he three times missed hold of the reins. His eyes were so dazed that he could see nothing. His face was ashy pale. With down-cast head he grasped the bar of his chariot, unable to find vent for his feelings.

Arriving outside the eastern gate of Lu, he met Liu Hsia Chi, who said, "I have not seen you for some days. From the look of your equipage I should say you had been travelling. I guess now you have been to see Chê."

Confucius looked up to heaven, and replied with a sigh, "I have."

"And did he not rebuff you," asked Liu Hsia Chi, "as I said he would?"

"He did," said Confucius. "I am a man who has cauterized himself without being ill. I hurried away to smooth the tiger's head and comb out his beard. And I very nearly got into the tiger's mouth."

Tzŭ Chang asked Man Kou Tê,

Which means "Full of the Ill-gotten."

saying, "Why do you not practise virtue? Otherwise, it is impossible to inspire confidence. And without confidence, no place. And without place, no wealth. Thus, with a view to reputation or to wealth, duty towards one's neighbour is the true key.

As leading to reputation, which was what Tzŭ Chang wanted.

If you were to discard all thoughts of reputation and wealth and attend to the cultivation of the heart, surely you would not pass one day without practising the higher virtues."

"Those who have no shame," replied Man Kou Tê,

Meaning himself.

"grow rich. Those who inspire confidence make themselves conspicuous.

Meaning Tzŭ Chang.

Reputation and wealth are mostly to be got out of shamelessness and confidence inspired. Thus, with a view to reputation or to wealth, the confidence of others is the true key.

As leading to wealth, which was what Man Kou Tê wanted.

If you were to discard all thoughts of reputation and wealth, surely the virtuous man would then have no scope beyond himself."

Beyond his own nature.

"Of old," said Tzŭ Chang, "Chieh and Chou sat upon the Imperial throne, and the whole empire was theirs. Yet if you were now to tell any common thief that his moral qualities resembled theirs, he would resent it as an insult. By such miserable creatures are they despised."

"Confucius and Mih Tzŭ, on the other hand, were poor and simple enough. Yet if you were to tell any Prime Minister of to-day that his moral qualities resembled theirs, he would flush with pride and declare you were paying him too high a compliment. So truly honourable is the man of learning.

"Thus, the power of a monarch does not necessarily make him worthy; nor do poverty and a low station necessarily make a man unworthy. The worthy and the unworthy are differentiated by the worthiness and unworthiness of their acts."

"A petty thief," replied Man Kou Tê, "is put in gaol. A great brigand becomes ruler of a State. And among the retainers of the latter, men of virtue will be found.

"Of old, Duke Huan, named Hsiao Poh, slew his elder brother and took his sister-in-law to wife. Yet Kuan Chung became his minister.

"T'ien Ch'êng Tzŭ killed his prince and seized the kingdom. Yet Confucius accepted his pay.

See p. 51.

"To condemn a man in words, yet actually to take service under him,—does not this show us practice and precept directly opposed to one another?

"Therefore it was written, 'Who is bad? Who is good? He who succeeds is the head. He who does not succeed is the tail.'"

"But if you do not practise virtue," said Tzŭ Chang, "and make no distinction between kith and kin, assign no duties to the worthy and to the unworthy, no precedence to young and old, how then are the Five Bonds and the Six Ranks to be distinguished?"

Commentators are divided as to these Bonds and Ranks. One makes the former calendaric. Another considers that the five cardinal virtues and six ranks of nobility are meant. Of the latter there are only five, but "sovereign" is added to patch the deficiency.

"Yao slew his eldest son," answered Man Kou Tê. "Shun banished his mother's brother. Was there kith and kin in that?

"T'ang deposed Chieh. Wu Wang slew Chou. Was that the duty of the worthy towards the unworthy?

"Wang Chi was the legitimate heir, but Chow Kung slew his elder brother. Was that precedence of young and old?

"The false principles of the Confucianists, the universal love of the Mihists,—do these help to distinguish the Five Bonds and the Six Ranks?

"You, Sir, are all for reputation. I am all for wealth. As to which pursuit is not in accordance with principle nor in harmony with right, let us refer to the arbitration of Wu Yoh."

"The mean man," said Wu Yoh, "devotes himself to wealth. The superior man devotes himself to reputation. The moral results are different in each case. But if both would set aside their activities and devote themselves to doing nothing, the results would be the same.

"Wherefore it has been said, 'Be not a mean man. Revert to your natural self. Be not a superior man. Abide by the laws of heaven.'

"As to the straight and the crooked, view them from the standpoint of the infinite.

All distinctions are thus merged.

Gaze around you on all sides, until time withdraws you from the scene.

"As to the right and the wrong, hold fast to your magic circle,

At the centre of which all positives and negatives converge. See ch. ii, p.8.

and with independent mind walk ever in the way of Tao.

"Do not swerve from the path of virtue; do not bring about your own good deeds,—lest your labour be lost. Do not make for wealth; do not aim at success,—lest you cast away that which links you to God.

"Pi Kan was disembowelled. Tzŭ Hsü had his eyes gouged out.

Better known as Wu Yüan. See p.52. He expressed a wish to be buried on the road to the Yüeh State that he might witness the defeat of the Wu State. Whereupon the prince of the latter State at once had him deprived of sight.

Such was the fate of loyalty.

"Chih Kung bore witness against his father. Wei Shêng was drowned. Such are the misfortunes of the faithful.

"Pao Chiao dried up where he stood. Shên Tzŭ would not justify himself.

He would not defend himself against a charge of putting poison in his father's food.

Such are the evils of honesty.

"Confucius did not visit his mother.

There is no authority for this statement.

K'uang Tzŭ did not visit his father.

By whom he had been turned out of doors.

Such are the trials which come upon the upright.

"The above instances have been handed down to us from antiquity and are discussed in modern times. They show that men of learning emphasized their precepts by carrying them out in practice; and that consequently they paid the penalty and fell into these calamities."

Discontent asked Complacency, saying, "There is really no one who does not either aim at reputation or make for wealth. If a man is rich, others flock around him. These necessarily take a subordinate position, and consequently pay him court. And it would seem that such subordination and respect constitute a royal road to long life, comfort, and general happiness. How is it then that you, Sir, have no mind for these things? Is it that you are wanting in wit? Or is it that you are physically unable to compete, and therefore go in for being virtuous, though all the time unable to forget?"

"You and your friends," replied Complacency, "regard all men as alike because they happen to be born at the same time and in the same place as yourselves. You look on us as scholars who have separated from humanity and cast off the world, and who have no guiding principle beyond poring over the records of the past and present, or indulging in the logomachy of this and that.

"Were we to lead the mundane lives you do, it would be at the sacrifice of the very conditions of existence. And surely thus we should be wandering far from the royal road to long life, comfort, and general happiness. The discomfort of wretchedness, the comfort of well-being, you do not refer to the body.

But to some external cause of which the body becomes subjectively conscious.

The abjectness of terror, the elation of joy, you do not refer to the mind itself. You know that such things are so, but you do not know how they are so. Wherefore, though equalling the Son of Heaven in power, and with all the empire as your personal property, you would not be free from care."

"Wealth," replied Discontent, "is of the greatest service to a man. It enables him to do good, and to exert power, to an extent which the perfect man or the true Sage could never reach. He can borrow the courage and strength of others to make himself formidable. He can employ the wisdom and counsels of others to add clearness to his own deliberations. He can avail himself of the virtue of others and cause it to appear as his own. Without being in possession of a throne, he can wield the authority of a prince.

"Besides, the pleasures of music, beauty, rich food, and power, do not require to be studied before they can be appreciated by the mind; nor does the body need the example of others before it can enjoy them. We need no teacher to tell us what to like or dislike, to follow or to avoid. Such knowledge is instinctive in man. The world may condemn this view, but which of us is free from the taint?"

"The wise man," answered Complacency, "acts for the common weal, in pursuit of which he does not overstep due limits. Wherefore, if there is a sufficiency, he does not strive for more. He has no use for more, and accordingly does not seek it. But if there is not a sufficiency, then he seeks for more. He strives in all directions, yet does not account it greed. If there is a surplus, he declines it. Even though he refused the whole empire, he would not account it honesty. To him, honesty and greed are not conditions into which we are forced by outward circumstances, but characteristics innate in the individual. He may wield the power of the Son of Heaven, but will not employ it for the degradation of others. He may own the whole empire, yet will not use his wealth to take advantage of his fellows. But a calculation of the troubles and the anxieties inseparable therefrom, cause him to reject these as injurious to his nature, not from a desire for reputation.

"When Yao and Shun occupied the throne, there was peace. They did not try to be beneficent rulers. They did not inflict injury by doing good.

They were simply natural, and good results followed.

"Shan Chüan and Hsü Yu both declined the proffered throne. Theirs was no empty refusal. They would not cause injury to themselves.

"In all these cases, each individual adopted the profitable course in preference to the injurious course. And the world calls them virtuous, whereby they acquire a reputation at which they never aimed."

"It is necessary," argued Discontent, "to cling to reputation. If all pleasures are to be denied to the body and one's energies to be concentrated upon health with a view to the prolongation of life, such life would be itself nothing more than the prolonged illness of a confirmed invalid."

"Happiness," said Complacency, "is to be found in contentment. Too much is always a curse, most of all in wealth.

"The ears of the wealthy man ring with sounds of sweet music. His palate is cloyed with rich meats and wine. In the pursuit of pleasure, business is forgotten. This is confusion.

"He eats and drinks to excess, until his breathing is that of one carrying a heavy load up a hill. This is misery.

"He covets money to surround himself with comforts. He covets power to vanquish rivals. But his quiet hours are darkened by diabetes and dropsy. This is disease.

"Even when, in his desire for wealth, he has piled up an enormous fortune, he still goes on and cannot desist. This is shame.

"Having no use for the money he has collected, he still hugs it to him and cannot bear to part with it. His heart is inflamed, and he ever seeks to add more to the pile. This is unhappiness.

"At home, he dreads the pest of the pilfering thief. Abroad, the danger of bandit and highwayman. So he keeps strict guard within, while never venturing alone without. This is fear.

"These six are the greatest of the world's curses. Yet such a man never bestows a thought upon them, until the hour of misfortune is at hand. Then, with his ambitions gratified, his natural powers exhausted, and nothing but wealth remaining, he would gladly obtain one day's peace, but cannot do so.

"Wherefore, if reputation is not to be enjoyed and wealth is not to be secured, how pitiable it is that men should harass their minds and wear out their bodies in such pursuits!"

CHAPTER XXX

On Swords

[Spurious.]

Of old, Wên Wang of Chao loved sword-play. Swordsmen thronged his halls, to the number of three thousand and more. Day and night they had bouts before the prince. In the course of a year, a hundred or so would be killed or wounded. Yet the prince was never satisfied.

Within three years, the State had begun to go to rack and ruin, and other princes to form designs upon it. Thereupon the Heir Apparent, Li, became troubled in mind; and said to the officers of his household, "Whosoever shall persuade the prince to do away with these swordsmen, to him I will give a thousand ounces of silver."

To this his officers replied, "Chuang Tzŭ is the man."

Thereupon the Heir Apparent sent messengers to Chuang Tzŭ with a thousand ounces of silver, which he would not accept, but accompanied the messengers back to their master.

"What does your Highness require of me," asked Chuang Tzŭ, "that you should bestow upon me a thousand ounces?"

"I had heard," replied the young prince, "that you were a famous Sage, and I ventured to send this money as a present to your servants.

Merely a ceremonious phrase.

But as you would not receive it, what more can I say?"

"I understand," answered Chuang Tzŭ, "that your Highness would have me cure the prince of his peculiar weakness. Now suppose that I do not succeed with the prince, and consequently with your Highness, the punishment of death is what I have to expect. What good would the thousand ounces be to me then?"

"On the other hand, if I succeed with the prince, and consequently with your Highness, the whole State of Chao contains nothing I could not have for the asking."

"You must know, however," said the young prince, "that my father will only receive swordsmen."

"Well," replied Chuang Tzŭ, "I am a good swordsman myself."

"Besides which," added the Heir Apparent, "the swordsmen he is accustomed to see have all dishevelled hair hanging over their temples. They wear slouching caps with coarse tangled tassels, and short-tailed coats. They glare with their eyes and talk in a fierce tone. This is what my father likes. But if you go to him dressed in your ordinary scholar's dress, the result is sure to be disastrous."

"I will accustom myself to the dress," replied Chuang Tzŭ; and after practising for three days, he went again to see the young prince, who accompanied him into his father's presence.

The latter drew a sharp sword and awaited Chuang Tzŭ's approach.

But Chuang Tzǔ, when he entered the door of the audience chamber, did not hurry forward, neither did he prostrate himself before the prince.

"What have you to say to me," cried the prince, "that you have obtained your introduction through the Heir Apparent?"

"I have heard," replied Chuang Tzǔ, "that your Highness loves sword-play. Therefore I have come to exhibit my skill."

"What can you do in that line?" asked the prince.

"Were I to meet an opponent," said Chuang Tzǔ, "at every ten paces, I could go on for a thousand li without being stopped."

"Bravo!" cried the prince. "There is not your match in the empire."

"When I fight," continued Chuang Tzǔ, "I make a show of being weak but push a vigorous attack. The last to start, I am the first to arrive. I should like your Highness to make trial of me."

"Rest awhile," replied the prince. "Stay here and await orders. I will arrange a day for you."

Thereupon the prince spent seven days in trying his swordsmen. Some sixty of them were either killed or wounded, but at length he selected five or six and bade them attend in the audience-chamber with their swords. He then summoned Chuang Tzǔ and said, "Now I will see what your swordsmanship is worth."

"I have been longing for this," replied Chuang Tzǔ.

"Does it matter to you," asked the prince, "of what length your weapon may be?"

"Not at all," replied Chuang Tzǔ. "I have three swords, of which I will ask your Highness to choose one. We will then proceed to the trial."

"Which are your three swords?" enquired the prince.

"There is the sword of the Son of Heaven," said Chuang Tzǔ, "the sword of the Princes, and the sword of the People."

"What is the sword of the Son of Heaven?" asked the prince.

"The stone wall of Yen-ch'i is its point," replied Chuang Tzǔ.

Some take "stone wall" as the name of a place.

"The mountains of Ch'i are its edge. Chin and Wei are its back. Chou and Sung are its hilt. Han and Wei are its sheath. It is enclosed in the four hordes of barbarians, wrapped in the four seasons, surrounded by the great ocean. It is made of the five elements. It is the arbiter of punishment and reward. It operates under the influence of the Yin and the Yang. In spring and summer it is at rest. In autumn and winter it moves abroad. Push it, it does not advance. Raise it, it does not go up. Lower it, it does not go down. Whirl it around, it does not change position. Above, it cleaves the floating clouds; below, it cuts through the density of earth. One flash of this blade, and the princes of the empire submit. Such is the sword of the Son of Heaven."

At this the prince seemed absorbed in his reflections. Then he enquired, saying, "And what is the sword of the Princes?"

"The Wise and brave," replied Chuang Tzǔ, "are its point. The incorruptible are its edge. The virtuous are its back. The loyal are its hilt. The heroic are its sheath. You may push this sword too, it will not advance. Raise it, it will not go up. Lower it, it will not go down. Whirl it around, it will not change position. Above, it models itself upon the round heaven, in order to keep in harmony with the sun, moon, and stars. Below, it models itself upon the square earth, in order to keep in harmony with the four seasons. It adapts itself to the wishes of the people, in order to diffuse peace on all sides. One flash of this blade is like a roaring clap of thunder. Between the boundaries of the State there is not left one but who yields and obeys the command of his prince. Such is the sword of the Princes."

"And the sword of the People?" enquired the prince.

"The sword of the People," replied Chuang Tzŭ, "has dishevelled hair hanging over its temples. It wears a slouching cap with coarse tangled tassel, and a short-tailed coat. It glares with its eyes and talks in a fierce tone. When it engages in conflict, above, it cuts off head and neck; below, it smites liver and lungs. Such is the sword of the People. It is like a gamecock. One day, its life is cut short, and it is of no more use to the State.

"Now you, great prince, wield sovereign power, and yet you devote yourself to this sword of the People. I am truly ashamed of it."

Thereupon the prince drew Chuang Tzŭ up on to the dais, and the attendants served food, the king three times assisting with his own hand.

The prince each time received the dish from the attendants, handed it to Chuang Tzŭ, and then walked round to his own seat again.

"Be seated, great prince," said Chuang Tzŭ, "and compose your mind. I have said all I have to say on swords."

After this the prince did not quit his palace for three months, while the swordsmen, submitting to the new order of things, died in their own homes.

One commentator says "killed themselves in their own dwellings." But if so, Chuang Tzŭ's influence was of small practical value as far as the swordsmen were concerned. They might as well have continued their profession of arms.

CHAPTER XXXI

The Old Fisherman

[Spurious.]

Confucius, travelling in the Black Forest, rested awhile at Apricot Altar. His disciples sat down to their books, and he himself played upon the lute and sang.

Half way through the song, an old fisherman stepped out of a boat and advanced towards them. His beard and eyebrows were snowy white. His hair hung loose, and he flapped his long sleeves as he walked over the foreshore. Reaching firm ground, he stood still, and with left hand on his knee and right hand to his ear, listened.

When the song was finished, he beckoned to Tzŭ Kung and Tzŭ Lu, both of whom went to him. Then pointing with his finger, he enquired, saying, "What is that man doing here?"

"He is the Sage of Lu," replied Tzŭ Lu.

"Of what clan?" asked the old man.

"Of the K'ung family," replied Tzŭ Lu.

"And what is his occupation?" said the old man.

"He devotes himself," replied Tzŭ Lu, "to loyalty and truth. He practises charity and duty towards his neighbour. He regulates ceremonies and music. He distinguishes the relationships of man. He is loyal to his prince above, a reformer of the masses below. Thus he will be of great service to the whole empire. Such is his occupation."

"Is he a ruler of a State?" asked the old man.

"He is not," said Tzŭ Kung.

"A minister?" said the old man.

"No," said Tzŭ Kung.

Then the old man laughed and walked away, saying, "Charity is charity, yet I fear he will not escape the wear of mind and tear of body which imperil the original purity of man. How far, alas, has he wandered from the true path!"

From Tao.

Tzŭ Kung went back and told Confucius, who, laying aside his lute, arose and said, "This man is a Sage!"

Thereupon he followed the old man down the shore, catching him up just as he was drawing in his boat with his staff. Perceiving Confucius, the old man turned round to receive him, at which Confucius stepped back and prostrated himself twice before advancing.

"What do you want, Sir?" asked the fisherman.

"Just now, venerable Sir," replied Confucius, "you left without finishing your remarks. In my stupidity I cannot make out what you mean. Therefore I have come in the humble hope of hearing any words with which you may deign to help me."

"Well," said the old man, "you are certainly anxious to learn."

At this Confucius prostrated himself twice, and when he got up said, "Yes, I have been a student from my youth upwards until now, the sixty-ninth year of my age. Yet I have never heard the true doctrine, which I am now ready to receive without bias."

"Like species follow like," answered the old man. "Like sounds respond to like.

See p.129, and the experiment of the two lutes, p. 145.

This is a law of nature. I will now with your leave apply what I know to what you occupy yourself with,—the affairs of men.

"The Son of Heaven, the princes, the ministers, and the people,—if these four fulfil their proper functions, the result is good government. If they quit their proper places, the result is unutterable confusion. When the officials mind their duties and the people their business, neither is injured by the other.

"Barren land, leaky roofs, want of food and clothing, inability to meet taxation, quarrels of wives and concubines, no precedence between young and old,—such are the sorrows of the people.

"Capacity unequal to one's duties, and inability to carry on routine work, absence of clean-handedness, and carelessness among subordinates, lack of distinction and want of preferment,—such are the sorrows of ministers.

"The Court without loyal ministers and the State in rebellion, the artisan unskilful and the tribute unsatisfactory, the periodical levées unattended and the Son of Heaven displeased,—such are the sorrows of the princes.

"The two great principles of nature working inharmoniously, heat and cold coming at irregular seasons so that men and things suffer, the princes rebellious and fighting among themselves so that the people perish, music and ceremonies ill regulated, wealth dissipated, the relationships of man disregarded, the masses sunk in immorality,—such are the sorrows which fall to the share of the Son of Heaven.

"But now you, Sir, occupying neither the more exalted position of ruler nor performing the subordinate functions of minister, nevertheless take upon yourself to regulate music and ceremonies and to distinguish the relationships of man, in order to reform the masses. Are you not travelling out of your own sphere?

"Further, men have eight blemishes, and there are four things which obstruct business. These should be investigated.

"Meddling with matters which do not matter to you, is prying.

"To push one's way in, regardless of neglect, is to be forward.

"To adapt one's thoughts and arrange one's words, is sycophancy.

"To applaud a person, right or wrong, is flattery.

"To love speaking evil of others, is slander.

"To sever friendships and break ties, is mischievousness.

"To praise people falsely with a view to injure them, is malice.

"To give ready assent with a view to worm out the wishes of others, good and bad alike, is to be a hypocrite.

"These eight blemishes cause a man to throw others into confusion and bring injury upon himself. The superior man will not have him for a friend; the enlightened prince will not employ him as his minister.

"To love the conduct of great affairs, and to introduce change into established order with a view to gain reputation,—this is ambition.

"To strive to get all into one's own hands, and to usurp what should be at the disposal of others,—this is greed.

"To know one's faults but not to correct them, to receive admonition but only to plunge deeper,—this is obstinacy.

"To suffer those who are like oneself, but as for those unlike not to credit them with the virtues they really possess,—this is bigotry.

"Such are the four things which obstruct business. And only he who can put aside the above eight and abstain from the above four is fit for instruction."

At this Confucius heaved a sigh of distress. Then having twice prostrated himself, he arose and said, "Twice was I driven from Lu. I was tabooed in Wei. My tree was cut down in Sung. I was surrounded by the Ch'êns and the Ts'ais. I know not what my fault is that I should have suffered these four persecutions."

"Dear me!" said the old man in a vexed tone, "How slow of perception you are.

"There was once a man who was so afraid of his shadow and so disliked his own footsteps that he determined to run away from them. But the oftener he raised his feet the more footsteps he made, and though he ran very hard his shadow never left him. From this he inferred that he went too slowly, and ran as hard as he could without resting, the consequence being that his strength broke down and he died. He was not aware that by going into the shade he would have got rid of his shadow, and that by keeping still he would have put an end to his footsteps. Fool that he was!

"Now you occupy yourself with charity and duty to one's neighbour. You examine into the distinction of like and unlike, the changes of motion and rest, the canons of giving and receiving, the emotions of love and hate, and the restraint of joy and anger. Yet you cannot avoid the calamities you speak of.

"Reverently care for your body. Carefully preserve your natural purity. Leave externals to others. Then you will not be involved. But as it is, instead of improving yourself you are trying to improve other people. Surely this is dealing with the external."

"Then may I enquire," said Confucius in a tone of distress, "what is the original purity?"

"Our original purity," replied the fisherman, "is the perfection of truth unalloyed. Without this, we cannot influence others. Hence, those who weep to order, though they mourn, do not grieve. Those who assume anger, though violent, do not inspire awe. Those who affect friendship, though they smile, are not in unison."

"Real mourning grieves in silence. Real anger awes without expression. Real friendship is unison without the aid of smiles. Our emotions are dependent upon the original purity within; and accordingly we hold the latter in esteem.

"If applied to human affairs, then in serving our parents we are filial, in serving our prince we are loyal, in the banquet hour we are merry, in the hour of mourning we are sad.

"The object of loyalty is successful service; of a banquet, mirth; of mourning, grief; of serving parents, gratifying their wishes. If the service is accomplished, it matters not that no trace remain.

In the way of kudos to the accomplisher.

If parents be gratified, it matters not how. If a banquet results in mirth, the accessories are of no importance. If there be real grief in mourning, it matters not what ceremonies may be employed.

"Ceremonial is the invention of man. Our original purity is given to us from God. It is as it is, and cannot be changed. Wherefore the true Sage models himself upon God, and holds his original purity in esteem. He is independent of human exigencies. Fools, however, reverse this. They cannot model themselves upon God, and have to fall back on man. They do not hold original purity in esteem. Consequently they are ever suffering the vicissitudes of mortality, and never reaching the goal. Alas! you, Sir, were early steeped in deceit, and are late in hearing the great doctrine."

Confucius, having again prostrated himself twice, arose and said,

"It has been a godsend to meet you, Sir, to-day. Pray allow me to follow you as your servant, that I may benefit by your teaching. I venture to ask where you live that I may enter upon my duties and learn the great doctrine."

"I have heard," replied the old man, "that if a man is a fit companion, one may travel with him into the uttermost depths of Tao. But that if he is not a fit companion, and does not know Tao, one must avoid his company, that no harm may befall. Excuse me, I must leave you." Thereupon he pushed off his boat, and disappeared among the reeds.

"Yen Yüan then brought up the chariot, and Tzŭ Lu offered the hand-cord to Confucius. But the latter paid no attention. He waited until the ripples on the water had smoothed down and the sound of the punt-pole had died away, before he ventured to get up.

Tzŭ Lu, who was at the side of the chariot, enquired saying, "Master, I have been in your service now for a long time, yet never did I see you treat any man like this. In the presence of a ruler of ten thousand or a thousand chariots, I have never seen you treated other than with great respect, while you yourself would wear a haughty air. Yet before this old fisherman, leaning on his punt-pole, you cringe and bow and prostrate yourself twice before answering. Is not this too much? The disciples do not know what to make of it. Why this behaviour to an old fisherman?"

"Yu!" cried Confucius, resting on the bar of the chariot; "it is difficult to make anything of you. You have long studied ceremonies and duty to your neighbour, yet you have not succeeded in getting rid of the old evil nature. Come here, and I will tell you.

"To meet an elder without respect is want of ceremony. To see a Sage and not to honour him, is not to be in charity with man. Unless you are in charity with man, you cannot humble yourself before a fellow-creature. And unless you can honestly do this, you can never attain to that state of original purity; but the body will constantly suffer. Alas! there is no greater evil than not to be in charity with man. Yet in such a plight, O Yu, are you.

"Further. Tao is the source of all creation. Men have it, and live. They lose it, and die. Affairs in antagonism thereto, fail; in accordance therewith, succeed. Therefore, wherever Tao abides, there is the reverence of the true Sage. And as this old fisherman may be said to possess Tao, could I venture not to respect him?"

CHAPTER XXXII

Lieh Tzŭ

Argument:—Outward manifestation of inward grace—Its dangers—Self-esteem—Its errors—Inscrutability of Tao—Artificiality of Confucius—Tests of virtue—Chuang Tzŭ declines office—His death.

When Lieh Tzŭ
Lieh Yü K'ou, a name well known in connection with Tao. But it is extremely doubtful if such a man ever lived. His record is not given by the historian Ssŭ-ma Ch'ien, and he may well have been no more than an allegorical personage created by Chuang Tzŭ for purposes of illustration. It was however thought necessary under the Han dynasty to supply his "Works"; and the treatise thus provided still passes under his name, though generally regarded as a forgery. See p. 2.
went to Ch'i, half way there he turned round and came back. Falling in with Poh Hun Wu Jen, the latter said, "How is it you are so soon back again?"

"I was afraid," replied Lieh Tzŭ.

"Afraid of what?" asked Poh Hun Wu Jen.

"Out of ten restaurants at which I ate," said Lieh Tzŭ, "five would take no payment."

"And what is there to be afraid of in that?" enquired Poh Hun Wu Jen.

"The truth within not being duly assimilated," replied Lieh Tzŭ, "a certain brightness is visible externally. And to conquer men's hearts by force of the external is to induce in oneself a disregard for authority and age which is the precursor of trouble.

"A restaurant keeper is one who lives by retailing soup. When his returns are counted up, his profit is but small, and his influence is next to nothing. But if such a man could act thus, how much more the ruler of a large State? His bodily powers worn out in the duties of his position, his mental powers exhausted by details of administration, he would entrust me with the government and stimulate me by reward. That is what I was afraid of."

"Your inner lights are good," replied Poh Hun Wu Jen; "but if you remain stationary at this point, the world will still gather around you."

Contrary to Tao.

Shortly afterwards Poh Hun Wu Jen went to visit Lieh Tzŭ, and lo! his court-yard was filled with boots.

Of the visitors come to hear him. These were left outside the door, in accordance with an ancient custom mentioned in the Book of Rites. See p.167.

Poh Hun Wu Jen stood there awhile, facing the north, his cheek all wrinkled by resting it on his staff. Then, without a word, he departed.

Upon this being announced to Lieh Tzŭ,

By the servant whose duty it was to receive guests.
he seized his shoes and ran out barefoot.
In his hurry.
When he reached the outer gate, he called aloud, "Master! now that you have come, will you not give me medicine?"

"It is all over!" cried Poh Hun Wu Jen. "I told you that the world would gather around you. It is not that you can make people gather around you. You cannot prevent them from doing so. Of what use would my instruction be? Exerting influence thus unduly over others, you are by them influenced in turn. You disturb your natural constitution, and are of no further account.

> *None of your companions*
> *Warn you of this.*
> *Their paltry talk*
> *Is but poison to a man.*
> *They are not awake, not alive to the situation.*
> *How should one of these help you?*

In the original, these lines rhyme.
"The shrewd grow weary, the wise grieve. Those who are without abilities have no ambitions. With full bellies they roam happily about, like drifting boats, not caring whither they are bound."

There was a man of the Chêng State, named Huan. He pursued his studies at a place called Ch'iu-shih. After three years only, he had graduated as a Confucianist; and like a river which fertilises its banks to a distance of nine li, so did his good influence reach into three families.
His father's, his mother's, and his wife's.
He caused his younger brother to graduate as a Mihist. But inasmuch as in the question of Confucianism versus Mihism,
The philosophy of Mih Tzŭ, who taught the doctrine of universal love, etc. See pp.8,199.
the father took the side of the Mihist, at the end of ten years Huan committed suicide.

Then the father dreamed that Huan appeared to him and said, "It was I who caused your son to become a Mihist. Why give all the credit to him who is but as the fruit of an autumn pine?"
Various interpretations of this simile are given: none satisfactory. E.g. (1) Like a dry cone. (2) Which another has planted and reared.
Verily God does not reward man for what he does, but for what he is.
I.e. for the natural, not for the artificial.
And it was in this sense that the younger brother was caused to become a Mihist.
He was naturally so inclined.
Whereas a man who should regard his distinctive abilities as of his own making, without reference to his parents, would be like the man of Ch'i who dug a well and then wanted to keep others away from it.
Forgetting that God put the spring there in the first instance.

Hence the saying that the men of to-day are all Huans.

Wherefore it follows that men of true virtue are unconscious of its possession. How much more then the man of Tao? This is what the ancients called escaping the vengeance of God.

Which would be incurred by aping his goodness.

The true Sage rests in that which gives rest, and not in that which does not give rest. The world rests in that which does not give rest, and not in that which does give rest.

The natural and the artificial.

Chuang Tzŭ said, "To know Tao is easy. The difficulty lies in the elimination of speech. To know Tao without speech appertains to the natural. To know Tao with speech appertains to the artificial. The men of old were natural, not artificial.

"Chu P'ing Man spent a large patrimony in learning under Chih Li I how to kill dragons.

To acquire Tao. There is no record of the persons mentioned.

By the end of three years he was perfect, but there was no direction in which he could show his skill.

Tao cannot be put into practice.

"The true Sage regards certainties as uncertainties; therefore he is never up in arms.

In a state of mental disturbance.

Men in general regard uncertainties as certainties; therefore they are constantly up in arms. To accustom oneself to arms causes one to fly to arms on every provocation; and to trust to arms is to perish."

"The intelligence of the mean man does not rise beyond bribes and letters of recommendation. His mind is be-clouded with trivialities. Yet he would penetrate the mystery of Tao and of creation, and rise to participation in the One. The result is that he is confounded by time and space; and that trammelled by objective existences, he fails to reach apprehension of that age before anything was.

"But the perfect man,—he carries his mind back to the period before the beginning. Content to rest in the oblivion of nowhere, passing away like flowing water, he is merged in the clear depths of the infinite.

"Alas! man's knowledge reaches to the hair on a hair, but not to eternal peace."

A man of the Sung State, named Ts'ao Shang, acted as political agent for the prince of Sung at the court of the Ch'in State. When he went thither, he had a few carriages; but the prince of Ch'in was so pleased with him that he added one hundred more.

On his return to Sung, he visited Chuang Tzŭ and said, "As for living in poverty in a dirty hovel, earning a scanty subsistence by making sandals, with shrivelled face and yellow ears,—this I could not do. Interviewing a powerful ruler, with a retinue of a hundred carriages,—that is my forte."

"When the prince of Ch'in is sick," replied Chuang Tzŭ, "and he summons his physician to open a boil or cleanse an ulcer, the latter gets one carriage. The man who licks his piles gets five. The more degrading the work, the greater the number of carriages given. You, Sir, must have been attending to his piles to get so many carriages. Begone with you!"

"Not," says Lin Hsi Chung, "from the pen of Chuang Tzŭ."

Duke Ai of Lu asked Yen Ho, saying, "Were I to make Confucius a pillar of my realm, would the State be profited thereby?"

"It would be most perilous!" replied Yen Ho. "Confucius is a man of outward show and of specious words. He mistakes the branch for the root.

Accessories for fundamentals.

He seeks to impress the people by an overbearing demeanour, the hollowness of which he does not perceive. If he suits you, and you entrust him with the welfare of the State, it will only be by mistake that he will succeed.

This passage is variously interpreted.

"To cause the people to leave the true and study the false does not so much affect the people of to-day as those of coming generations. Wherefore it is better not to have Confucius.

"The difficulty of governing lies in the inability to practise self-effacement. Man does not govern as God does.

Regardless of self.

"Merchants and traders are altogether out of the pale.

Of Tao.

Or if chance ever brings them within it, their rights are never freely admitted.

"External punishments are inflicted by metal and wood. Internal punishments are inflicted by anxiety and remorse. Fools who incur external punishment are treated with metal or wood. Those who incur internal punishment are devoured by the conflict of emotions. It is only the pure and perfect man who can succeed in avoiding both."

Confucius said, "The heart of man is more dangerous than mountains and rivers, more difficult to understand than Heaven itself. Heaven has its periods of spring, summer, autumn, winter, daytime and night. Man has an impenetrable exterior, and his motives are inscrutable. Thus some men appear to be retiring when they are really forward. Others have abilities, yet appear to be worthless. Others are compliant, yet gain their ends. Others take a firm stand, yet yield the point. Others go slow, yet advance quickly.

"Those who fly to duty towards their neighbour as though thirsting after it, drop it as though something hot. Thus the loyalty of the superior man is tested by employing him at a distance, his respectfulness by employing him near at hand. His ability, by troublesome missions. His knowledge, by unexpected questions. His trustworthiness, by specification of time limits. His integrity by entrusting him with money. His fidelity, by dangerous tasks. His decorum, by filling him with wine. His morality, by placing him in disreputable surroundings. Under the application of these nine tests, the inferior man stands revealed.

"Chêng K'ao Fu, on receiving his first appointment, bowed his head. On receiving his second appointment, he hunched his back. On receiving his third appointment, he fell upon his face, walking away at the side of the path.

Instead of in the middle as any blustering braggart would have done.

Who would not try to be like him?

"Yet ordinary men, on their first appointment, become self-important. On their second, they give themselves airs in their chariots. On their third, they call their own fathers by their personal names.

As we should say, "by their Christian names." The term "fathers" includes uncles.

Which of them can be compared with Hsü Yu of old? "There is nothing more fatal than intentional virtue, when the mind looks outwards.

Spontaneity is the essence of real virtue.

For by thus looking outwards, the power of introspection is destroyed.

"There are five sources of injury to virtue.

Eyes, nose, mouth, ears, and thought.

Of these, that which aims at virtue is the chief. What is it to aim at virtue? Why a man who aims at virtue practises what he approves and condemns what he does not practise.

> *Compounds for sins he feels inclined to*
> *By damning those he has no mind to.*

"There are eight causes of failure, three certain elements of success. There are six sources of strength and weakness.

"Beauty, a long beard, size, height, robustness, grace, courage, daring,—these eight, in which men surpass their fellows, are therefore passports to failure.

"Modesty, compliance, humility,—these three are sure roads to success.

"Wisdom manifests itself in the external.

Whereby the internal suffers.

Courage makes itself many enemies. Charity and duty towards one's neighbour incur many reproaches.

Three sources of weakness.

"To him who can penetrate the mystery of life, all things are revealed. He who can estimate wisdom at its true value,

Sc. at nothing.

is wise. He who comprehends the Greater Destiny, becomes himself part of it.

Of the great scheme of the universe, seen and unseen.

He who comprehends the Lesser Destiny, resigns himself to the inevitable."

Referring to life as ordinarily regarded by mortals. Three sources of strength.

A man who had been to see the prince of Sung and had been presented with ten chariots, was putting on airs in the presence of Chuang Tzŭ.

"At Ho-Shang," said the latter, "there was a poor man who supported his family by plaiting rushes. One day his son dived into the river and got a pearl worth a thousand ounces of silver. The father bade him fetch a stone and smash it to pieces, explaining that he could only have got such a pearl very deep down from under the nose of the dragon, which must have been asleep. And he said he was afraid that when the dragon waked, the boy would have a poor chance.

If found with it in his possession.

"Now the State of Sung is deeper than a deep river, and the prince of Sung is fiercer than a dragon. To get these chariots, you must have caught him asleep. And when he wakes, you will be ground to powder."

Some prince having invited Chuang Tzŭ to enter his service, Chuang Tzŭ said in reply to the envoy, "Sir, have you ever noticed a sacrificial ox? It is bedecked with ribbons and fares sumptuously. But when it comes to be slaughtered for the temple, would it not gladly exchange places with some neglected calf?"

Quoted, with variants, by the historian Ssŭ-ma Ch'ien, in his biographical notice of Chuang Tzŭ. See Introduction.

When Chuang Tzŭ was about to die, his disciples expressed a wish to give him a splendid funeral. But Chuang Tzŭ said, "With Heaven and Earth for my coffin and shell; with the sun, moon, and stars as my burial regalia; and with all creation to escort me to the grave,—are not my funeral paraphernalia ready to hand?"

> *And had he not high honour?—*
> *The hillside for his pall;*
> *To lie in state while angels wait*
> *With stars for tapers tall;*
>
> *And the dark rock pines like nodding plumes*
> *Above his bier to wave,*
> *And God's own hand in that lonely land*
> *To lay him in the grave.*
> *The Burial of Moses (Mrs. Alexander).*

"We fear," argued the disciples, "lest the carrion kite should eat the body of our Master"; to which Chuang Tzŭ replied, "Above ground I shall be food for kites; below I shall be food for mole-crickets and ants. Why rob one to feed the other?

With this may be compared the reply of Diogenes on a similar occasion. When the old cynic asked to be left unburied, his friends objected that he would be eaten by dogs and birds.

"Place my staff near me," said Diogenes, "that I may drive them away."

"How will you manage that?" enquired the friends. "You will not be conscious."

"What then will it matter to me to be torn by beasts," cried Diogenes, "if I am not conscious of it?"

"If you adopt, as absolute, a standard of evenness which is so only relatively, your results will not be absolutely even. If you adopt, as absolute, a criterion of right which is so only relatively, your results will not be absolutely right. Those who trust to their senses become slaves to objective existences. Those alone who are guided by their intuitions find the true standard. So far are the senses less reliable than the intuitions. Yet fools trust to their senses to know what is good for mankind, with alas! but external results."

As the genuine text of the Spring and Autumn ends with the appearance of the ch'i lin (or kilin) and the death of Confucius, so have disciples of Chuang Tzŭ agreed that the genuine text of Chuang Tzŭ comes to a fitting close at the death-bed of their great Master.

The final chapter is but a summary of the whole, compiled by the early editors of the work.

CHAPTER XXXIII

The Empire

[Summary by early editors.]

Systems of government are many. Each man thinks his own perfect. Where then does what the ancients called the system of Tao come in? There is nowhere where it does not come in.

It may be asked whence our spirituality, whence our intellectuality. The true Sage is born; the prince is made. Yet all proceed from an original One.

He who does not separate from the Source is one with God. He who does not separate from the essence is a spiritual man. He who does not separate from the reality is a perfect man. He who makes God the source, and Tê the root, and Tao the portal, passively falling in with the modifications of his environment,—he is the true Sage.

These are but four different denominations of the ideal man.

He who practises charity as a kindness, duty to one's neighbour as a principle, ceremony as a convenience, music as a pacificator, and thus becomes compassionate and charitable,—he is a superior man.

We sink here to a lower level, though still a high one. The "superior man" is the ideal man of Confucian ethics. In him divinity finds no place.

He who regulates his conduct by law, who regards fame as an external adjunct, who verifies his hypotheses, who bases his judgment upon proof,—such men rank one, two, three, four, etc. It is thus that officials rank. In a strict sense of duty, in making food and raiment of paramount importance, in caring for and nourishing the old, the weak, the orphan, and the widow, they all exemplify the principle of true government.

Partly, if not wholly. This the dead level of ordinary mortality, still within the operation of Tao.

Thus far-reaching was the extension of Tao among the ancients.

The companion of the gods, the purifier of the universe, it nourishes all creation, it unites the empire, it benefits the masses. Illuminating the fundamental, it is bound up with the accessory, reaching to all points of the compass and to the opposite extremes of magnitude. There is indeed nowhere where it is not!

How it enlightened the polity of past ages is evidenced in the records which historians have preserved to us. Its presence in the Canons of Poetry, History, Rites, and Music, has been made clear by many scholars of Chou and Lu. It informs the Canon of Poetry with its vigour, the Canon of History with its usefulness, the Canon of Rites with its adaptability, the Canon of Music with its harmonising influence, the Canon of Changes with its mysterious Principles, and the Spring and Autumn with its discriminations. Spread over the whole world, it is focussed in the Middle Kingdom, and the learning of all schools renders constant homage to its power.

But when the world is disorganised, true Sages do not manifest themselves, Tao ceases to exist as One, and the world becomes cognisant of the idiosyncrasies of the individual. These are like the senses of hearing, sight, smell, and taste,—not common to each organ. Or like the skill of various artisans,—each excellent of its kind and each useful in its turn, but not equally at the command of all.

Consequently, when a mere specialist comes forward and dogmatises on the beauty of the universe the principles which underlie all creation, the position occupied by the ancients in reference to the beauty of the universe, and the limits of the supernatural,—it follows that the Tao of inner wisdom and of outer strength is obscured and prevented from asserting itself. Every one alas! regards the course he prefers as the infallible course. The various schools diverge never to meet again; and posterity is debarred from viewing the original purity of the universe and the grandeur of the ancients. For the system of Tao is scattered in fragments over the face of the earth.

Not to covet posthumous fame, nor to aim at dazzling the world, nor to pose as a benefactor of mankind, but to be a strict self-disciplinarian while lenient to the faults of others,—herein lay the Tao of the ancients.

Mih Tzŭ and Ch'in Hua Li

A disciple of Mih Tzŭ.

became enthusiastic followers of Tao, but they pushed the system too far, carrying their practice to excess. The former wrote an essay Against Music, and another which he entitled Economy.

To be found in the collection which passes under the name of Mih Tzŭ.

There was to be no singing in life, no mourning after death. He taught universal love and beneficence towards one's fellow men, without contentions, without censure of others. He loved learning, but not in order to become different from others. Yet his views were not those of the ancient Sages, whose music and rites he set aside.

The Yellow Emperor gave us the Hsien-ch'ih. Yao gave us the Ta-chang. Shun, the Ta-shao. Yü, the Ta-hsia. T'ang, the Ta-hu. Wên Wang, the P'i-yung. Wu Wang and Chou Kung added the Wu.

Famous musical compositions.

The mourning ceremonial of old was according to the estate of each, and determined in proportion to rank. Thus, the body of the Son of Heaven was enclosed in a seven-fold coffin. That of a feudal prince, in a five-fold coffin. That of a minister, in a three-fold coffin. That of a private individual, in a two-fold coffin. But now Mih Tzŭ would have no singing in life, no mourning after death, and a single coffin of only three inches in thickness as the rule for all alike!

Such doctrines do not illustrate his theory of universal love;

They betray a want of sympathy with human weaknesses.

neither does his practice of them establish the fact of his own personal self-respect. They may not suffice to destroy his system altogether; though it is unreasonable to prohibit singing, and weeping, and rejoicing in due season.

He would have men toil through life and hold death in contempt. But this teaching is altogether too unattractive. It would land mankind in sorrow and lamentation. It would be next to impossible as a practical system, and cannot, I fear, be regarded as the Tao of the true Sage. It would be diametrically opposed to human passions, and as such would not be tolerated by the world. Mih Tzŭ himself might be able to carry it out; but not the rest of the world. And when one separates from the rest of the world, his chances of developing an ideal State become small indeed.

Mih Tzŭ argued in favour of his system as follows:—Of old, the great Yü drained off the flood of waters, and caused rivers and streams to flow through the nine divisions of the empire and the parts adjacent thereto,—three hundred great rivers, three thousand branches, and streams without number. With his own hands he plied the bucket and dredger, in order to reduce confusion to uniformity,

Make all streams flow to the sea.

until his calves and shins had no hair left upon them. The wind bathed him, the rain combed him; but he marked out the nations of the world, and was in very truth a Sage. And because he thus sacrificed himself to the commonwealth, ages of Mihists to come would also wear short serge jackets and straw sandals, and toil day and night without stopping, making self-mortification their end and aim, and say to themselves, "If we cannot do this, we do not follow the Tao of Yü, and are unworthy to be called Mihists."

The disciples of Hsiang Li Ch'in,

A professor of Mihism.

the followers of the five princes, Mihists of the south, such as K'u Huo, Chi Ch'ih, and Têng Ling,—all these studied the canon of Mih Tzŭ, but their disagreements and agreements were not identical. They called each other schismatics, and quarrelled over the "hard and white," the "like and unlike," and argued over questions of "odd and even." Chü Tzŭ was their Sage, and they wanted to canonise him as a saint, that they might carry on his doctrines into after ages. Even now these differences are not settled.

Thus we see that Mih Tzŭ and Ch'in Hua Li, while right in theory, were wrong in practice. They would merely have taught mankind to vie with each other in working the hair off their calves and shins. The evil of that system would have predominated over the good. Nevertheless, Mih Tzŭ was undoubtedly a well-meaning man. In spite of failure, with all its withering influences, he stuck to his text. He may be called a man of genius.

But not a true Sage.

Not to be involved in the mundane, not to indulge in the specious, not to be overreaching with the individual, nor antagonistic to the public; but to desire the tranquillity of the world in general with a view to the prolongation of life, to seek no more than sufficient for the requirements of oneself and others, and by such a course to purify the heart,—herein lay the Tao of the ancients.

Sung Hsing and Yin Wên became enthusiastic followers of Tao. They adopted a cap, shaped like the Hua Mountain, as a badge. They bore themselves with kindly discrimination towards all things. They spoke of the passive qualities of the heart as though they had been active; and declared that whosoever could bring joy among mankind and peace within the girdle of ocean should be made ruler over them.

They suffered obloquy without noticing the insult. They preserved the people from strife. They prohibited aggression and caused arms to lie unused. They saved their generation from wars, and carried their system over the whole empire, to the delight of the high and to the improvement of the lowly. Though the world would have none of them, yet they struggled on and would not give way. Hence it was said that when high and low became tired of seeing them, they intruded themselves by force. In spite of all this, they did too much for others, and too little for themselves.

"Give us," said they, "but five pints of rice, and it will be enough." The master could not thus eat his fill; but the disciples, although starving, did not forget the world's claims.

This is not satisfactorily explained by any commentator. Kuo Hsiang says that these two men regarded the world as their "master."

Day and night they toiled on, saying, "Must we necessarily live? Shall we ape the so-called saviours of mankind?"

"The superior man," they say, "is not a fault-finder. He does not appropriate the credit of others. He looks on one who does no good to the world as a worthless fellow. He regards prohibition of aggressive actions and causing arms to lie unused, as external; the diminution and restraint of our passions, as internal. In all matters, great or small, subtle or gross, such is the point to which he attains."

To be public-spirited and belong to no party, in one's dealings not to be all for self, to move without being bound to a given course, to take things as they come, to have no remorse for the past, no anxiety for the future, to have no partialities, but to be on good terms with all,—herein lay the Tao of the ancients.

P'êng Mêng, T'ien P'ien, and Shên Tao, became enthusiastic followers of Tao. Their criterion was the identity of all things. "The sky," said they, "can cover but cannot support us. The earth can support but cannot cover us. Tao can embrace all things but cannot deal with particulars."

They knew that in creation all things had their possibilities and their impossibilities. Therefore they said, "Selection excludes universality. Training will not reach in all directions. But Tao is comprehensive."

Consequently, Shên Tao discarded all knowledge and self-interest and became a fatalist.

It is about as difficult to apprehend Tao apart from fatalism as the omniscience of God apart from predestination.

Passivity was his guiding principle. "For," said he, "we can only know that we know nothing, and a little knowledge is a dangerous thing.

"Take any worthless fellow who laughs at mankind for holding virtue in esteem, any unprincipled vagabond who reviles the great Sages of the world, and subject him to torture. In his agony he will sacrifice positive and negative alike. If he can but get free, he will trouble no more about knowledge and forethought. Past and future will cease to exist for him, in his then neutral condition.

"Move when pushed, come when dragged. Be like a whirling gale, like a feather in the wind, like a mill-stone going round. The mill-stone as an existence is perfectly harmless. In motion or at rest it does no more than is required, and cannot therefore incur blame.

"Why? Because it is simply an inanimate thing. It has no anxieties about itself. It is never entangled in the trammels of knowledge. In motion or at rest it is always governed by fixed laws, and therefore it never becomes open to praise. Hence it has been said, 'Be as though an inanimate thing, and there will be no use for Sages.'

"For a clod cannot be without Tao,"—at which some full-blooded young buck covered the argument with ridicule by crying out, "Shên Tao's Tao is not for the living, but for the dead!"

It was the same with T'ien P'ien. He studied under P'êng Mêng; with the result that he learnt nothing.

Tao cannot be learnt.

P'êng Mêng's tutor said, "Those of old who knew Tao, reached the point where positive and negative ceased to exist. That was all."

Now the bent of these men is one of opposition, which it is difficult to discuss. They act in every way differently from other people, but cannot escape the imputation of purpose.

Which takes the place of spontaneity.

What they call Tao is not Tao; and what they predicate affirmatively cannot escape being negative. The fact is that P'êng Mêng, T'ien P'ien, and Shên Tao, did not know Tao. Nevertheless they all had a certain acquaintance with it.

To make the root the essential, to regard objective existences as accidental, to look upon accumulation as deficiency, and to meekly accept the dispositions of Providence,—herein lay the Tao of the ancients.

Kuan Yin and Lao Tzŭ became enthusiastic followers of Tao.

For Kuan Yin, see p. 105.

They based their system upon nothingness, with One as their criterion. Their outward expression was gentleness and humility. Their inward belief was in unreality and avoidance of injury to all things.

Kuan Yin said, "Adopt no absolute position. Let externals take care of themselves. In motion, be like water. At rest, like a mirror.

Receptive, but not permanently so.

Respond, like the echo.

Only when called upon.

Be subtle, as though non-existent. Be still, as though pure. Regard uniformity as peace. Look on gain as loss. Do not precede others. Follow them."

Lao Tzŭ said, "He who conscious of being strong, is content to be weak,—he shall be a cynosure of men.

This is quoted by Huai Nan Tzŭ as a saying by Lao Tzŭ, and appears in ch. xxviii of the Tao-Tê-Ching. See The Remains of Lao Tzŭ, p. 21.

"He who conscious of purity, puts up with disgrace,—he shall be the cynosure of mankind.

"He who when others strive to be first, contents himself with the lowest place, is said to accept the contumely of the world.

"He who when others strive for the substantial, contents himself with the unsubstantial, stores up nothing and therefore has abundance. There he is in the midst of his abundance which comes to him without effort on his part. He does nothing, and laughs at the artifices of others.

"He who when others strive for happiness is content with security, is said to aim at avoiding evil.

Compare the Tao-Tê-Ching, ch. xxii.

"He who makes depth of fundamental importance and moderation his rule of life, is said to crush that which is hard within him and temper that which is sharp.

"To be in liberal sympathy with all creation, and not to be aggressive towards one's fellow-men,—this may be called perfection."

O Kuan Yin! O Lao Tzŭ! verily ye were the true Sages of old.

Silence, formlessness, change, impermanence, now life, now death, heaven and earth blended in one, the soul departing, gone no one knows where: suddenly, no one knows whither, as all things go in turn, never to come back again;—herein lay the Tao of the ancients.

Chuang Tzŭ became an enthusiastic follower of Tao. In strange terms, in bold words, in far-reaching language, he gave free play to his thoughts, without following any particular school or committing himself to any particular line.

He looked on the world as so sunk in corruption that it was impossible to speak gravely. Therefore he employed "goblet words" which apply in various directions; he based his statements upon weighty authority in order to inspire confidence; and he put words in other people's mouths in order to secure breadth.

See ch. xxvii ad init.

In accord with the spirit of the universe, he was at peace with all creation. He judged not the rights and wrongs of mankind, and thus lived quietly in his generation. Although his book is an extraordinary production, it is plausible and harmless enough. Although the style is most irregular, it is at the same time ingenious and attractive.

As a thinker, he is endlessly suggestive. Above, he roams with God. Below, he consorts with those who are beyond the pale of life and death, who deny a beginning and an end. In relation to the root,

The origin of all things.

he speaks on a grand and extensive scale. In relation to Tao, he establishes a harmony between man and the higher powers. Nevertheless, he yields to the modifications of existence and responds to the exigencies of environment. His arguments are inexhaustible, and never illogical. He is far-reaching, mysterious, and not to be fully explored.

It is impossible for a European critic to believe that Chuang Tzŭ penned the above paragraphs. See post, p 206.

Hui Tzŭ was a man of many ideas. His works would fill five carts. But his doctrines are paradoxical, and his terms are used ambiguously.

He calls infinite greatness, beyond which there is nothing, the Greater One. He calls infinite smallness, within which there is nothing, the Lesser One.

Recognising two absolute extremes.

He says that that which is without dimensions measures a thousand li.

On the principle that mathematical points, though themselves without dimensions, collectively fill up space.

That heaven and earth are equally low. That mountain and marsh are equally level.

It depends upon the point of view.

That the sun at noon is the sun setting.

To people living farther east.

That when an animal is born, it dies.

As regards its previous state it dies when leaving it for a new state.

That the likeness of things partly unlike is called the lesser likeness of unlikes. That the likeness of things altogether unlike is called the greater likeness of unlikes. That southwards there is no limit, and yet there is a limit. That one can reach Yüeh to-day and yet be there before. That joined rings can be separated. That the middle of the world is north of Yen and south of Yüeh.

It is wherever the speaker is. The space between Yen and Yüeh is as zero compared with the infinite.

That he loves all creation equally, just as heaven and earth are impartial to all.

In covering and supporting all.

Accordingly, Hui Tzŭ was regarded as a great philosopher and a very subtle dialectician; and became a favourite with the other dialecticians of the day.

He said that there were feathers in an egg.

Because on a chicken.

That a fowl had three feet.

The third being volition.
That Ying was the world.
As you cannot say it is not the world.
That a dog could be a sheep. That a mare could lay eggs. That a nail has a tail.
Names being arbitrary in all cases.
That fire is not hot.
It is the man who feels it hot.
That mountains have mouths.
As evidenced by echoes.
That wheels do not press down the ground.
Touching only at a point.
That the eye does not see.
It is the man.
That the finger does not touch. That the uttermost extreme is not the end. That a tortoise is longer than a snake.
Because longer lived!
That a carpenter's square is not square.
Like Horace's Whetstone which makes other things sharp, "exsors ipsa secandi."
That compasses will not make a circle.
It is the draughtsman.
That a round hole will not surround a square handle. That the shadow of a flying bird does not move. That there is a moment when a swiftly-flying arrow is neither moving nor at rest. That a dog is not a hound.
Two things cannot be identical unless even their names are the same.
That a bay horse and a dun cow are three.
Taken separately they are two. Taken together they are one. One and two make three.
That a white dog is black.
If his eyes are black. Part standing for the whole.
That a motherless colt never had a mother.
When it had a mother, it was not an orphan.
That if you take a stick a foot long and every day cut it in half, you will never come to the end of it.
Compare "Achilles and the Tortoise," and the sophisms of the Greek philosophers.
And such was the stuff which dialecticians used to argue about with Hui Tzŭ, also without ever getting to the end of it.

Huan T'uan and Kung Sun Lung were of this class. By specious premises they imposed on people's minds and drove them into false conclusions. But though they won the battle in words, they did not carry conviction into their adversaries' hearts. Theirs were but the snares of the sophist.

Hui Tzŭ daily devoted his intelligence to such pursuits, purposely advancing some preposterous thesis upon which to dispute. That was his characteristic. He had besides a great opinion of his own wisdom, and used to say, "The universe does not hold my peer."

Hui Tzŭ makes a parade of his strength, but is devoid of any sound system. An eccentric fellow in the south, named Huang Liao, asked why the sky did not fall and the earth sink; also, whence came wind, rain, and thunder.

Hui Tzŭ was not backward in replying to these questions, which he answered unhesitatingly. He went into a long discussion on all creation, and talked away without end, though to himself he seemed to be saying very little. He supplemented this with most extraordinary statements, making it his chief object to contradict others, and being desirous of gaining fame by defeating all comers. Thus, he was never popular. Morally, he was weak; physically, he was violent. His was a dark and narrow way.

Looked at from the point of view of the Tao of the universe, the value of Hui Tzŭ may be compared with the efforts of a mosquito or a gadfly. Of what use was he to the world? As a specialist, he might have succeeded. But to let him put himself forward as an exponent of Tao, would have been dangerous indeed.

He would not however be content to be a specialist. He must needs roam insatiably over all creation, though he only succeeded in securing the reputation of a sophist.

Alas for the talents of Hui Tzŭ! He is extravagantly energetic, and yet has no success. He investigates all creation, but does not conclude in Tao. He makes a noise to drown an echo. He is like a man running a race with his own shadow. Alas!

As to the genuineness of this concluding chapter, every one may form his own opinion. The question has been hotly fought, and great names could be mentioned on each side. Wang An Shih and Su Tung P'o both thought that it might well have come from the hand of Chuang Tzŭ. Lin Hsi Chung thought not, and on his side the majority of Western students will in all probability be ranged.

Lightning Source UK Ltd.
Milton Keynes UK
UKHW010154240123
415813UK00001B/35